LIBRARY PROGRAMS

How to Select, Plan

and Produce Them

by

John S. Robotham

and

Lydia LaFleur

The Scarecrow Press, Inc.

Metuchen, N.J.   1976

Library of Congress Cataloging in Publication Data

Robotham, John S   1924-
    Library programs: how to select, plan, and produce
them.

        Bibliography: p.
        Includes index.
        1. Libraries--Cultural programs.   I.   LaFleur, Lydia,
joint author.   II.   Title.
Z716. R62   021'. 4   76-2033
ISBN 0-8108-0911-7

ACKNOWLEDGMENTS

Many librarians, and others, have contributed information to this book. We cannot name them all, but we would particularly like to recognize the generosity of the following librarians in giving their time and knowledge: Margaret Benjamin, Elizabeth Goldfarb and Norma Herz, children's librarians of The New York Public Library; Marilyn Iarusso, assistant coordinator of children's services for The New York Public Library; Athena Kendris, young adult librarian, The New York Public Library; William Sloan, film librarian of The New York Public Library; L. A. Moore, director, and the staff of the Plainfield, N.J., Public Library; Katherine Z. Armington, readers' advisor librarian of the Rockville Regional Library, Rockville, Md.; Julia Losinski, coordinator of young adult services for Prince George's County Memorial Library System, Hyattsville, Md.; Mary Flournoy, young adult specialist, Office of Work with Adults and Young Adults, Free Library of Philadelphia.

Special thanks go to Lillian Morrison, coordinator of young adult services for the New York Public Library. She has given us much advice and encouragement, and has helped us in many ways.

Finally, it must be said that, although many people have helped us, any errors are our own.

TABLE OF CONTENTS

INTRODUCTION

In late summer, 1973, the fact that libraries not only lent books, but also put on puppet shows, showed films and conducted discussion groups, was front-page news for The New York Times (Sept. 17, 1973, p. 1). It was not, however, news to the hundreds of librarians who had struggled to do such things for many years. Still, many librarians do not have programs, or they do programming in a tentative, halfhearted way as though it is a frill that they flutter when they have time. There are many reasons for this attitude. Libraries are short of money, staff, space and time. If they had more money, they would buy more of the materials they lack. If they had more staff, they could better do the jobs for which they now have so little time. And few libraries have sufficient space even for the books, not to mention programs. Furthermore, some librarians don't think programming is part of the library's function. We do! We also think the other problems can be overcome.

There are several reasons for having programs in a library, or, as so many libraries are now doing, producing library-run programs outside the library. The traditional reason--and the reason given by many librarians in the New York Times article--is to lure people into the library. It is a good reason. Many people never enter a library. Some of them have the wrong idea about what is inside; they think public libraries are for children--that they're an adjunct to the schools; or they think it's only a place to get best sellers and mystery stories; or, for a variety of reasons, they think it is too forbidding. Libraries never enter the consciousness of some people. They are surprised when it is suggested that they try the library for an answer to their questions. So, programs are a form of publicity. People are enticed into the library, discover all the things libraries have to offer, and begin to use them. Programs sometimes work in this way (we will give examples) and sometimes they create ripples--that spread out, as ripples will, in all directions; ripples that lead to other programs or exhibits; ripples that

vii

create good will, and that spread the library's fame by word of mouth. However, librarians who produce programs, at the cost of some hard work and some valuable time, are often disappointed when a lot of the people who come to the programs don't start using the library; many times they do not. Others who come to programs are people who were using the library anyway.

Those librarians should not be disappointed. There are other reasons for having programs; they are extensions of the material on library shelves. A film on Karel Appel or Robert Frost, a rock or jazz concert, modern or interpretive dance programs, poetry readings, plays, a speaker on spiders, a discussion group dealing with ecology or war all add dimensions to the books, periodicals, pamphlets and recordings that are the library's stock in trade. Such an extra dimension (the performance of a play, the reading of a poem) is often necessary to complete the experience or understanding that comes from reading a book (the play or poem). Is it not ideal to have the components of this experience available in one place? We do not suggest competing with other institutions, commercial or public, but a library can often be more flexible and offer more variety than other institutions.

Furthermore, we, as a society, are beginning to realize that people learn in different ways. A macrame demonstration or a film on the population explosion might be more meaningful to some people than reading about those subjects, and we, as librarians, must learn to use any medium to achieve our goals. As one librarian put it, "we are in the business of information and ideas--whether they come in printed form (books, magazines) or audio- (records, cassettes, musical programs) or visual (films, exhibits, etc.) or human (personal contact, rapping, programs) ... [Young Adult Alternative Newsletter, Oct. 15, 1973, pp. 7-8].

There is another reason to do programs. In many places, little or nothing of a cultural nature is available, or is being offered to the general public. Even in places such as New York City that do offer many cultural experiences there is a need for many kinds of programs. There are a lot of films, for example, that are rarely, if ever, seen by the general public, and most people are probably not even aware they exist. Even in colleges, or large cities with museums and film associations, one's chances of seeing them are few. A beautiful film, such as White Throat (Dan Gibson

Productions), that follows a white-throated sparrow through the woods, or <u>Wholly Communion</u> (Contemporary/McGraw-Hill), that captures the excitement of a poetry reading by Ginsberg, Ferlinghetti, Voznesensky and many others in London's Albert Hall, are only two examples of many kinds of films that would be enjoyed by many people, if they could be seen. Dance programs and discussion groups, lectures and poetry readings may, in some places, be difficult to find, if they are given at all. For all of these reasons, library programs can, if they are well presented, provide a valuable free public service.

Presenting a program may well sound easier, or harder, than it is. It is our intention, therefore, to describe the techniques we have learned and the pitfalls we have encountered--and sometimes fallen into--on the way to successful programming. We have also tried to describe as many kinds of library programs as we have been able to find or to dream up. By the phrase "library program" we mean any activity, in or out of the library, in which a librarian and two or more members of the public are involved. (We are reminded by a children's librarian that she has more than once read to only one child. That is also a program.)

Programs in libraries now cover a tremendous range of activity. Libraries are not only engaged in the traditional activities of telling stories to children, showing films, and leading discussion groups; they are flying kites, demonstrating karate, teaching people how to repair motorcycles, and doing anything that seems important to any group of people.

To gather the information presented in this book, we have talked to many librarians, written them letters, and visited their libraries. We have also read all the published or unpublished material on the subject we could find in books, pamphlets, periodicals and reports. But, most importantly, we have been through the mill. During the last twenty years, we have led discussion groups and planned and produced film programs, poetry readings, plays, musical programs, lectures, and workshops, and worked out combinations of these as well. We have learned much, and we hope we can pass on what we have learned to those who would like to do some programs but who feel that because of one limitation or another they cannot.

The emphasis in this book is on public libraries and they are the ones that will do the most programming. The material should be useful, however, to schools, colleges, museums and other organizations and institutions that have, or want to have, programs. It should also be useful to library school students who will do the programs in the future, and who will be free of the fixed ideas of the past about library service.

In organizing the material, we followed a logical sequence of events. That is, we thought of the librarian who wanted to begin having programs or the librarian who wanted to do more programs. He or she would first try to think of all the possible programs. So, in the seven chapters of Part I we describe every kind of program, or variation on a program, that we could think of, or find out about. In this part, we also describe how libraries handled many of the different programs, because we wanted to give actual experiences wherever possible, and because we thought it useful to describe the entire experience of some programs in one place. With this method, we have included some material in this part that might have more properly belonged in Part III--on producing and publicizing the program. The material in those chapters is more general in nature and applies to all kinds of programs.

Once a librarian has thought of all the kinds of programs possible, he must then think about where he can get them; usually, he must think about where he can get them for nothing. We have indicated in Chapter 8 of Part II the kinds of places from which one can get successful programs, and we have told how we, and others, have gone about getting them. These are mostly free sources, but we have included ways to raise money, if you want to go into programs on a larger scale, or on a regular basis.

When you know the kinds of programs there are, and what is available in the community, you then have to think about which programs are suitable for your library. In Chapter 9 of Part II we describe a variety of techniques for finding out what programs would interest the library's users as well as others in the community. We discuss the demographic factors that must be taken into account. We discuss how to find out what is already being done (and what is not being done) in the community. And we talk about practical matters: such things as staff, space and equipment must be considered. We conclude Part II by discussing the reactions of the community, or segments of the community, to the programs (and how to elicit those reactions); there may be complaints and librarians will want to be ready for them.

After the program has been selected, it must be planned and produced. Part III is mostly devoted to mundane, but important, details. First one faces the decision of whether to have the program in the library or somewhere else in the community. Then there is the complicated business of scheduling, the necessity for checking up on equipment and other details, the importance of audience comfort, and the planning of the format of the program. We also discuss related exhibits, introductions, receptions and other things one does or can do at a program. There is also a discussion of the problems that can arise and what can be done about them--mainly, foreseeing them.

Publicity properly belongs with planning and producing the program and is discussed in Chapter 11. Planning the publicity, its kind and distribution, is discussed first. Then we describe the easiest and least expensive ways to have publicity designed and reproduced. (Appendix E contains numerous samples of flyers and posters.) The writing and use of press releases is discussed at some length. We then describe other means of publicizing the program, ways of getting publicity distributed, and the use of tickets in publicity.

For the convenience of those readers who want a handy recapitulation of steps to be taken in planning and administering a program as given in the various chapters on various subjects, and for users who are in the midst of actual preparation for a library program and do not have time to read the general advice of the chapters, a "summary and checklist of preparations" is provided at the ends of chapters 1, 2, 3 (four different ones for the four different performing arts covered), 4, 5, and 10.

We thought it would be helpful to have one program described from beginning to end. In Chapter 12, the end of Part III, is a case history of the Paul Zindel program, which brings out many of the problems involved in programming. It also shows how successful a library program can be.

Appendix A presents three lists of books suitable for discussion groups; Appendix B gives a brief list of films suggested for discussion groups; Appendix C gives sample film programs arranged as to suitability for teenagers, adults and children; Appendix D lists sources for both free loan and commercially distributed films. All materials and sources suggested in the Appendices have been successfully used in library programs. A Bibliography cites articles and books that are further sources of ideas or information on library programs in general, plus three brief sections of specific references on film programs, puppet shows, and storytelling. In addition a section on materials relating to videotaping has been included.

In the Index you will find all the kinds of programs mentioned anywhere in the text.

Part I

KINDS OF PROGRAMS

The kind of program one can have in a library is only limited by one's imagination--plus such mundane matters as money, staff, space and equipment. The important thing to remember is that one should not be limited by what has been done; librarians need to think freely about programming, and to explore the needs and possibilities, both in form and in content. We will describe many of the programs that have been presented in libraries, and will suggest some things that might be done. We hope librarians will use these ideas as launching platforms for their own imaginations, and will develop programs that fit the needs of their own libraries.

Chapter 1

DISCUSSION GROUPS

Discussion groups were probably the earliest kind of
library program for adults, and they used to be the most
common. They usually consist of a series of sessions, although it is possible to have a one-session discussion. It is
desirable to have more or less the same people attend all
sessions, but it is not always possible and is not absolutely
necessary. The ideal number of discussants is from ten to
twenty-five, but discussions can be held with five or six and
in some programs, especially the one-shot discussions, the
number has been much larger.

There are usually one or two trained leaders--often
a librarian and/or a member of the community. In some
cases, when special information is needed, a guest expert,
to act as a resource person, may be desirable. It is important that such a resource person not be regarded as a
teacher, because they can easily, if unintentionally, inhibit
discussion.

Discussion groups can be centered around any medium
of communication. Any printed material, such as books,
pamphlets or periodicals, can be used, or one can use combinations of these. Recordings (discs, cassettes, tapes),
films, filmstrips, or videotapes can be used. Or any combination of media might be tried. The choice should be dic-
tated by which media best illuminate the subject, and which
stimulate thought and provoke discussion. The potential discussants will also incline you to one medium or another.

One thing about library discussion groups should be
stressed; one should not expect, or necessarily even want,
to convert the participants to a particular point of view, or
to teach them anything; they are not classes. They can, however, stimulate the participants and give depth to their thought,
and they can be intellectually exciting and rewarding for both
the participants and the leaders.

A discussion group is a very flexible kind of program. It can be used in any library from the largest to the smallest, with almost any age, deal with many kinds of subjects, and can engage many kinds of people.

THE LEADER is an essential ingredient in a discussion group; without him, a discussion will quickly degenerate and you might as well have a group of people talking in your living room--which is all right, but it will not be a discussion. It is sometimes useful to have two leaders, especially if they are inexperienced; they can give each other support, and if one is sick, or otherwise unavailable, the other will be there. An experienced leader, however, can easily handle a group alone.

Leading a group is something one learns to do mainly through experience. There are some pointers, though, that can help the beginner. The leader may first have to inform the group that he is not a teacher; people often think they are attending a class in whatever it is you are discussing. A leader should have a relaxed, friendly attitude which encourages people to talk. He will also, at times, have to be firm. People always wander off the subject (a little bit is all right), talk too long or too much, don't talk at all, become belligerent, and do other things that hinder good discussion. The leader must, in a firm but friendly way, stop them from doing these things, and he must lead them back, or on, to a good discussion. Beginning leaders are most afraid of silences. This fear is usually unjustified. If there are short silences, that is all right; people need time to think when they are seriously discussing something.

The preparation of questions is important. The questions should not be long or involved. They should require more than a yes or no answer. The leader should be prepared to follow up answers with more probing questions, so that the discussion will go deeper; many discussions remain on a superficial level. He should have some provocative questions ready when the discussion lags. Occasionally the entire group will be of the same opinion about something. Then the leader must ask questions that will bring out arguments for the other side.

A discussion should not be allowed to die; if it has gone on for an hour or more, and the topic seems to be about used up, end the session; participants are left with a better feeling about the session, and will look forward to the

next one. Finally, the leader does not enter the discussion.
He may supply factual information, but he doesn't express
his own opinions. He also doesn't allow himself to talk too
much; if questions are unnecessary, he doesn't ask them.

THE NUMBER OF SESSIONS will depend on the content
and on the potential interest of the participants. Groups have
lasted from one session to fifteen or sixteen, and some
groups have continued year after year. One-session discussions would probably use films or recordings, since readings
must be done in advance. And they would be best used with
some particularly hot topic, which would be fairly narrow in
scope. Sometimes one book or narrow subject area would
call for a series of three or four sessions. These short-
term groups are also useful if one wants to test the validity
of having discussion groups or of discussing a particular subject; if it works, a longer series can be planned. If there
is reason to believe the interest of the participants will wane,
one would not want to plan a long series. In an area where
people get into their gardens with the approach of good weather, Plato may lose the battle to petunias. The possibility of
blizzards and the certainty of Christmas are some other factors that may limit the number of sessions. In any case, go
over the calendar and do some forecasting from what you
know of your public and your area. The number of available
staff members and the preparation time required will also be
a factor, as will the availability of materials.

THE SPACING OF SESSIONS must be considered.
Spacing is partly related to the number of sessions and to
the content. If it is a long series, or if long readings are
used, every other week is good spacing. Having sessions
further apart then two weeks makes it difficult to maintain
continuity of either people or ideas. Weekly sessions are
good for use with films, for short series, and when the subject is of immediate interest. Meetings would not be scheduled more often than once a week, in most cases.

Notice the phrases, "in most cases," "probably," and
others that are used throughout this book: there are always
exceptions to rules.

THE SIZE of the group can vary from as few as six
or seven to twenty-five or more. And some, particularly
the one-shot groups, have had much larger attendances.
More than twenty-five, though, gets to be unwieldy. Not
everybody will be able to participate and the discussion prob-

ably won't get into any depth. Also if books must be charged
out, the mechanics become difficult with a large group.
Small groups have other problems. People stimulate each
other and a small group runs out of ideas too quickly. That
might be a good test of your leadership ability, but you have
to ask yourself if it will benefit the participants. It also
may not be desirable for the library to invest so much time
and effort in a small group. But, if no extra scheduling is
involved, if materials can be used that are already in the library, and if the group doesn't take up needed space, one
could justify spending time with five or six people; certainly
the time is justified if the participants derive something of
great value from the discussion. Sometimes they do. The
best size, allowing for a full participation and a lively discussion, seems to be about twelve to fifteen.

        THE AGES of the participants must be considered.
There have been discussion groups for senior citizens, for
young teenagers, for older teenagers and for all ages. Although libraries don't usually keep anyone out of a program--
unless she is a drunk, or otherwise obstreperous--some librarians feel that it is best, if possible, to limit some
groups to the same age category. Both teenagers and the
elderly have been said to feel more comfortable with their
age peers. There is evidence both for and against this
idea, and the choice probably depends on the subject, the
sophistication of the participants, and their relationship to
the librarian or leader. The Los Angeles Public Library has
a general policy regarding teenagers: "Young Adult Services
ordinarily discourages adults and parents from attending the
programs in order to encourage good discussion participation
from the young people."[1] The New York Public Library has
no hard and fast rule, but if because of the subject, or because there might not be enough room, there are indications
that adults will interfere with the teenagers' enjoyment of a
teenage program, they also discourage the adults from attending. In a program on venereal disease, for example, some
adults monopolized the discussion. In another program, on
sex, however, some adults did attend and the teenagers still
entered fully into the discussion; in this case, the adults--as
well as the leader--were young, and that may have made a
difference. Other programs that included adults and teenagers have been very successful. A program for parents
about the problems of dealing with teenage children was attended by a number of teenagers and an excellent discussion
took place. A poetry discussion group was attended mostly
by elderly people and teenagers and it was very successful.

Some programs have been arranged especially for the elderly, but again if the leader is sympathetic and they aren't overwhelmed by the rest of the audience, there seems to be no reason to segregate them.

Although there have not been as many discussion groups for teenagers as there have for adults, there have been some successful ones. The Racine, Wisconsin, Public Library has had a lot of success with a Great Books group for seventh and eighth graders.[2] The program began in 1960 and had run for a number of years at last report. It was conceived to try to keep the teenagers reading independently before they became too involved in high school and to acquaint them with some books they might not read on their own. Teenagers also need to be able to express themselves freely, away from a structured school, and the program was geared to that purpose. A different leader was used for each session, to give flexibility and to make the discussions seem less like school. The leaders, as in discussion groups for any age, were asked not to lecture; the opinions of the teenagers were considered most important. And an informal atmosphere was the goal "to achieve a free flow of ideas and exchange of opinions." This goal was apparently achieved; "although the meetings frequently have begun stiff and formal, the participants soon realize that no one is being graded or degraded for what he says, and the ice melts."

Participants were chosen from lists submitted by librarians and English teachers. Selection was made on reading capability and interest. There was a seventh-grade series of five sessions, and an eighth-grade series of six. Groups met every other week, to allow reading time. Paperbacks were used and were furnished by the library. Each session lasted 50 to 80 minutes, depending on enthusiasm. Teachers, librarians and other community residents were enlisted as leaders, and many found it a rewarding experience. The following books were used:

Seventh grade

London. Call of the Wild
Twain. Huckleberry Finn
Poe. Great Tales
Crane. Red Badge of
    Courage
Shaw. Pygmalion
Frank. Diary of a Young
    Girl

Eighth grade

Crane. Red Badge of
    Courage
Shaw. Pygmalion
Dickens. Oliver Twist
Ullman. Banner in the Sky
Thoreau. Walden
Stowe. Uncle Tom's Cabin

Some of the most successful were Call of the Wild, Huckleberry Finn, Red Badge of Courage, Pygmalion, Diary of a Young Girl and Poe's short stories. Although the Great Books Foundation puts out a Junior Great Books list, this library found that its own selections worked well, and did not use it.

A less traditional discussion group for teenagers was held in New York City. Using The New York Public Library's Books for the Teenage as the basic reading list. the teenagers selected the subject they wanted to discuss, and read a book from that section of the list. Espionage, Africa and art were some of the subjects discussed. Guest experts were sometimes invited and the librarian who ran the group says they added a good deal of vitality to the sessions. Among the guests were a staff member who had been a member of the O.S.S. during World War II, two teenage art students from the neighborhood who demonstrated painting and sculpture, and a young woman who was a native of Dahomey.

In New Carrollton, Maryland, the County library ran a film discussion series for teenagers that dealt with some of the problems teenagers face. The flyer describing the series gives the following description:

Brian at Seventeen   Some times in the life of a typical
    teenage boy.
Claude, and Ivan and His Father   A funny and serious
    look at the generation gap.
Changing   A young family changes its lifestyle.
Bunny, Tom, Guy and Teddy   The youth culture from
    four different viewpoints.
Nobody Waved Goodbye   At odds with his family, Peter
    strikes out on his own.

ADVANCE REGISTRATION is a useful device for discussion groups. For one thing, it will give you some idea of how many will attend; always figure in a certain amount of attrition, when estimating potential attendance. If registration is becoming too large, one can then cut it off when an agreed-upon point is reached; some groups do this, because a large enrollment is not usually conducive to good discussion or to participation by most members. On the other hand, if registration is going slowly, one can grind out more publicity. And advance registration allows you to give the participants the first title for a book discussion.

Registrants can also be urged to attend all meetings; such continuity makes for more meaningful and less superficial discussion.

Discussion groups can, of course, be held without any registration, and with people drifting in and drifting out from meeting to meeting. Much depends on the kind of people you plan to attract, and on the materials you select. If you are trying to attract a group of new library users, you may prefer an informal arrangement. Or, if the materials in each session can be discussed independently, it is not so important to have the same people each time. It is, however, usually better to have the same group; they get to know each other and to talk more freely, and there will be continuity. Even if there is advance registration, don't be too rigid about it; it is only a guideline, and people are there for pleasure, after all.

If there is registration, and other rules, put them in the publicity. A registration form can be part of the publicity flyer. It is also a good idea to describe a discussion group on the flyer. People often arrive at a first session thinking it is a class and you are the teacher. This is what one library put on its flyer:

> PLEASE NOTE:
>
> Register in advance; enrollment is limited.
> Books are provided by the Library.
> Participants are expected to attend each session thoroughly prepared by having read completely the book to be discussed.
> Discussion is limited only to the material assigned. No outside sources are permitted.

The use of the word "assigned" and the general tone of this flyer were, perhaps, unfortunate, since an image of school is evoked. Another flyer was less formal:

> This book discussion program is open to people who are interested in the Black man's part in the nation, his future, his rights, and discussion of methods by which he may attain his goals. It is based on readings in old and new books and is concerned with questions of power, priorities and dissent in the United States.
> During the discussion each person is invited

to express fully his reactions, opinions, beliefs on the ideas and questions raised by the reading.

In the library discussion programs, the leader encourages the exchange of ideas, he does not lecture. Members of the group are expected to prepare reading assignments in advance and to play an active part in the discussion. Copies of all readings will be supplied by the Library.

There is that word "assigned" again, or in this case "assignment," which brings on visions of homework. But the tone is good and seems likely to appeal to the independent learner.

The form, the content, the problems and the audience aimed at will vary somewhat with the medium used for discussion, and we will now describe discussion groups using books, films, recordings, other media, and combinations of these.

Book discussion groups

These have been the most common kind. In this format, a copy of the book is loaned to each participant, and it is returned and discussed at the following session. Paperbacks are usually used now, since they can be inexpensively purchased in quantity. Readings are chosen by the availability of quantities of the titles, and the discussability of the material.

Clearly, not all books are useful for discussion purposes. So, as librarians are always doing, we must select the books we are going to use. Some books are too long; it is too much to expect a normally busy person (people who attend programs are usually those who do a lot of other things) to read and digest a thousand pages in a week or two. You could, of course, devote a whole series to one book. Or you could have the group read passages from a long book. One of the series of Great Books readings, for example, lists six chapters of Veblen's Theory of the Leisure Class, three chapters of The Education of Henry Adams, and two books of Plato's Republic. Rarely, on the other hand, are readings too short. Beginning discussion leaders are often afraid the discussion will peter out. But since, in everyone's experience, people can talk for hours about nothing, they can also talk for hours about something; that is, they can if the discussion leaders keep digging in. Short readings

can also be packed with ideas, and only one or two fruitful
ideas are needed to keep a discussion going. The Declaration of Independence can keep a group going all night. This
kind of discussion is probably the most fruitful, because the
ideas can be explored in depth--something that is rarely
done, even in the best of circles.

More important than the length are the contents; that
is, the book or other material must raise some question that
is not subject to scientific proof--some metaphysical, moral,
artistic, or socioeconomic question. It may be something as
vital to the life of the discussants as welfare rights or the
right to have an abortion. It may be on a somewhat more
removed plane, such as secrecy in government. Or it may
be something that doesn't really affect our lives, but is still
fascinating, such as free will versus determinism. Some
books are particularly apt, because they raise questions that
touch on current situations. Such a book is Robert Bolt's
A Man for All Seasons which raises questions of individual
conscience in relation to governmental power. George Orwell's 1984, too, seems more appropriate with every passing
year.

The difficulty of the material must also be considered;
if a reading requires a background in physics, you must
think whether your potential group might have such a background. The readability of the material is important. No
matter how difficult are the ideas, they can be expressed in
a way that is clear, concise and interesting. If the writing
is turgid or dull, the group will tire of it. The bias of the
writing must be examined: the presentation should not be
slanted or distorted (as nearly as this is possible). You
might, of course, want to discuss slanted writing; an examination of propaganda can be very interesting and could be the
basis for an excellent discussion.

The form of the reading in a book discussion group
can be anything. Plays, poems, novels, short stories, essays, biographies, journalism and anything else you can think
of can be used if it illuminates the subject or fuels the fires
of discussion. Book discussion groups (maybe they should be
called printed materials discussion groups) can also use pamphlets, newspaper clippings and magazine articles. A reading
list for a particular subject--say, the destruction of the en-
vironment--might well include several of these forms.

Book discussions take many forms. They can be on

subjects, forms of writings, countries, ideas. The familiar
Great Books series, with its fifteen years of readings (see
Appendix A), was probably the earliest book group. Selections cover thousands of years, many parts of the world, and
a great variety of ideas. Subjects such as the American
Heritage and the American Idea later became popular. Now
all kinds of subjects and ideas are discussed. Significant
Modern Books is a useful title for a discussion group that The
New York Public Library has developed. The list of readings
(see Appendix A) is revised regularly so that important new
titles or subjects can be included. Novels, plays, poetry,
essays, biographies and books dealing with social issues are
used. The Feminine Mystique, Clockwork Orange, Ceremonies in Dark Old Men and Cat's Cradle are examples.

Any debatable topic can be used--even broad subjects
such as war and education. All the current problems have
been discussed; among them are drugs, youth in America,
dissent in America, women's rights, mental health, the black
experience, American Indians, ecology, advertising, and
foreign affairs. Among the forms of writing that have been
bases for discussion series are science fiction, poetry and
plays. Series involving broad philosophical or moral questions have centered around the Eastern religions, science and
modern man, and such a catchall as "Love or Will? Questions of Morality." Variations on, and parts of, these large
subjects can be used. Play discussions have used "Significant
Modern Plays" and "The Tragic Theme in Greek Drama and
Shakespeare." Modern poetry, American poetry or almost any
subdivision could be used.

Film discussion groups

With this type of program, the group views and then
discusses the film on the spot. Film discussions have some
advantages over books: you don't have to supply the reading
material; no preparation time is necessary for the participants (the leader will have to prepare though); and the discussion material (the film) will be fresh in the minds of the
group. The film discussion may be more lively and more
spontaneous for those reasons, although the leader will have
to allow the group time to gather its thoughts after viewing
the film. Printed material, on the other hand, allows re-
flection prior to the meeting. It also lets you consult the
text during the discussion, which is often helpful and even
necessary, and further, it allows the participant to read the

text again after he has had the benefit of the discussion.
The choice of film or book will depend on the availability
of materials, the subject to be discussed (some subjects are
better served by film and others by print), and the kind of
audience you aim for (some young people, for example, may
prefer a film to a book). One thing to consider with any use
of film is that they add technical complications (the details
will be described later).

Films for discussion should not be too long, since
there must be time left to talk. More than thirty minutes
seems undesirable, although some absorbing and provocative
films that were much longer have been successfully used.
Fortunately, there are a lot of good, short films that are
packed with stimulating ideas. The Hand, a 19-minute
Czechoslovakian film from Contemporary/McGraw-Hill,
could lead to a discussion of dissent, privacy, rebellion, and
a whole range of problems involving citizens and the government. Neighbors, an animated, nine-minute film from International Film Bureau is about the use of force to settle dis-
putes, and That Rotten Tea Bag is only three minutes long;
this film, from Children's Cultural Foundation, was made by
teenagers and is about patriotism and protest, and about the
environment.

Film discussion groups have been held with all kinds
of people. They are useful for people who are nonreaders
or those who are highly visually oriented. They can be used
with any age or any group. A branch of The New York Public
Library held a film discussion group for teenagers. It was
entitled "Talking About Sex." They used the film, About Sex
(Texture Films), and staff members of a youth services organization were on hand to act as resource persons. A library in New Jersey held a film discussion group for senior
citizens. They showed films like Norman Rockwell's World,
Helen Keller, Fun Factory (about the Keystone Cops, Charlie
Chaplin and others), and some of the films of W. C. Fields.
The elderly people discussed their experiences and life in the
past. That library purposely avoided films dealing with the
problems of the elderly, feeling that that was not what they
wanted to talk about. At another program, in the same library, the elderly people watched Televisionland, a film of
short clips from television programs, and they were shown
some videotape equipment by the audiovisual specialist. They
then discussed modern means of communications, in the light
of their experiences.

Film discussion series have been held on the black experience in the United States. One of these covered such subjects as slavery, the black soldier, the generation gap, a film about a black teenager who is torn between her black and white friends, and a film about teaching the problems of prejudice. Other intergroup relations can be the subjects for film discussion groups. There are many films about the American Indian experience, such as Ballad of Crowfoot (National Film Board of Canada), Charley Squash Goes to Town (Learning Corporation) and The Pride and the Shame (Time-Life), that present the problems and provide material for discussion. Films about labor problems, such as Decision at Delano (Q-Ed Films) and Harvest of Shame (McGraw-Hill), present another intergroup conflict. The destruction of the environment is very filmable and very discussable. There are films on every aspect of the subject and some of them can evoke very strong feelings--feelings that can be channeled by a discussion leader into enlightening discussion.

Violence is another subject that is a film discussion natural. Violence, in its outward manifestations, can easily be presented by visual means. Violence takes many forms, and it seems to be pandemic. There is much debate, among experts, about the nature of human violence and there is a lot of good material available. For these reasons, violence seems to be an ideal subject for film discussion. Toys (Contemporary/McGraw-Hill) is a seven-minute color film in which children's toys become alive; they conduct a full-scale war, which is inter-cut with the faces of children. This short, powerful film provides much discussion material. Culloden (Time-Life) recreates the battle of that name and shows war, and the effects of war, in all their horror. Other aspects of violence--in the family, in the street--can be brought into the picture.

Another discussion group wrinkle could be used for this subject (and for others). Since much has been written on the various theories of violence, readings could be used along with the films. This method would allow you to bring together those aspects of the subject that are best presented visually, and those that are best presented verbally. As in book discussion groups, participants could be assigned a reading beforehand, and, at the session, they could watch a complementary film.

A librarian who has led a discussion group of this

kind said she thought the amount of material contained in a film plus a book was too much to discuss at one session. She suggested the possibility of alternating films and books. Shorter readings might be another answer. (This librarian wanted to try, but never had, another variation; participants would each be given a reading on a different aspect of the subject; they would then become, for purposes of the discussion, experts, and would be used as resource persons; the film would be shown to the group as a whole.)

The program of readings along with films mentioned above follows. It will be seen that, although the materials do complement each other, there would be a great many ideas and a great deal of information to be absorbed and discussed. Nevertheless, it represents an interesting experiment that has possibilities.

First session:

Film: 12-12-42 (Grove Press)
Reading: Norman Mailer, Armies of the Night

Second session:

Film: Two Men and a Wardrobe (Contemporary / McGraw-Hill)
Reading: Leonard Lewin, ed., Report from Iron Mountain on the Possibility and Desirability of Peace

Third session:

Film: My Childhood: James Baldwin (Benchmark Films)
Reading: W. H. Grier and P. M. Cobbs, Black Rage

Fourth session:

Film: Culloden (Time-Life)
Reading: Ernest Hemingway, A Farewell to Arms

Fifth session:

Film: Very Nice, Very Nice (Contemporary /McGraw-Hill)
Reading: Tom Wolfe, Kandy-Kolored, Tangerine-Flake Streamline Baby

Many other subjects are usable for film discussion groups. Banks and the Poor (Indiana University) presents a variety of viewpoints on banking practices. The Woman's Film (Newsreel) and Women on the March (Contemporary /

McGraw-Hill) present aspects of women's liberation. The
National Endowment for the Humanities and the City University of New York have put together several film discussion
programs. "The Identity Crisis" uses The Hand (Contem-
porary/McGraw-Hill), A to B (Time-Life), and such feature
films as Loneliness of the Long Distance Runner, The Overcoat and Member of the Wedding. "The Uses of the Past"
uses Black History: Lost, Stolen or Strayed (BFA), The
Island Called Ellis (McGraw-Hill), All the King's Men and
others. "Freedom and Responsibility" uses films about
Socrates, Galileo, and the Nuremberg trials, and one about
an important case in law in which a ship was abandoned. A
difficulty with many of these films is that they are very long.
They have, however, been successfully used in library discussion groups.

Recordings and books

The use of recordings with books in discussion groups
presents several interesting possibilities. Since poetry should
be heard as well as seen, the use of recordings in a poetry
discussion group is highly desirable. There are many excellent recordings of poetry on the market; the poems are
often read by the poets themselves, or they are read by some
of the best actors, and these readings bring the poetry to life
--completing the poetic process.

A music discussion group would obviously need to use
recordings. One group used LeRoi Jones's book, Black
Music. There were four sessions: "New Wave in Jazz,"
"John Coltrane," "Black Mysticism," and "Rhythm and Blues
and the New Black Music." Participants borrowed a copy of
the book and a variety of recordings for each subject.
Twenty-five enthusiastic adults and teenagers attended.

Another music discussion group ran for several years
at the same library. It was entitled "Music, History and
Ideas," and it followed the same pattern; a book, or books,
was available for each member, and they could also borrow
recordings related to the subject under discussion. (Records
were also played during the sessions.) Some of the books
used were Music, History and Ideas by Hugo Leichentritt,
Beethoven; His Spiritual Development by John W. Sullivan,
French Music; From the Death of Berlioz to the Death of
Faure by Maring Cooper, Schumann and the Romantic Age by
Marcel Brion, and the essays of Romain Rolland. Each

session was devoted to either a musical period, or to a major composer such as Bach or Beethoven. The discussion leader had to be musically knowledgeable; in both these cases, librarians were the leaders, but potential leaders could probably be found in the community.

There are other possibilities for music discussion groups. The development of American music, for example, could be covered, tying in the literature and art of each period with the music. The development of rock music alone would make material for a series of discussions. All kinds of folk music could be used as bases for discussion; it could be tied in with the historical events, personalities, or customs that it celebrates.

Other media that could be the bases for discussions are painting, drawing and sculpture. One would probably have to either use slides or obtain very good reproductions. An artist or other knowledgeable person might be wanted as a resource person. The works of an artist, a school of artists, a period in art history, or a theme could be the basis for a discussion. The historical and social backgrounds could be explored as well as the artists' techniques. Such a discussion could be very beneficial, since most people don't explore a work of art in any depth or for any length of time. Supplementary readings might be used in place of, or in addition to, a resource person.

In the East Meadow (N.Y.) Public Library there is a discussion group that is not tied to any medium or group of media; they use records, tapes and "whatever else is relevant" to stimulate discussion. It is a morning group entitled "Mental Encounters," and they talk about films, the theatre, contemporary problems and other things that interest them.

Discussion groups: a summary and checklist of preparations

KINDS (media)

Print media--can use books, pamphlets, magazines, newspapers or any combination

Film

Film and one or more print media

Recordings

Recordings and one or more print media

Paintings, drawings, sculpture, etc. and one or more print media

Other--any combination of above

MATERIALS

Print media--readings for each participant and for leaders

Film--films to be shown to group at the session

Recordings--to be played for group at session, and to be borrowed

Paintings, drawings, sculpture, etc.--reproductions and slides to be viewed at session, readings for each participant

EQUIPMENT

Chairs

Tables--desirable but not essential

Ash trays--if smoking allowed

Pencils and paper

Projector(s)

Record player

STAFF

One or two trained leaders--allow several hours of preparation time for each session, as well as time at session (staff can often be supplemented with outside leaders, from, e.g., schools and colleges, library users)

Projectionist--unless leaders are experienced, probably desirable to have projectionist separate

Clerk--to charge out materials, if large group and only one leader

AUDIENCE

Best for ten to twenty participants, but groups work with five to twenty-five or thirty

Adults and teenagers

SESSIONS

Number--one, or a series of three or four, or longer series up to fifteen or sixteen (some groups continue year after year)

Spacing--one or two weeks apart

Length--from one to two hours

SPACE

Size--400 sq. ft. adequate for most groups (even a film can be shown in a small space to a small group)

Location--quiet and away from public use area, or in such an area when not used by public

SUBJECTS (Examples)

Economic, social and political problems--foreign affairs, women's rights, destruction of the environment, urban problems, mental health, drugs, sex, capital punishment, war, intellectual freedom, democracy, privacy, minority groups, violence

Philosophical problems--free will and determinism, illusion and reality, beauty, truth, morality

Poetry--modern American, English, Black, American Indian, Romantic, war, individual poets

Drama--Greek, modern, American, tragedy, comedy, theatre of the absurd, individual dramatists

Fiction--modern, great, American, European, science fiction, women novelists, protest novels, experimental

Music--Romantic, rock, American, Black, European, individual composers, avant garde

Art--modern, European, American, great art of all ages, primitive, avant garde, individual artists

General series--Great Books, Significant Modern Books, American Idea, Black Experience, Oriental Thought

NOTES

1. Sigler, Ronald F. "A Study in Censorship: The Los Angeles 19," Film Library Quarterly, Spring 1971, p. 37.
2. Elsmo, Nancy. "Junior High Book Discussions," Wisconsin Library Bulletin, Sept. 1966, pp. 279-80.

Chapter 2

FILM SHOWINGS

　　Films are useful in many kinds of programs. They
appeal to all ages, and have been successfully used in programs with preschool and elementary school children, teenagers, the middle-aged and the elderly. Films can be used
by themselves, or in combination with music, dance, drama,
poetry readings and lectures. They can be the basis for a
discussion group, or the subject of a workshop. In this
chapter, we are dealing with film showings of interest to
teenagers and adults only. (Their use in discussion groups
is covered in Chapter 1; their use in film workshops is
covered in Chapter 5; and in combination with other media,
Chapter 6. Film programs for children are discussed in
Chapter 7.)

Popularity of film programs

　　Film showings are the most usual kind of library program. One reason is that films are widely available, many
thousands having been produced in the last fifteen years.
Furthermore, the art of the film has become tremendously
popular, especially with the young. There are some indications that, now, films are being thought of as old hat--cer-
tainly live performers are often more popular--but film programs continue, and will continue, to be very popular.

　　Another reason for the popularity of film programs is
that they seem to be an easy kind of program to produce.
They can be simple and successful, if one is careful--or they
can be disasters. The reason for this proclivity to disaster
is that, with films, attention must be paid to many details
that are not present in other programs.

The projectionist

First, one must have an experienced projectionist--
one who is thoroughly familiar with the projector and who
will know what to do in an emergency. In spite of all precautions things can go wrong. They usually don't, if one
has prepared well, but they can. Films break. They jam
in the projector. Bulbs burn out. So the more knowledgeable the projectionist is, the better.

If possible, the projectionist should be a separate
staff member. He should have no other duties while films
are running, so he can watch for developing problems. He
must watch the focus and the sound, loss of the film loops,
trouble developing in the projector, etc. These things can
happen very quickly, and they must be quickly attended to
or both film and projector can be badly damaged. It is also
wise to have a backup projectionist, in case of sickness,
death or any other adversity. One library that was presenting many film programs trained every staff member to
run a projector. Fortunately, it is easy to learn.

The projector

If the library doesn't own a projector, there are
several possibilities. For a few showings--if, for example,
one wanted to test the potential popularity of film showings--
a projector could be borrowed. Other libraries, museums,
schools and colleges are some possible sources of 16mm projectors. Individuals often own 8mm projectors. New, 16mm
projectors are expensive, but if film showings are to become
part of a library's permanent programming schedule, it would
be important to have two or more. Consult various issues
of Previews and consumer magazines for ratings and discussion of makes and models.

It is possible to buy a used projector, but as a recent
article on the subject says, "the rule is a definite buyer
beware."[1] The article gives some rules for testing the projector. Listen to the projector and see if it squeaks,
whistles, clatters or jerks through the motions. Take 100
feet of unused black leader (from a processing laboratory)
and run it through. If there are scratches on the film, don't
buy. Look at the film gate for rough spots. Be sure the
projector can take the strain of running the length of films
you want to show. Check the focus and look for cracked

condensers in front of the projector lamp. Check the sprockets for missing points and the pull-down claw movement for missing pins. Run a sound film through without picture and listen to sound. Run the picture without the sound. Adjust the framer so the frame line shows on the screen; it should be steady. If the projector has only sound speed, have it converted, in the shop where you buy it, to run at silent speed too. It will only cost a little if it is done when you buy it, but a lot more later. The article ends with a final caveat; "Get a good guarantee and check it out before you finally accept any piece of equipment and part with your money."

Other equipment

In addition to the projector itself, one should have several extra pieces of equipment. An extra projection lamp is essential, since they don't last long. Be sure the projectionist knows how to change it quickly. The electrical outlet may be some distance from where the projector must be placed so an extension cord is necessary. A set of take-up reels of the right size is important. Otherwise the films may have to be rewound during the program, causing delays and annoyance.

Acquisition of films

The next thing a film showing needs is films. They can be acquired in several ways: they can be purchased, leased, rented, or borrowed free of charge. If films are being bought, one would naturally want to be sure they are going to be used fairly frequently over a long period of time. Most films can be previewed by would-be purchasers. When films are going to be used for a lot of programs, but it appears that they might date or that interest in the subject will wane, they can be leased. One company leases films for one year for a third of the purchase price. After three years, you have bought the film.

Rental Films. Many films will be shown only once or twice; these can be rented. Experience has shown that the companies that rent films are usually efficient; that is, the films come a day or two ahead of the program, and they are the right films. That doesn't mean that one shouldn't be watchful, however. When films are rented, there are rules

about their showing. Some companies are fussy about these
rules, and some are not. Often, for instance, one is not
allowed to advertise rental films. Sometimes, each showing
must be paid for, so if the film is going to be shown twice
in one day, additional fees would be paid. Sometimes the
rental is for a day, or for two or three days. Usually the
film must be shown at a specified place and time. The library pays the return postage, and should insure the film
even if it is not required. Fortunately postal insurance
rates are cheap, as are mailing rates for library materials.
The package can be marked, Library Rate--16mm Films, or
Special Fourth Class Rate--16mm Films. Library rate is
cheaper and can be used by specified organizations only.
They should also be sent special delivery. The company's
catalog will give their rules and will often provide an order
form. Most libraries will probably not want to rent a lot of
films as that would be very expensive. But many films are
available for from $10 to $20 and when a film that costs
$300 can be rented for $15, rentals are worth a look.

Free-Loan Films. The category of most interest to
many libraries is that of the free-loan film. As with most
free things, there are some drawbacks, but if the emptor
caveats, there are many good free films to be found. The
first thing to know is that free films are not always entirely
free. Usually, one must pay the postage--sometimes both
ways--and sometimes a deposit is required. Then, those
lending the films are often inefficient. Some will send substitute films that you won't want. Sometimes the films are
late. Sometimes the wrong film is sent by mistake. Occasionally a film won't come at all. And whenever films are
used, one must be sure they are not on the reels backward
or upside down. So when using films, alertness is a pre-
requisite; check in plenty of time to be sure the right film,
on the reel the right way, arrives at the right time. If the
distributor is close enough, some of these problems can be
avoided by picking up and returning the film in person.

There may be other problems with free films. Sometimes films from commercial sources have, not unnaturally,
commercials included. If the commercials are at the beginning or end of a film, one can avoid showing them. Sometimes they are not so blatant or objectionable that it would
matter anyway. Even if there are no commercials, a film
from a commercial source (or any source) may be propaganda
for a particular point of view. Whether or not it is shown
depends on the objective of the program. The program may be

designed to show different points of view, or to show examples of propaganda.

The availability of the films is important. Rental films, possibly because the renting agency has more than one copy, usually seem to be available. With free-loan films it varies. If the film is a popular one, or the subject is of seasonal interest, it is best to book a couple of months in advance. With rental films, they can sometimes be booked as little as two weeks ahead. All distributors, even of free-loan films, will confirm bookings. As far as the efficiency of the distributor is concerned, it is best to experiment and find the efficient ones.

Sources of free films

The sources of free films are many. State and regional libraries may have circuit collections of films and they will be the first places to check for free films. Professional baseball, basketball, football and hockey leagues and teams offer free films. They may cover a team's highlights for a season or cover a World's Series, Super Bowl or Stanley Cup playoff. Or they may be how-to-play films, with one or two players showing how to shoot baskets or play the infield. These films tend to be slightly chauvinistic but they have a lot of action. The consulates, information bureaus or airlines of some countries may provide free films--and sometimes speakers--for programs. Large corporations (Shell Oil Co., Ford Motor Co. and others) and some smaller companies produce and loan films to groups and organizations. These films may be well-produced and have some useful information, in spite of their obvious propaganda purpose.

The United States Government is a big producer of films. More than 1500 films are available free from 47 different Federal agencies. Colleges and universities use films and libraries may be able to borrow from them. Museums, scientific and historical associations sometimes have films they will lend. Religious organizations, labor unions and organizations, such as environmental groups, that are promoting a cause may have films to lend. National health organizations such as the American Cancer Society and the National Multiple Sclerosis Society have free films. Films dealing with social and economic problems may be available from such organizations as Planned Parenthood and similar groups, agencies concerned with drug abuse and prevention, organizations working with the elderly, and consumer agencies. Youth organizations like the Boy Scouts and Girl Scouts have films available.

Film clubs and individual collectors are an important source of free films. These are usually 8mm or super 8mm films, and often include such unfailingly popular films as those of Charlie Chaplin and Laurel and Hardy. Sometimes the collectors will come along with the films, and they are often very knowledgeable. One student of films, who also collected them, not only provided his films free, but also provided an enriching commentary.

Then there are the individuals who make their own films. Sometimes they are in college or high-school film courses. Often they are experimenting on their own or they have formed clubs. They produce animated films, documentaries and films with actors; many of them are imaginative, funny, thoughtful and well-photographed. To find them one should contact the teachers of film or photography in the schools and colleges, contact youth centers, talk to library users (particularly those borrowing books on film making), watch local newspapers, and talk to the proprietors of stores that sell the necessary equipment.

Getting the room ready

There are a number of important things to do before projecting. The room must be made dark. During the day, one may have to fasten some opaque materials, such as construction paper or heavy cloth, over the windows. Chairs must be arranged so the audience will have a clear, full view of the screen. Avoid putting chairs in front of the projector. The screen should be raised as high as it will go, and it should be placed so that an opening door won't cast light on it.

The placing of the projector speaker is important. Check the acoustics when the film is running. Often the speaker is best placed in front of and at the center of the screen, and raised off the floor. But experimentation might show it is better raised high and off to one side of the screen. Put it on something solid and steady such as a stool or table. Remember the best spot and always use it. If power lines must be placed so the audience will have to

step over them, tape them to the floor; one can't afford to
lose a member of the audience with a broken neck.   The
projector should be placed so that the picture exactly fills
the screen.   If the room is too small for that, changing to
a lens with a longer focal length might do it.   But sometimes there is no alternative, and it might be better to show
a film under less-than-ideal conditions than not show it at
all.   Except that if you can't get a sharp picture, or clear
sound, don't show films; that will send audiences away, never
to return.   If the audience is small, one can show a film in
a very small space.   During a high school "career night,"
the authors showed a film to small groups of teenagers, in
a space of not more than 100 sq. ft.   They just sat up close
to the small clear picture, and enjoyed it.   (There is a more
detailed discussion of seating at the end of this chapter.)

Projecting

The projectionist should clean the film gate on the
projector with a soft lintless cloth before running each film.
When threading the film, the end should not be allowed to
fall on the floor where it will collect dust.   Pinched reels
should not be used as they can damage the film.   Avoid as
much as possible, stopping and reversing the film, as the
film can be torn in that way.   Never put the films on a
radiator.   Films and take-up reels should be put in the
order in which they will be shown so time won't be lost between films.   Have the first film threaded and focused before the audience arrives.   Help the projectionist adjust the
sound.   Long, narrow rooms are a problem, since the sound
is often too loud near the front and too soft at the back.   Be
alert to changes in focus and tell the projectionist.   Silent
films made before 1920 should be run at "silent speed."
Silent films made after 1920 are usually run at "sound speed,"
in which case the amplifier should be turned off.

When running sound films, be sure the sound switch is
on.   If the voice is not synchronized with lip movements, the
lower loop of the film may be too big.   If the sound is indistinct, one can try adjusting the treble dial; spoken words
are often more distinct if the treble is fairly high.   If there
is a manual with the projector, it will pay to study it.   If
there isn't one, try to get it.

All these technical details should be checked in plenty
of time before the program so that any deficiencies can be

corrected. One might need to borrow another projector, to
buy an extension cord, or to get more room-darkening materials. Know in advance where you can get those things
you might need, and allow time to get them. The foregoing
might seem formidable to the uninitiated, but if a little care
is exercised, film programs usually run very smoothly, and
with a little practice it will all seem routine.

Previewing films

Something else needs to be done before one has a
film program, and it is very important; if it is at all possible, the film should be previewed; one can not and should not
depend on reviews. There may be some exceptions to this
rule. A well-known film like Man of Aran, for example,
about which much has been written, might not have to be previewed. But even then, it would be helpful for the person
introducing the program to see it himself.

There are several excellent reasons for previewing.
First, one needs to check the technical qualities: color,
sound, focus. Then, the effectiveness of the film in presenting its subject should be considered. Is it original?
Does it raise questions? Does the filmmaker show a bias?
Will it be offensive to anyone? These are all questions that
the previewer might ask, depending on the film and the purpose of the program. Having a bias, or being offensive,
doesn't necessarily exclude the film from the program, but
at least one will want to be aware of these qualities, and
either prepare the audience for what is coming, or be ready
for audience reaction.

The authors had an experience that emphasizes the
importance of previewing. They were showing what they
thought to be a perfectly harmless Pearl White film. It was
being shown to a racially mixed audience, and, to the authors'
horror, some of the characters in that film displayed all the
worst stereotypes that have been associated with black people.
If the film had been seen first, they would have either substituted another film, or carefully introduced the Pearl White
film.

Introducing the film

One of the main reasons for previewing is to prepare

to introduce it. All films should be introduced, but some
should be introduced more than others. A brief, well-pre-
pared introduction can add to the audience's appreciation and
understanding of the film. At the same time, one can mention, or describe, library materials that will also add to
their understanding or enjoyment. Furthermore, these things
will make them feel more at home in the library, and make
them more conscious that this is a library program. If the
audience just comes, watches the film, and then leaves, the
program has not achieved its full potential. Of course, if
one can get a guest expert to introduce the films, that would
be great. But by viewing the film first, and possibly doing
some background reading, one can make a satisfactory introduction. It might also be useful to consult experts on the
subject of the film, or filmmakers, or film librarians.
Sometimes members of the audience can make enlightening
comments and they should be encouraged. Sometimes they
can make boring, pointless or too long comments (so can
experts and librarians) but it is worth giving them a chance.

Experimental and avant garde films particularly need
to be introduced, since audiences will often not feel at home
with the new techniques or styles of filmmaking. One can
give some background on the film, describe the filmmaker's
techniques or tell what he is trying to achieve. Renais-
sance (Pyramid Films) is an example of fascinating special
effects; a room explodes and puts itself together again. The
audience will certainly want to know how the filmmaker
achieved these startling effects. Moon, 1969 (Scott Bartlett)
is a poetic interpretation of a trip through space, using video-
graphic techniques. The sound and images are purposely
garbled and indistinct. The audiences should be warned about
that and the techniques should be described. Around Perception (National Film Board of Canada) is a computer-made
film that may arouse feelings of annoyance or anger in the
audience, and unless that is the purpose of the program, it
may be wise to tell them in advance.

Films that are important in film history and films
dealing with early filmmakers, such as La Fantasie de
Méliès (Blackhawk) or Abel Gance, Yesterday and Tomorrow (Contemporary/McGraw-Hill) are enhanced by some
background on the techniques used, and on the filmmaker's
place in film history. Controversial films may need introduction, and one should assess the potential audience. It
may be useful to explain to them why a film is being shown,
or even to tell them in advance that they may not agree with

it. Veronica (Jason Films) is about a black, middle-class
teenager who is trying to find herself and is trying to relate
to both black and white friends. Some black teenagers have
not liked it, but it can provide good discussion material if
it is introduced.

Many films are, of course, technically good, have no
special qualities that need introduction, and are not controversial. But they still should be previewed. They may be
moving, thought-provoking, sad, funny or beautiful and still
not fit into the program. They need to be examined with an
eye to style, content, mood, up-to-dateness, age level,
background needed by the audience and other factors to see
if they are exactly what is wanted for a particular program,
and for a particular audience. One of the authors needed a
film in a hurry, for a program for a woman's club.
Clouds (New Line Cinema) was recommended as a beautiful film. It is a film about Crow Indians; they talk about
their heritage, and they are seen at work and at an all-
Indian rodeo. It is a beautiful film, but it was a ho-hum
film for that group, and if it had been previewed, that fact
would have been recognized.

Where to show films

As with other programs, the where and when of a
film program is important. In spite of needing projectors
and an electrical power source, film showings can be given
in many places. Libraries have had film programs in vacant lots, playgrounds, parks, parking lots, on sidewalks,
in hospitals, nursing homes, drug rehabilitation centers,
churches and in many other places, as well as in libraries.
The Iowa State Traveling Library has taken films to county
fairs; they have devised a simple, efficient set of equipment,
and they have spread film showings, and news of the library,
far and wide.[2] They would get permission to use a small
space--as small as 10' x 20'--in a dark corner of one of
the tents. They carried ten to fifteen folding chairs, a six-
foot collapsible aluminum table for the projector, a collapsible typewriter table for the screen which was made from a
cardboard box two feet square with a black interior and a
white poster board. One staff member at a time was needed
for the program, which ran from noon to 9 p.m. each day of
the fair. Silent comedies, horror films, films about war
and natural history were among those shown. They attracted
people of all ages and occupations. The librarian talked

about the library's services, and there were discussions,
eagerly participated in, of the films.

When to show films

Just as film programs have been produced in every
imaginable place, they have been run at most imaginable
times. Libraries have shown films during mornings, afternoons and evenings, in every day of the week, and in every
season of the year. Some libraries, in business areas, have
had success with noontime programs. Others, in residential
areas, have attracted large audiences of housewives to
morning programs. Late afternoon programs have drawn
both teenagers and adults, in some places. Sometime Saturday or Sunday afternoon is a good time. So one can be
flexible in planning, and, considering the audience and other
factors, pick the best potential site and time.

The length of the program, the number of films used,
and the order in which they are to be shown are all factors
to be considered in deciding when to show them. The length
of the program will vary somewhat with the age of the audience. The very young, the elderly, and the sick may not
want to sit as long as the rest of us. The subject and the
nature of the films will also have a bearing on the length of
the program. Only the most devoted filmaniac would want to
sit through two hours of computer-made films, but a four-
and-a-half-hour film like The Sorrow and the Pity does
not seem long. On the average, from one to one and a half
hours seems like a good length for a film program.

Number of films on program

Film showings will usually be comprised of from one
to no more than four films. (There are exceptions.) With
more than four films, one would be using more time changing
the films than showing them, unless more than one projector
is available. Of course, if somebody is commenting on the
film, that time could be put to good use. Again, the number
of films depends on the kinds of films and on the kind of
audience. One fairly long film such as Robert Flaherty's
Man of Aran makes a good program by itself at 70 minutes.
A three-film program on New York City might include Summer Days (20 minutes), a portrait of two teenagers at
liberty during the summer in New York City; Golden Mountain on Mott Street (34 minutes), about the Chinese in New

York City; and Harlem Wednesday (10 minutes), which
evokes the mood and activities of a Wednesday in Harlem.
Or one might want one long film and a short opener. For
a program on art, The Louvre, a 45-minute film, could
be used, and the program could be opened with God Is Dog
Spelled Backwards, a four-minute film in which hundreds
of the world's great works of art flash by.

Order of showing

The order in which films are shown is important.
Pace, style, and length should be varied so that rigor mor-
tis doesn't start in the audience. With a short film and a
long one, the short one would probably be used as a curtain
raiser. A fast-moving film, or a light film, might be shown
after one that was more serious or slow-moving. On the
other hand, if a particularly impressive, thought-provoking
film is being shown, that could be the finale so that the audience would go out thinking about it. Think about the audience
and the purpose of the program. One might not want to
show several animated films together, unless one was trying
to compare styles of animation. Or one might show different
kinds of films together for ironic contrast. The point is that
the order should be thought out. A haphazard arrangement
may work, but why not make the program better?

Selection of films

But before films can be arranged in a particular
order, they must be selected. They are, of course, selected with an eye to that order, as well as to the length
of the films, the length of the program and the technical
qualities of the films. Other bases for selection might be
age, educational level, race, religion, national origin and
sex. These factors are clues to the interests of the potential audience. But they are not conclusive. Interests cut
across all these lines, and interest, after all, is of para-
mount importance in the selection. Methods of determining
interests are discussed in another section.

Known interest is not the only criterion for selection,
however. Sometimes people don't know they will like something until they see it, and, in fact, they often don't know
that that thing exists. Even with television, colleges, film
societies, film festivals and individual collectors showing

more and more films, there are still many films that one
might never see. And in many parts of the country--except
for television--even these outlets do not exist. Film programs are, therefore, a chance for libraries to provide useful, interesting, stimulating, humorous and moving filmic
experiences to persons that would not otherwise have been
aware of them. Of course, getting the public to attend these
films may be difficult, but that's where canny selection comes
in.

If one is showing the films of Charlie Chaplin or
Laurel and Hardy (both very popular with all ages) one might,
at the same time, show such silent film stars as Harry Lang-
don, Charlie Chase or Snub Pollard; these comedians are
little-known to the general public, but would be enjoyed.
For a program of traditional films, one can slip in one unusual or experimental film. Not everybody will like it, but
if it is a short film, they will tolerate it, and some will be
surprised. If the program deals with the United States, An
American Time Capsule (Pyramid) can be shown as a change
of pace. This film covers all of American history by showing 1300 pictures in less than three minutes. If the program
is on dance, Dance Squared (National Film Board of
Canada) could be shown; it is a four-minute film using animated geometric shapes.

Variety programs

The possible subjects for a film showing are almost
limitless. At least, there are enough to fill any librarian's
programming lifetime. One possible subject is no subject.
If the library is in an area where people will readily attend
film programs, or the time is right, or the program can be
made attractive enough, imaginative, variety film showings
can be very successful. This is often true when people have
a lot of spare time, such as vacationers, retired persons,
people wanting to fill up lunch hours, Saturdays and Sundays,
some housewives, the unemployed and the ill or disabled.
This kind of programming allows for flexibility of choice.
If one is not confined to a subject, the most imaginative,
humorous, beautiful or moving films available can be chosen.
It also allows more freedom if last minute substitutions must
be made, or if one wants to respond quickly to an event by
getting a film on the subject.

There are innumerable combinations. A silent comedy,

an animated film, a computer-made film, and a documentary might make a program. Or a showing could include a nature film, a travel film, and a film about some historical event or period. One actual program included: People Soup (Learning Corporation), a 13-minute film in which two boys, in a kitchen, mix some odd ingredients into their food, which turns them into animals; Rock in the Road (BFA), a 10-minute, animated film on the need for tolerance; K-9000 (Creative Film Society) an 11-minute, animated spoof of 2001; Barber Shop (Blackhawk), a 23-minute W. C. Fields film. Another program included: Charley Squash Goes to Town (Learning Corporation), a 5-minute, animated film about an Indian who tries to follow everybody's advice; Minestrone with Music (Grove Press), a 6-minute animated film that touches various aspects of modern life; The National Flower of Brooklyn (out of print), a 12-minute evocation of the history of the Brooklyn Bridge through the use of old pictures, newsreels and radio broadcasts; The Ride (Contemporary/McGraw-Hill), an 8-minute slapstick comedy.

Subjects for showings

Usually, film showings are built around a particular subject. Often, a library will present a series of showings, with each showing devoted to a different subject. That kind of program will draw both those people with special interests, and those with a variety of interests who just want to see some films. For film showings built around subjects, there are many kinds of possibilities. Programs of topical interest are useful. Films on such subjects as China, American Indians, women's liberation, consumerism, the destruction of the environment or impeachment can be shown when interest in the subject arises. Films on art do well in some places, and there are many kinds of arts and many excellent films to choose from. Music, dance, theatre, poetry, painting, sculpture, and printmaking are some subjects.

A poetry series could include films on William Butler Yeats, Robert Frost, Dylan Thomas, James Dickey, Allen Ginsberg and Lawrence Ferlinghetti. For sculpture, there are films available on Michelangelo, Giacometti, Barbara Hepworth, Henry Moore, Jose de Creeft and others. There are many fine films on painters and painting, including Rembrandt, Picasso, Frans Hals, Jackson Pollock, Marc Chagall and Paul Klee. There are films dealing with popular, classical and folk music, such as It Ain't City Music (Tom Davenport Films) and Andrés Segovia (Irving Lesser), as well as such narrower categories as blues and jazz.

Dance is a subject that lends itself naturally to filmic treatment and there are many films on classical, modern and folk dancing. A program on modern dance might include such imaginative films as Capriccio (James Seawright), which is a special effects film made with television equipment that produces multiple exposures of two modern dancers, and Nine Variations on a Dance Theme (Radim), which explores the movements of a modern dancer. A ballet program could include Behind the Scenes with the Royal Ballet (Warner Brothers/Seven Arts), Dance: New York City Ballet (Indiana University) and Galina Ulanova (Audio/Brandon), a film about a Russian ballerina. A program on folk dancing could include Norwegian, African, Scottish and Spanish dances.

Natural history films make beautiful and fascinating programs and although many are now being shown on television, many are not. They are also much better when seen on a big screen. There are fine films about white-throated sparrows, monarch butterflies, animals of the Arctic and life in sand dunes among other more usual nature films.

Films about places are often popular, and showings can be organized in a number of ways. One might do a series about cities, and again there are many films in this category. Rome, London, Paris, Venice, and Kuala Lumpur can all be brought into the library, and they have been filmically treated in many ways. A good program could be produced about Paris alone. 1848 (Radim), a 22-minute film about the uprising of that year in Paris, could start the program. Eugene Atget (Contemporary/McGraw-Hill), a 10-minute poetic evocation of a Paris morning at the turn of the century, could follow. Then would come In Paris Parks (Contemporary/McGraw-Hill), a $13\frac{1}{2}$-minute, 1955 film about the day of some children in a Parisian park. And the pièce de résistance would be The Louvre (EBEC), a 45-minute film in color, that presents the evolution of that museum and some of the magnificent works of art it contains. So many films have been made about New York City that several series could be done on that subject. (For example, The New York Public Library's film catalog lists 35 films on New York City.) Showings can be given about countries, groups of countries and continents. Many films are available on Brazil, Great Britain, Africa and South America, to name a few. One library had a program about places of the past, with films about Pompeii, ancient Peru and Angkor Wat. Another library showed films of island life, including Pitcairn Island, Easter Island, Trinidad and the Queen Elizabeth Islands of the Arctic.

Biographical films suggest some ideas. For instance, there are a number of films on women; they include such diverse people as Angela Davis, Eleanor Roosevelt, Grandma Moses, Frances Flaherty (the wife of Robert), Madalyn Murray O'Hair (the advocate of atheism) and Imogen Cunningham (a photographer). There is a wide range of other biographical films from Gandhi to Ulysses S. Grant, and including Daniel Berrigan, Bertrand Russell, Dr. Ernest Jones and Wilfrid Thesiger. From the available biographical films one could make a number of interesting combinations.

Religion is a possible subject for a series of showings. There are films on Buddhism, Hinduism, Atheism, Judaism, various forms of Christianity and others. There are a number of films about child care, mathematics, railroads, and migrant workers, indicating the diversity of available films.

Another possibility is to group films by form. One could have showings on abstract, animated or avant-garde films. And, in fact, these categories often contain the most interesting films, but they are not usually classifiable by subject. They are also not widely shown, and that makes them ideal for library programs. A librarian in Atlanta, Georgia, for example, was told by a film critic that, "Atlanta movie theaters simply do not offer the more complicated and sophisticated films at their theaters because the general public is not educated in film language and has no appreciation for the cinema as an art form."[3]

One example of this kind of program was given at the Boulder (Colorado) Public Library.[4] It was a Norman McLaren festival. Sixteen films of this indefatigable animater were shown. The films were arranged chronologically to give a feel for his developing techniques. The program was shown on three consecutive days and drew two hundred people--a respectable number for any library film program. This program also, incidentally, indicates another idea for a film showing: the works of one filmmaker or director. Or, one could have programs devoted to an actor, such as Buster

Keaton or Charlie Chaplin (who was his own director--and
producer and scriptwriter). For filmmakers, one could
show the work of such greats as Robert Flaherty, modern
documentary filmmakers like Julien Bryan, avant garde
filmmakers like Stan Brakhage, or young filmmakers like
Scott Morris.

Films popular with teenagers

There are several kinds of films that teenagers like.
"Sports above all," says one librarian who works with teenagers. And what they like most are those films that show
action; films that are borrowed from the professional basketball, baseball, football and hockey leagues and teams, and
those that show those teams in actual games; and films of
action from other sources, such as Sports Action Profiles:
Calvin Murphy (Oxford) and The Professionals: Basketball
(Warner Brothers/Seven Arts), that shows Wilt Chamberlain
and Jerry West in action. Films that teach one how to play
a game are not, says this librarian, as popular as the action
films, although teenagers do attend them. A film of this
kind, such as Willis Reed: Center Play (Schloat Productions), might be included on a program with an action film.
Aikido, judo and karate are subjects that have become very
popular in recent years and one might have a program including Aikido (Japan Publications Trading Co.), a demonstration of the techniques of that sport, and San Nukas
(Black Horizon Films), a film that shows students learning
judo and karate, and the instructor of a school in Harlem
discussing the importance to black people of learning these
sports as a means of developing pride, dignity and self-
discipline. Here again, one can include the unusual or
avant-garde film with the more popular, to develop an appreciation of films. If Tokyo Olympiad (Jan-Or) were
being shown, the short, beautiful diving sequence from Leni
Riefenstahl's poetic documentary of the 1936 Olympic Games
could be slipped in.

Science fiction and horror films are attended by
teenagers in large numbers. Many of these are feature
films and must, usually, be rented. But there are shorter,
often humorous, films, many made by young filmmakers,
that teenagers like. Invasion of the Teacher Creatures
shows ghoulish teachers rampaging through a school. Curse
of the House of Horrors is about the investigation of a
creepy old house which results in a series of murders, and

it is a spoof on old horror movies. And Flash is about a boy from another planet who saves the earth from an invader from outer space. All three films are made by teenagers and distributed by Youth Film Distribution Center.

Also available are clips of many of the famous horror movies. A librarian in the tiny town of Joice, Iowa, used these to put on film programs for the horror film addicts of that community.[5] She found that the younger teenagers were engrossed in horror comics, movies and models of the characters. So she decided to try some programs that would show the history of the horror film and would encourage discussion of the techniques used in making those films. She collected books on filmmaking and some of the classic horror stories for the teenagers to borrow. Some of the films were The Mummy, The Mummy's Tomb, The Bride of Frankenstein, Dracula, Dr. Jekyll and Mr. Hyde, Tarantula, My Son the Vampire and The Curse of Frankenstein. The audiences entered fully into the spirit of the programs; they played games and did pantomimes (sometimes on their own) related to the films, and they discussed the films.

Films on crafts, such as Macrame (produced by Stelios Roccos), and films about their special interests, such as oceanography and archeology, will draw some teenagers. Films about their problems are also of interest. About Sex (Texture Films) is such a film; it is also a good example of a film that should be previewed, because of the language used by the teenagers and because of one explicit scene; one could then be ready for any reactions to the film. VD Questions, VD Answers (produced by Herbert Bernard and Harry Robin) and Phoebe (McGraw-Hill), about the problems of a pregnant teenager, are other films in this category. Films of this kind are best used with a guest expert, to clear up any questions the films may provoke and to lead further discussion of the subjects.

One librarian had an especially interesting experience with teenagers in a New York State reformatory.[6] This reformatory held many black and Puerto Rican teenagers, aged 14 to 17. Their usual film fare, in the reformatory, had been the sappy, harmless television-type movies, which finally caused a near-riot. The librarian, finally, was able to bring in other kinds of films, and made the immediate discovery that what they liked were the best and most sophisticated films. Among those they particularly liked were

Un Chien Andalou, Potemkin, Two Men and a Wardrobe, Neighbors, The Hand, The General, The Gold Rush and Nanook of the North. They found none of the drug films good, except a couple made by teenagers. If nothing else, this shows the folly of generalization, and the folly of under-estimating anybody.

Not a few teenagers are interested in the art of film-making. One could have programs of films like The Sound-men, The Stuntman, and Special Effects which show how the professionals do those things, and include films made by other teenagers to show them what their contemporaries have accomplished.

Teenagers, and children, as well as most adults, like the films of the old-time comedians. The people in rural Iowa mentioned earlier, the black and Puerto Rican teenagers in the reformatory, and middle-class suburbanites all like the films of such favorites as Buster Keaton, Charlie Chaplin, Laurel and Hardy and W. C. Fields. Many of these films are short and are available to libraries at reasonable prices, both to buy and to rent. If a sure-fire program is wanted to bring the crowds into the library, this is it.

Aside from the subjects of the films, there are several ways to have a film showing. One could have a single showing for a special purpose, such as celebrating a holiday or an occasion, or because a special film is avail-able, or because the filmmaker or other person is available. One library, for example, every year during the Christmas season, shows The Nutcracker (Warner Brothers /Seven Arts). This is a 60-minute film of Tchaikovsky's ballet featuring famous dancers from around the world, and it makes a fine holiday program, drawing a family audience. Libraries often present a series of film showings. These can all be on one general subject such as the arts, or each showing can be devoted to a different subject. A series can be designed to appeal to a particular group such as mothers of pre-school children, businessmen, teenagers, the elderly or others. They could be seasonal programs designed to take advantage of good weather or leisure time. One might have a spring series or a summer series, or a Saturday afternoon series.

Film showings can also be unplanned or unstructured, to take advantage of special situations. One library showed films, during the summer, to any group that appeared in the library and asked for them. Another library had continuous film showings during a school strike.

Guest experts

Having an expert present to comment on the films
and to answer questions is another variation from the straight
showing. This can either be an expert on filmmaking, or a
subject expert, depending on the program. The authors
found a film editor who was persuaded to talk about the
work of an editor at a showing of some avant-garde films,
and who also, incidentally, answered the questions of some
teenagers about opportunities in the film industry. At another program, a film historian showed some of the mile-
stones of film history and commented on their significance.
Used in this series were The Great Train Robbery (Film
Classic Exchange), one of the first films to tell a story;
Abel Gance, Yesterday and Tomorrow (Contemporary/Mc-
Graw-Hill), about the innovative French director; and The
Great Director (Time-Life), about the work of D. W.
Griffith. In the Oak Park (Illinois) Public Library, an independent filmmaker showed some of his films, and talked
about the use of the camera. He then moved among the
audience and made a film of them, which they returned a
week later to see.[7]

Showcase for the young and unknown

As with other media, libraries have an admirable opportunity to show the work of young or unknown filmmakers.
This can be in the form of a festival or contest, or it can
be a series of straight film showings. The authors have
several times presented programs of films made by local
college students, always to overflow crowds. The Randalls-
town (Md.) Public Library has, for several years, been presenting programs of films made by teenagers, and it has become a regular feature of their programming. A file of
about forty young filmmakers has been built up, through the
years.[8]

Contests

The Los Angeles Public Library has had several successful contests for teenage filmmakers, and they have a
number of suggestions for those who wish to try one.[9] They
had some difficulty in finding films at first. They contacted
film organizations, recreation centers, high schools (teachers
and students), and they asked around among the teenagers

they saw; gradually they built a list of films and contacts. Once one has the contacts succeeding festivals become easier. They needed judges and they found the colleges a good source. Entry blanks were found to be useful. They provide material for publicity, and they can give such information as the age and experience of the filmmaker if one wants to divide the entries into categories. In Los Angeles, they showed the films in the order of the ages of the participants. This was found to be helpful when there were many participants.

Equipment presented some problems. They had several projectors lined up so they could show the films one after another. This was also useful since the projectors were getting long hard use, and several broke down during the festival. Most beginning filmmakers don't use sound films and to supply sound, use records, cassettes, and reel-to-reel tape of different sizes and speeds. It was therefore desirable to ask the entrants to bring their own sound equipment. It was felt that the library should supply, at least, a three-speed record player. Shears and splicing tape (8mm, super-8, and 16mm) were needed, as was an adapter so that super-8 film could be threaded on an 8mm projector. Since many of the teenagers were knowledgeable about films, they could be used as projectionists. Teenagers also helped with the publicity, handing out flyers and writing articles for school newspapers. They found that the room needed to be especially dark, since some of the films were under-exposed or were less sharp than professional films.

Prizes added greatly to the interest. The prizes were contributed by a music store, a book store, a camera shop and a gift shop; they were records, paperbacks, reels of film and posters of horror movies. There was no consensus about the value of the prizes and it was thought best to display them all and let the winners choose the prize they wanted in the order that they won. One festival was attended by two hundred people. Thirty-eight films were collected but only 21 could be shown because of projector breakdowns. Twenty-one films were shown at another festival, and although it lasted four hours, seventy people stayed to the end. Clearly both were successes.

The Providence Public Library is also sponsoring a film competition. 10 This contest was open to filmmakers of all ages and levels of experience and the films were to focus

on community problems and their solutions. Prizes were to
be awarded in the following categories: eighth grade and
under, ninth through twelfth grades, college, hobbyist and
professional. The winning entries would then be shown to
the public.

The room

For film showings, the subject of space deserves
some extra discussion. This is so because of the equipment involved. Factors that must be considered are the
size and type of screen, the size of the film, the type and
wattage of the projection lamp, and the focal length of the
lens. These things are considered in relation to the size
and shape of the room, and the size of the audience.

There are two main problems: where to place the
audience in relation to the screen; and where to place the
projector in relation to the screen. One film librarian suggests that experimentation is the best way. Simply move a
chair around to determine how close to the screen, how far
back from the screen, and how far to the sides the audience should sit. The same can be done for projection distance. Move the projector or screen back and forth to
determine the best distances. But there are some guidelines. A rule-of-thumb is that the minimum viewing distance is twice the height of the picture, and the maximum
viewing distance is eight times its height. The size of the
audience determines the width of the picture. And the width
of the picture is determined by its distance from the projector, and the focal length of the lens. The tables shown
on pages 42-43 are guides. But remember they are only
guides. College and high school students have crammed
themselves into every available space at some film showings
--breaking all the rules of audience seating but enjoying the
films. And with projection distances, there may be factors,
such as light leaking into the room, that make the rules
invalid. "In the final analysis," says the film librarian we
consulted, "you have to depend on your eyes." And, of
course, libraries--not commonly having a lot of money--may
not be able to buy all the lenses, projection lamps, screens
and projectors necessary for excellent viewing in every situation. In some cases, it may be better to show the films
under less than ideal conditions than not show them. If the
words can't be heard or the picture is too dark, naturally you
won't show the film. But for some kinds of films and some
audiences, perfect viewing conditions are secondary.

Screens

If a library is lucky enough to have a choice of screens, a screen can be chosen to fit the shape of the room, thus enhancing the viewing and in some cases allowing a larger audience to view the film. One film periodical gives the following advice:

> If you have a wide viewing area the matte screen is probably the best for bright projection because it reflects light evenly in all directions providing an adequate image when viewed from an oblique angle.
>
> If you have a narrower room you can use a lenticular screen, which is made up of a series of tiny cylindrical lenses that are embossed on the screen itself. It is quite bright over a fairly broad angle of viewing.
>
> If the audience sits directly in front of the screen, a beaded screen reflects light in a narrower angle, about 30 degrees. For a very narrow room, the best screen to use is the silver screen, coated with metallic aluminum, for it has a very narrow brightness reflection angle. It is also good for stereo projection with polarizing filters for its narrow angle of view will not result in double images.
>
> If you cannot darken the room properly for ideal projection conditions, there is the Kodak Ektalight Screen which gives good brightness for narrow angle viewing.[11]

Film showings (adults and teenagers): a summary and checklist of preparations

KINDS

Straight showing

Showing with commentary--by a director, editor, et al. or by a subject expert

Contest or festival--of locally made films

Showing as part of a larger celebration--e.g., an open house or a group of activities celebrating the culture of a country

(cont'd. on p. 44)

SEATING GUIDE

THEATER-STYLE SEATING FOR DIFFERENT ROOM SIZES

(FOR CONFERENCE-STYLE SEATING, USE ONE-HALF THE SEATING CAPACITY SHOWN)

Room Ratio 1:1				Room Ratio 4:3				Room Ratio 3:2				Room Ratio 2:1				Room Ratio 3:1			
Room Size—ft L x W	Viewing Angle* 50°	60°	90°	Room Size—ft L x W	Viewing Angle* 50°	60°	90°	Room Size—ft L x W	Viewing Angle* 50°	60°	90°	Room Size—ft L x W	Viewing Angle* 50°	60°	90°	Room Size—ft L x W	Viewing Angle* 50°	60°	90°
	Seating Capacity				Seating Capacity				Seating Capacity				Seating Capacity				Seating Capacity		
16x16	10	11	13	16x12	8	8	8	16x11	6	6	6	16x8	–	–	–	16x5	–	–	–
20x20	18	21	25	20x15	15	16	17	20x13	13	13	13	20x10	7	7	7	20x7	–	–	–
24x24	28	33	41	24x18	24	26	28	24x16	22	23	23	24x12	14	14	14	24x8	5	5	5
28x28	41	48	60	28x21	36	39	43	28x19	33	34	36	28x14	22	23	23	28x9	9	9	9
32x32	56	66	83	32x24	50	55	60	32x21	46	48	51	32x16	33	33	33	32x11	16	16	16
36x36	73	87	109	36x27	66	73	80	36x24	61	65	69	36x18	45	46	46	36x12	23	23	23
40x40	95	111	139	40x30	85	93	104	40x27	78	84	90	40x20	59	60	61	40x13	32	32	32
44x44	115	137	173	44x33	106	116	130	44x29	98	105	113	44x22	74	77	77	44x15	42	42	42
48x48	139	167	210	48x36	129	141	159	48x32	119	128	139	48x24	92	95	96	48x16	53	53	53
52x52	166	199	252	52x39	154	169	191	52x35	143	154	167	52x26	111	115	117	52x17	66	66	66
56x56	195	234	296	56x42	181	200	226	56x37	169	182	198	56x28	132	137	139	56x19	80	80	80
60x60	226	272	345	60x45	211	233	264	60x40	197	212	232	60x30	155	161	164	60x20	96	96	96
64x64	259	313	397	64x48	243	269	305	64x43	227	245	268	64x32	180	187	191	64x21	112	112	112
68x68	295	356	453	68x51	277	307	348	68x45	259	280	307	68x34	206	214	219	68x23	131	131	131
72x72	334	402	512	72x54	313	347	395	72x48	293	318	349	72x36	234	244	250	72x24	150	150	150
76x76	374	452	576	76x57	352	390	445	76x51	330	357	393	76x38	264	275	283	76x25	171	171	171
80x80	417	504	642	80x60	393	436	497	80x53	368	399	440	80x40	296	309	317	80x27	193	193	193
84x84	462	558	713	84x63	436	484	552	84x56	409	444	489	84x42	330	344	354	84x28	216	216	216

*The 90-degree figures should be used only with screens capable of producing good brightness characteristics in that range, and then only when maximum seating capacity is necessary.

This chart and the explanation on the facing page are from Kodak Publication No. S-16, copyright © 1969 by Eastman Kodak Company, and are reproduced by permission.

HOW TO USE THE SEATING GUIDE

Figure 1 illustrates the arrangement used for rooms listed in the guide. The screen location was selected to cover the maximum seating area for a room.

Capacity figures in the table are based on the use of two side aisles (each 3 feet wide), and a rear aisle 4 feet deep. Six square feet of space is allowed per person, which includes provision for a 42-inch aisle, front-to-back, after every fourteenth seat.

For legibility, members of the audience should be seated within the specified angles for the screen material being used and should not be seated closer to the screen than two times, nor farther than eight times, the *height* of the projected image. Minimum image height, for legibility, can be determined by dividing by eight the distance from the screen to the rear of the back row of seats. For visual effect, it is sometimes desirable to project an image somewhat larger than legibility standards specify. To avoid obstruction of the screen by the seated audience, and to establish minimum *ceiling* height, add 4 feet to the minimum image height. In addition, it may be necessary to add extra height to allow positioning of the screen to clear overhead obstructions.

Determination of the maximum viewing area depends on the material used for the screen. The KODAK EKTALITE Projection Screen has excellent brightness characteristics within a viewing area of 60 degrees. Most matte, and a few lenticular, front-projection screen materials can provide good brightness levels for viewing areas up to 90 degrees wide. Beaded front-screen projection materials, and the most commonly used rear-projection screen materials, can give good brightness in a viewing area of up to 50 degrees. Examples follow:

1. Known:

   a. Screen material—matte (60-degree viewing area).

   b. Room size—28 x 21 feet.

Find:

   a. Seating capacity for theater-style and for conference-style seating.

   b. Minimum image height.

   c. Minimum ceiling height.

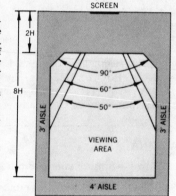

SCREEN

Figure 1

The room has a 4:3 ratio. Using a 60-degree viewing area, you find in the table that theater-style capacity is 39. Conference-style capacity, half that of theater-style, is 19. Allowing 4 feet for the rear aisle, the distance to the rear of the last row of seats is 24 feet. Dividing this distance by eight gives you a minimum image height of 3 feet. Adding 4 feet to the minimum image height gives you a minimum ceiling height of 7 feet.

2. Known:

   a. You plan to build a meeting room with theater-style seating for 90 people.

   b. Screen material—beaded.

Find:

Room dimension that will be suitable.

Fifty degrees is the recommended maximum viewing angle for beaded screens. In the table, under the 50-degree columns, you find that a 40 x 40-foot room will accommodate 93 seats, a 48 x 24-foot room will seat 92, and a 60 x 20-foot room—96. Your ultimate choice will depend on such factors as the dimensions of available rooms or space, the ceiling height required, etc.

How to Use the Seating Guide

Seating Arrangements

Matte, Lenticular, or KODAK EKTALITE Projection Screen

The diagram directly below shows the best viewing area for matte, lenticular, and KODAK EKTALITE screens.

The seats nearest the screen should not be closer than twice the height of the picture (2H); the rear seats should not be farther than 8 times the height of the picture (8H).

Beaded Screen

The diagram below shows the best viewing area for beaded screens.

The seats nearest the screen should not be closer than 2½ times the height of the picture (2½H); the rear seats should not be farther than 8 times the height of the picture (8H).

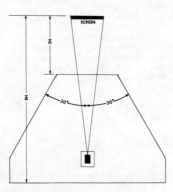 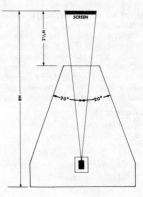

These diagrams and the chart with text on the facing page are from "How to Use the Kodak Pageant Sound Projector Model AV-126-TR," and are reproduced by permission by the Eastman Kodak Company.

MATERIALS

Films--8mm, super 8mm, or 16mm

Books, pamphlets, periodicals, recordings on the subject, or on film making--for display, for use in introduction or by commentator, or to be borrowed by audience

EQUIPMENT

Projector(s)--appropriate to film size (8mm projector has adapter for super 8 film); an extra projector is always desirable

(cont'd. on p. 48)

Screen · Lamp · Lens Combinations

Proper selection of screen, lamp, and lens for your particular setup is important. The screen image should be of adequate size and brilliance for comfortable viewing. With the wide variety of lamps and lenses available for your PAGEANT Projector, you can tailor your equipment to meet this requirement.

The chart shows the relation between projection distances and screen sizes for each of the currently available lenses. It is best to use a lens that provides a screen image of a height that is not less than one eighth of the distance from the screen to the back row of seats. If the image is smaller than this, the viewers in the back rows will not be able to see the fine detail in the pictures.

Make sure that the screen image is neither too bright nor too dark. If it is too bright, flicker may become objectionable; if too dark, detail will be lost in the shadow areas of the pictures.

Shown in the table are the maximum image widths or heights for adequate illumination on matte screens and on lenticular or beaded screens with those lamps recommended for use. These maximum widths or heights are for good projection conditions in a darkened room; they will have to be somewhat less if there is much stray light in the room.

Projection Lamp Wattage	Maximum Image Width or Height in Inches in a Darkened Room*							
	Shutter in 3-Blade Position				Shutter in 2-Blade Position			
	Matte Screen		Lenticular or Beaded Screen		Matte Screen		Lenticular or Beaded Screen	
	W	H	W	H	W	H	W	H
750	60	45	85	64	70	53	100	75
1000	70	53	100	75	80	60	120	90
1200	75	56	110	83	90	68	130	98

*With 2-inch lens alone, or with CINE-KODAK Bifocal Converter.

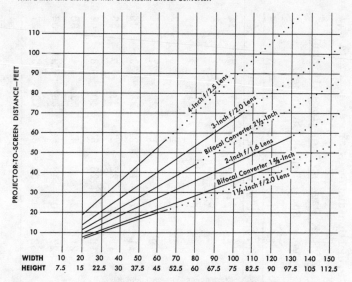

Solid lines equal or exceed recommended brightness.
SCREEN IMAGE—INCHES

Projection Distance Tables for KODAK Motion Picture Projectors

(Projection distances are approximate and are measured from projector gate to screen.)

KODAK Pageant Projectors (16 mm)								Screen-Image Dimensions (inches)	KODAK Super 8 Projectors						
Lens Focal Length (in inches)									Lens Focal Length (in millimeters) — Zoom —						
$\frac{1}{2}$	1	$1\frac{1}{2}$	$1\frac{5}{8}$	2	$2\frac{1}{2}$	3	4		15	$17\frac{1}{2}$	20	22	25	28	32
Projection Distances (in feet)									Projection Distances (in feet)						
$1\frac{1}{2}$	$2\frac{3}{4}$	$4\frac{1}{4}$	$4\frac{1}{2}$	$5\frac{1}{2}$	7	$8\frac{1}{2}$	11	9 x 12	3	$3\frac{1}{2}$	4	$4\frac{1}{2}$	5	$5\frac{1}{2}$	$6\frac{1}{2}$
$1\frac{3}{4}$	$3\frac{3}{4}$	$5\frac{1}{2}$	6	$7\frac{1}{2}$	$9\frac{1}{4}$	11	15	12 x 16	4	$4\frac{1}{2}$	$5\frac{1}{4}$	$5\frac{3}{4}$	$6\frac{1}{2}$	$7\frac{1}{2}$	$8\frac{1}{2}$
$2\frac{1}{4}$	$4\frac{1}{2}$	$6\frac{3}{4}$	$7\frac{1}{2}$	9	11	14	18	15 x 20	5	$4\frac{1}{2}$	$6\frac{1}{2}$	$7\frac{1}{4}$	$8\frac{1}{4}$	$9\frac{1}{4}$	$10\frac{1}{2}$
$3\frac{1}{2}$	$6\frac{3}{4}$	10	11	14	17	20	27	$22\frac{1}{2}$ x 30	$7\frac{1}{2}$	$8\frac{1}{2}$	$9\frac{3}{4}$	11	12	14	16
$4\frac{1}{2}$	9	13	15	18	22	27	36	30 x 40	$9\frac{3}{4}$	11	13	14	16	18	21
$5\frac{1}{2}$	11	17	18	22	28	33	45	$37\frac{1}{2}$ x 50	12	14	16	18	20	23	26
$6\frac{3}{4}$	13	20	22	27	33	40	53	45 x 60	15	17	20	21	24	27	31
8	16	24	26	32	40	48	64	54 x 72	18	20	23	26	29	33	37
11	21	32	35	42	53	64	85	72 x 96	23	27	31	34	39	44	50
13	27	40	43	53	66	79	106	96 x 120	29	34	39	43	49	54	62
16	32	48	52	64	79	95	127	108 x 144	35	41	47	51	58	65	75

Projection Distance Tables for KODAK EKTAGRAPHIC and CAROUSEL Slide Projectors
(Projection distances are approximate and are measured from projector gate to screen.)

Lens Focal Length (in inches)									Screen-Image Dimensions (in inches)			
1.4	2	3	4	5	7	9	11	4 to 6 (Zoom)	135-35mm	126	Super-Slide	Single-Frame Filmstrip
Projection Distances (in feet)												
2	3	4	$5\frac{1}{2}$	7	10	$12\frac{1}{2}$	$15\frac{1}{2}$	$5\frac{1}{2}$ to $8\frac{1}{2}$	$13\frac{1}{2}$ x 20	$15\frac{1}{2}$ sq	22 sq	10 x $13\frac{1}{2}$
3	4	6	8	10	14	18	$22\frac{1}{2}$	8 to 12	20 x 30	23 sq	$33\frac{1}{2}$ sq	15 x 20
$3\frac{1}{2}$	$5\frac{1}{2}$	8	$10\frac{1}{2}$	13	$18\frac{1}{2}$	24	29	$10\frac{1}{2}$ to 16	27 x 40	31 sq	$44\frac{1}{2}$ sq	20 x 27
$4\frac{1}{2}$	$6\frac{1}{2}$	10	13	$16\frac{1}{2}$	23	$29\frac{1}{2}$	36	13 to $19\frac{1}{2}$	$33\frac{1}{2}$ x 50	39 sq	$55\frac{1}{2}$ sq	26 x $33\frac{1}{2}$
$5\frac{1}{2}$	8	$11\frac{1}{2}$	$15\frac{1}{2}$	$19\frac{1}{2}$	27	35	$42\frac{1}{2}$	$15\frac{1}{2}$ to $23\frac{1}{2}$	40 x 60	45 sq	60 sq	30 x 40
$6\frac{1}{2}$	9	$14\frac{1}{2}$	18	23	$32\frac{1}{2}$	$41\frac{1}{2}$	51	$18\frac{1}{2}$ to $27\frac{1}{2}$	48 x 72	56 sq	80 sq	36 x 48
$8\frac{1}{2}$	12	$18\frac{1}{2}$	$24\frac{1}{2}$	$30\frac{1}{2}$	$42\frac{1}{2}$	55	67	$24\frac{1}{2}$ to $36\frac{1}{2}$	64 x 96	75 sq	87 sq	48 x 64
$10\frac{1}{2}$	15	23	$30\frac{1}{2}$	38	53	69	84	$30\frac{1}{2}$ to $45\frac{1}{2}$	80 x 120	93 sq	132 sq	60 x 81
$12\frac{1}{2}$	18	27	$36\frac{1}{2}$	$45\frac{1}{2}$	64	82	100	$36\frac{1}{2}$ to 55	96 x 144	112 sq	160 sq	72 x 96

This table and the one on the preceding page are from Kodak Publication No. S-49 and are reproduced with the permission of the Eastman Kodak Company.

Reels--a set of all sizes for taking up film

Extension cord

Screen--get the library to install a built-in screen, if possible; but everything from window shades to poster board has been used; weigh the alternatives of showing or not

Projection lamp--at least one extra

Chairs--some librarians have found that teenagers like to sit on the floor, and you can get more in that way

Lectern--for speaker or commentator

Flashlight--it's dark in there

Record player--one might wish to play appropriate music before program, during intermissions, or as part of program

STAFF

Projectionist--the more experienced the better, and have a backup

Librarian--to introduce the program and films, and to relate films and program to the library's other services

Clerk(s)--to charge out materials being borrowed; could be same as projectionist

Ushers, ticket takers--as needed (the projectionist should have no other duties while films are running)

AUDIENCE

Age--any; some programs are for one age group only, some for combinations, some for all ages

Size--from twenty to capacity, ordinarily; for some purposes, might show to smaller groups; audience size also depends on size of film (8mm, 16mm), size of screen and other factors

SESSIONS

Number--one, a short or long series, or a regular part of library's programming continuing each year

Spacing--one or two weeks apart, once a month, several in a year (if major programs), many in a short space of time (a day or a week) for special purposes, such as open house, festival, etc.

Length--one to two hours, unless film or reason is unusual

SPACE

Must be able to be made dark, have electrical outlets within reach of extension cord, and away from public use area so readers won't be disturbed; a minimum of outside noises is desirable, but films have been shown under all conditions; again, the alternatives should be weighed

SUBJECTS (Examples; see Appendix C for sample film programs)

The film as an art form--animation, abstract, avant garde, documentaries, silents, films without narration, film history, films of a director, films of an actor, horror, Westerns, science fiction, works of local filmmakers

The arts--architecture, painting, printmaking, sculpture, crafts, dance (ballet, folk, modern), music (popular, folk, black, classical), mime, theatre, poets, novelists, photography

Travel--cities, countries, continents, islands, ancient places, groups of people

Science--archeology, astronomy, mathematics, medicine, biology

Natural history--birds, mammals, ocean life, insects, life of a region (Africa, Australia, the Arctic)

Sports--archery, automobile racing, fishing, judo, karate, track and field, gymnastics, baseball, basketball, boxing, football, hockey, golf, tennis, the Olympics

Social problems--abortion, sex, venereal disease, homosexuality, destruction of the environment, population, poverty and unemployment, minority groups, city problems, consumer education, housing, the handicapped, mental health, the elderly, prisons, protest, crime, war, disease, work (migrants, assembly line)

Other--biography, religion, railroads, cowboys, humor

and satire, family life (in various parts of the world), history, youth, films from books

SOURCES (of films; see Appendix D for names and addresses of sources)

Libraries (state and regional), sports leagues and teams, agencies of foreign countries (consulates, airlines, information bureaus), colleges and universities, museums, scientific associations, historical associations, labor unions, U.S. government, national health organizations, businesses (particularly large corporations), religious groups, organizations that are promoting a cause (environmental groups, etc.), consumer agencies and organizations, youth organizations (Boy Scouts, Girl Scouts), individual collectors, independent filmmakers

How to find the sources--visit film libraries, attend film festivals, get on mailing lists of distributors, watch newspapers for reports of films available to groups, look at film magazines, explore the telephone directory's Yellow Pages for some of the organizations listed above, talk to library users, contact youth centers, contact teachers of film or photography in schools

PLANNING AND PRODUCING

Select target audience (general public or special group)

Decide where to show films (in library or elsewhere in community)

Be sure space can be darkened, has electrical outlets, outside noise won't spoil films, won't disturb library users

Check projector, and be sure you have necessary equipment (see above)

Find a projectionist, and learn to run projector yourself

Make preliminary list of possible subjects for showing

Survey potential sources of films

Preview films, if at all possible

Select dates and times for showings (if outdoors, it must be dark enough and not too cold); consider the occupations of potential audience, other community activities

Plan introduction

Plan related displays

Checkup--in plenty of time before showing (several hours to several days), be sure right films have arrived, projectionist is available, equipment is working, chairs and other furniture in place, any visiting speaker has been reminded

PUBLICITY

Use flyers and posters (with film annotations, color, running time), announcements in newspapers, on radio and television, in community calendars

Distribute to schools and colleges, other libraries, film societies, groups interested in subjects of films (ethnic, religious, literary, artistic, scientific organizations), centers for age groups (elderly, teenagers)

Use mailing list to individuals

NOTES

1. Hoelcl, Gisela. "Projection," University Film Study Center (Box 275, Cambridge, Mass.) Newsletter, Suppl. vol 3, no. 4, p. 4.
2. Vaughn, Susan Beach. "8mm at the County Fair," Film Library Quarterly, Spring 1970, pp. 33-6.
3. Le Clercq, Anne. "Featuring Films: A Children's Librarian's Programmatic View," Library Journal, May 15, 1972, p. 1510.
4. Heckel, James. "McLaren Film Festival," American Libraries, Dec. 1971, pp. 1195-7.
5. Vaughn, Susan. "Monster Movies," Library Journal, Oct. 15, 1971, p. 231.
6. Halleck, DeeDee. "Films in the Joint," Film Library Quarterly, Spring 1972, pp. 34-5.
7. American Libraries, Oct. 1973, p. 542.
8. Library Journal, March 15, 1972, p. 1120.
9. Campbell, Patty and Jane Brooks. "The Media Novice Plans a Young Film-makers' Festival," Wilson Library Bulletin, Jan. 1973, pp. 440-5.
10. Library Journal, May 1, 1974, p. 1263.
11. Hoelcl, op. cit.; reprinted by permission of the University Film Study Center.

Chapter 3

THE PERFORMING ARTS

POETRY READINGS

Poetry is said to have become popular, and poetry readings are said to draw crowds. Sometimes they do. The Poetry Center in Manhattan's Y.M.H.A. can draw large crowds for well-known poets. (They draw less well for those who are less well-known.) Some colleges and some other places get good audiences for poets. But libraries are not likely to have Robert Lowell read at one of their programs, and public libraries, at least, do not have audiences that are concentrated as do schools and colleges. Furthermore, most librarians will tell you that the borrowers of poetry are not many.

Locating the audience

Nevertheless, one can build audiences for poetry readings, even for the lesser-known poet giving a reading in a less densely populated area than Manhattan; also, for libraries, audiences of thirty or forty people may make very successful programs. It does take, in our experience, some intensive, selective publicity to find that scattered audience for poetry readings. We have used selective mailing lists (to special groups and individuals), carefully selected quotations from the poet's work on the publicity, and other devices such as newspaper pictures of the poet before the event, and a good deal of person-to-person talk.

Selecting the poet

The selection of the poet is very important--if you have a choice. And the poet you get will indicate how and

when and where you publicize. Choosing a black poet for a
black audience may not be enough. Robert Hayden, an excellent poet, may be too traditional in both form and content for a young audience. Imamu Amiri Baraka (formerly,
LeRoi Jones), even if you can afford him, may not go over
in some other communities. So, the poet should, to some
extent, be geared to the age, race, sophistication and other
factors of the potential audience. You must, therefore,
read, beforehand, some of his or her poems to gain a
feeling for the style and content. How well a poet reads is
very important, unless his name is big enough so that people
will just come out to look at him; that doesn't make a very
satisfactory program, however. One of the twentieth-cen-
tury's leading poets read very poorly and his considerable
charm could not overcome that problem.

If a published poet with an established reputation is
living in the area, he may well be willing to read at the
local library. The chances are, though, that you will have
to rely on poets without big reputations. But, that is all
right. Libraries can serve an important function by giving
space to the new, the different and the unknown. This
function is especially important for poets who are likely to
have small audiences for their works in any case.

If the poet merely reads his poetry and leaves, that
may be enough. You can have a much more varied, interesting and meaningful program, however, if he will also talk
about his poetry and himself, or if he will answer questions,
or carry on a dialogue with the audience. In a library program entitled a "Poetry Jam Session," three young friends--
published, but not well established poets--read their poems,
played some music, and talked about themselves and their
poetry.

Much poetry is difficult to grasp on first hearing it.
If the poet will tell you in advance what he is going to read,
it may be desirable to have copies made for distribution to
the audience prior to the program. This was done when
Hugh MacDiarmid read in New York City a few years ago,
and even with the Scottish dialect words (a glossary was included) he was readily understood.

If you can't get a poet, or even if you can, you may
want to get an actor (or other ham) to read the works of a
poet or group of poets. That way, with the reader's agreement, you can dream up your own program, and you will
have the world's poets to choose from.

There are many possibilities for poetry programs, depending on who makes up your public, what subjects are of current interest, and who or what is available. Forms, styles, schools and other groupings can be the nuclei of programs. Love poems, light verse, the New York school, sonnets or other metrical forms could make programs, or parts of programs. Concrete poetry, with the poem written on a blackboard in back of the speaker, might be used. The work of a particular poet could be celebrated with a program. Tu Fu, Keats, Pablo Neruda and many poets in between can be so celebrated, for any excuse you can think of. A Robert Burns night would make an excellent evening of poetry and song; his poems are easily understood (in spite of the dialect), popular, and of very high quality. The public library of East Meadow, New York, celebrated the poetry of Gabriela Mistral. Her poems were read in English and Spanish, and one who had known her talked about her and showed slides of her life.

Ethnic poetry

The poetry of a country or culture makes a good program. Lithuanian, Portuguese, Puerto Rican, American Indian, Chilean, Australian, or Japanese poetry might be tried, if the circumstances warranted it. The poetry of many of these countries may be relatively little known, even to people whose ancestors came from them, and that alone makes such a program desirable. Many people are now interested in the culture of the country of their origin; and of course there are many who are simply interested in other cultures. Scotland, for example, has a rich poetic tradition that is practically unknown in this country, and the Scottish poets from Dunbar and Henryson to MacDiarmid and McCaig might be successfully presented. One of us recently presented two programs of ethnic poetry (Italian, Greek, Puerto Rican, Russian and Polish) with the poets talking about the effect of their backgrounds on their poetry.

A library in Flushing, New York, has shown what can be done with ethnic poetry programs. For two consecutive years, they have conducted a series of programs featuring poetry around the world. Each session is devoted to the poetry of one or more languages. The reader for the evening starts out by giving some information about the poet and his poetry--biographical details, poetic style and themes. Then she or he reads the poem in an English translation, and follows that with a reading in the original language. They used to read the poem in the original language first, but they have found that since many in the audience did not know the languages well, they tended to get lost. Usually about eleven or twelve short poems are read, and the program lasts from forty-five minutes to an hour. The readers are local residents, poets, students, housewives, librarians, who know the language. At many of the sessions, a college student supplied background music on a guitar. The readers wear native costumes, and in some cases the food of the country is served. The walls are often hung with works of art from the appropriate country. The small costs have been met from fine money and from donations of materials by librarians.

Programs were held at four o'clock in the afternoon and were thus geared to teenagers. They were, some of them, very popular with the teenagers, but adults also attended. The black poetry reading was the most popular with teenagers because, it was felt, of the themes of the poems. Some poems in this session were dramatized and some were sung. A great deal of discussion followed this particular program, and attendance increased for the following session. (Which probably means you should lead with your best punch.) Following is a sample list of some of the programs:

"Hebrew and Yiddish Poetry"--read by the wife of a local poet

"Seven Centuries of Italian Poetry"--read by an Italian-American poet residing in the neighborhood

"World Poetry Reading"--Pakistani poems read by a 12-year-old student; Spanish and Italian poems read by a high school Spanish teacher

"Black Poetry Reading"--works of Nikki Giovanni, Imamu Amiri Baraka, Don L. Lee, Langston Hughes, Countee Cullen, Claude McKay, Linda and Dennis Robinson--read by a library trainee

"Chinese Poetry Reading"--read by a librarian

"Federico Garcia Lorca, El Poeta en Nueva York--Celebration of New York City"--read by a community resident and college Spanish major who had visited South America

One of the authors has conducted, in New York City's Harlem, several programs of teenagers reading their own

poetry, and she has shown how useful and successful such
programs can be.   They provided a showcase for the young
poets, a chance to try out their work on other people.   They
stimulated others to self-expression.   They provided the
audience with the catharsis of having their own strong feelings
expressed by others.   They stimulated an interest in poetry
and an interest in, and good feeling for, the library.   Here
is what she wrote about the programs at the time:

> "Like other teenagers, the young Negro poets
> write about love and their awareness of beauty; but
> more often they write about the indignities and the
> suffering that they and previous generations of Afro-
> Americans have experienced for having been born
> black.   It is through poetry that they can express
> their frustrations, bitterness and especially rage at
> the white man, a rage which the Negro has been
> forced to suppress for centuries....   It is also through
> poetry that they can extol the beauty of 'black'; the
> young women write about the beauty of the black man
> and the young men write about the beauty of the black
> woman, always with the emphasis on 'Black.'   They
> use poetry to celebrate their ancestors and the home
> of their ancestors, Africa.   Therefore, it is not sur-
> prising that some of the most successful programs at
> the North Manhattan Project in Harlem have been
> Poetry Evenings for Young Adults....   The idea for
> such a program was a long time coming to me, be-
> cause I did not know how much young people like
> poetry, nor did I know when I first began working in
> Harlem how much poetry meant to its young adults as
> a means of self-expression.   Then one day at the li-
> brary I watched a group of boys listen with reverence
> and complete involvement to a reading of Negro poetry
> on a record.   Frequently from then on, we played
> this record to classes visiting the library, and always
> the reaction, even of boys who were considered
> 'troublemakers' was intense.   Another time I was
> given a copy of What's Happening, a magazine put out
> entirely by teenagers with about a third of it devoted
> to poetry written by young adults.   I was stunned by
> it.   This poetry, coming straight from the teenagers,
> without editing and without any reservations was sim-
> ple, direct and very moving.   They told it exactly
> 'like it is.'

> "It was probably then ... that I began thinking of

doing a program on poetry by young adults. At first I
was afraid there would not be enough interest, but as
it turned out, lack of participation was not a problem
at all. We contacted the teenagers who wrote for
What's Happening, and some of the teachers and English
chairmen at several junior and senior high schools,
requesting them to tell any young poets in their schools
about the program. A large sign was put up in the
library inviting young adults to read their own poetry
or to come and hear poetry by their contemporaries.
In no time we had eleven poets for the program. We
thought that it would be stimulating for the audience,
and especially for the participants, to have on the
same program a published adult poet who would talk
about his development as a poet and comment on the
work of these young people. The book New Negro
Poets: U.S.A. proved to be a gold mine of a source,
for from the biographical material in the back, we
learned that several of the poets in the anthology were
living in New York. Among these was G. C. Oden.
All it took was one phone call; she seemed delighted
to be asked and accepted immediately. (Once I had
misgivings about asking adults to give of their time to
a library program without a fee, but I have learned
that most will accept such an invitation if they feel
that they will be of help to young people.)

"Because I still had no idea of how much appeal
poetry had and thought, mistakenly as I was soon to
find out, that the audience would be small, I decided
to use a meeting room that could hold fifty people instead of the auditorium. When the program began,
the room was completely filled up, and people kept
coming until they were standing outside the door. The
audience consisted of both teenagers and adults, some
of whom were friends or relatives of the young poets.
Many with no personal ties to the participants came
solely for the poetry. It was an exciting and unfor-
gettable evening for both poets and audience.

"The following day when I telephoned the program
director of the radio station in Harlem asking him to
make announcements about coming programs at the library, I told him about the Poetry Evening. He was
interested immediately in having it done on radio.
Several days later the eleven young poets read their

poetry and discussed it on an hour-length program
which was broadcast several times....

"In the days that followed a number of readers,
both adult and young adult, asked us when the next
Poetry Evening would take place.... This time we
had fourteen young poets reading and as the guest
poet, Jay Wright, who is also in New Negro Poets:
U.S.A. This time we used the auditorium. Again
the program was an overwhelming success, perhaps
even more exciting than the first.

"From the response to these programs I believe
that there is enough interest in poetry to warrant doing
a series of monthly programs.... There is a lot of
work involved in putting on a Poetry Evening or any
other type of program, but the returns to those who
take part--the poets, the audience, and the librarians--
make the effort, no matter how great, worthwhile...."[1]

For these poetry readings, there was no screening of
the poems for either their quality or their content. Some of
the poems were moving, even powerful, and some of poor
quality. Some of them were also very strong in their use
of language. She did not find it necessary, in that neighborhood, to screen out anything; everything was accepted as
natural. Depending on the audience, the neighborhood, and
the purpose of the program, other librarians, having such
programs, might feel the need for some process of selection.

A series of poetry programs would have been warranted
in the Harlem project described above. The librarian was,
however, transferred to another area of the city before she
was able to get more programs together. This illustrates one
problem with library programming. A librarian will frequently build up an audience, a list of performers, and good
publicity, and then change jobs. Then if her or his replace-
ment is not inclined in this way, the programs languish. To
be effective, they should be built into the library's activities,
just as is book selection, or any other ongoing activity.

DRAMA

Libraries and the theatre have had a long connection--

particularly in children's theatre--but also in workshops and
play production for teenagers and adults. Probably the outstanding relationship between the theatre and a library
started in the late nineteen thirties when the Rose McClendon
Workshop Theatre was created in the auditorium of The New
York Public Library's 125th Street Branch.[2] Many prominent actors came from that workshop, including Canada Lee
and Dooley ("Play it again Sam") Wilson. The N.Y.P.L.'s
Port Richmond Branch has an excellent theatre (actors rave
about its acoustics) that was built by the W.P.A. at about
the same time. Theatrical programs have flourished in libraries in Philadelphia, Yonkers, N.Y., Minneapolis, and
Ontario. So there are plenty of precedents (if anybody needs
a precedent) for plays in libraries.

Plays also, not incidentally, always seem to draw
good crowds, even in New York City which abounds in all
kinds of theatres; and that is a pretty good reason to have
a program. With drama, as with other kinds of programs,
libraries can turn their small meeting spaces and flexibility
(they don't have to draw large crowds) to good advantage.
Seldom-performed plays by established playwrights and the
works of new and known playwrights can be given for those
relatively few persons who are interested. The Tinker's
Wedding and In the Shadow of the Glen by John Millington
Synge or Eugene O'Neill's Bound East for Cardiff would be
most welcome to some. Short plays are especially suited
for library programs; they fit into a library's scheduling
problems, and they are not often produced elsewhere.

There is also always room for the more popular
plays. Plays like No Exit, Look Back in Anger and The
Glass Menagerie have been very successfully performed in
a number of libraries. Even though such plays have been
shown many times, there is always an audience for them.
If the library doesn't have a full-fledged theatre and you
are only going to have an occasional play--and assuming the
playing area is small--you will probably want a play that
requires only a few actors and little in the way of props.
(No Exit is ideal for those reasons.) The space or the
furniture problem may allow you to have only play readings;
they can certainly be very effective, however, and are well
worth the while; they are also, of course, much simpler to
produce.

Dramatic readings have been performed in many New
York City libraries. A group called the New York Shavians,

Inc., has for many years performed readings of the plays
of GBS: he is particularly suited to such a presentation.
Another group has done readings of Finnish, Swedish, Danish,
and Norwegian plays. Dramatic readings need not be confined to plays. In a Staten Island, N.Y., library an actor
gave a very dramatic reading of a short story by Charles
Dickens. The Asia Society in New York City has sponsored
dramatic readings of a variety of selections from Asian
literature. Other groups have done readings from Three
Lives by Gertrude Stein and Creatures Great and Small by
Colette. No doubt, many other ideas will suggest themselves. Even if you think the space is too small, don't
give up without further investigation. Plays have been produced in some remarkably small places.

Scenes and combinations of art forms

Possibilities for theatrical programs, other than
giving a full play, are to put on several scenes from different plays by one playwright. Scenes from a group of
playwrights that are in some way connected (Irish, Black,
poetic drama), or scenes that have a common theme are
other ideas. For the common theme idea, poetry, music
and drama mix very well. One such program, entitled "Re-
lationships of Man," combined a wide variety of poets, playwrights and composers. Following are two examples.

I. LOVERS

Cummings, E. E. "my sweet old etcetera" (poem)
Masters, Edgar Lee "Knowlt Hoheimer" and "Lydia
    Puckett" from Spoon River Anthology (poems)
"Someday She Go" (folk song)
"Love Has So Many Strings" (folk song)
Beckett, Samuel Krapp's Last Tape (play), excerpt
Packard, William "O Lady of Long Days" (poem)
Shakespeare Romeo and Juliet (motion picture), theme
    from--Nino Rota
Shakespeare Romeo and Juliet (play), Juliet's soliloquy,
    III, ii
"Young and Innocent Days" (folk song)
Shakespeare Sonnet XVIII "Shall I compare thee to a
    summer's-day?"
Shakespeare Sonnet CXXX "My mistress' eyes are
    nothing like the sun"
Shakespeare Love's Labour's Lost (play) V, ii, excerpts

Vanbrugh, John The Relapse (play) IV, iii
"Colors" (folk song)
Eliot, T. S. "The Love Song of J. Alfred Prufrock"
  (poem)
"The Water Is Wide" (folk song)
Shakespeare Hamlet (play) III, i

II. MY FAMILY, THE WORLD

Shaffer, Peter Five Finger Exercise (play) III, excerpt
Osborne, John Look Back in Anger (play) I, excerpt
"Pretty Saro" (folk song)
Masters, Edgar Lee "Minerva Jones," "Dr. Meyers"
  and "Mrs. Meyers" from Spoon River Anthology
  (poems)
"Farther Along" (traditional hymn)
Williams, Tennessee The Glass Menagerie (play), iii
  (Tom and Amanda)
Masters, Edgar Lee "Searcy Foote" from Spoon River
  Anthology (poem)
Packard, William "Duty" (poem)
Williams, Tennessee The Glass Menagerie (play), vii
  (Tom, final speech)
The Beatles "Dear Prudence" (song)
Wesker, Arnold Roots (play) I, excerpt (Beatie and
  Jimmy)
Miller, Arthur All My Sons (play) II, excerpt (father
  and Chris)
"The Horse Named Bill" (folk song)
Williams, Tennessee The Glass Menagerie (play) vi,
  excerpt (Tom)
"I Know Where I'm Going" (folk song)
Shakespeare Hamlet (play) II, ii
"In the Night" (folk song)
Miller, Arthur All My Sons (play) III (father, final
  speech)

Original plays

   One theatre group that produced original plays had as
part of their program a discussion with the audience after
the play; both director and playwright were always present
for these discussions. Dramatic workshops are still another
kind of theatrical program and they will be treated, with
other kinds of workshops, at the end of the chapter.

Most theatre groups will have prepared certain programs and you may have to accept those or not have that group. On the other hand, they may welcome some imaginative suggestions. All programs dealing with the theatre present great possibilities for the use of library materials in connection with them. Recordings of plays, biographies of theatre people, books about acting, directing and producing plays and the plays themselves can all be made useful.

Your own theatrical group

One possibility for exploring drama is to form a group of your own. This can take several forms: reading of plays, workshops, discussions, full-fledged productions of plays. One librarian formed some teenagers into a play-reading group, and she gives some general rules to follow. Such a group, she says, should have no more than fifteen members, because plays with larger casts are hard to find. Each participant should read a part every time. A variety of plays, and kinds of plays, can be used. They tried comedies, tragedies, histories, and musicals. For the musicals, it was useful to have recordings of the songs to play at the appropriate times. [3]

The Salt Lake City (Utah) Public Library has also formed forty-five teenagers from junior and senior high schools into a theatre company. The teenagers not only act, but also design the costumes, make-up, lighting and scenery. A staff member with theatrical experience directs them. The enthusiastic response to this venture has led the young adult department to sponsor a playwriting contest for teenagers. The best plays will be performed by the company. [4]

MUSIC

Musical programs have a wide appeal and they can be very successful, if the content is well chosen. They have the advantage of, usually, coming to you pre-packaged; all you have to do is present them. In this kind of program, there is an existing musical group that chooses what to play or what to do on the program. On the other hand, if you have the time and the will, you can dream up some very imaginative programs that you can put together yourself.

The size and location of the playing space is very important. Library meeting spaces are usually very small, rarely seating more than 200 and often much less. The level of sound is also a problem in libraries. For these reasons, intimate musical programs usually work best. Also one can present programs for those minorities that like special forms of music. Because it is the quietest of musical forms, and because it is not the most popular, chamber music is especially suitable for libraries. (Although it is not widely popular, we have seen up to 200 people at a chamber music concert in a library.) String quartets, recorder groups and even chamber orchestras have been successfully used. Individual artists such as pianists, flautists, and guitarists make good program material. Folk singers, usually accompanying themselves, are often available and are popular. Small jazz groups can also be used. Rock groups can, of course, be very popular, but they present the problem of excessive noise--although there are a lot of softer rock sounds around now. One library was able to have a concert of fully amplified hard rock, because the auditorium was several levels and some distance removed from the public area.

Another solution to the sound problem is to have the concert when the library is closed. One library has very successful musical programs on Sunday afternoons; they have been a regular feature of that library, several times a year, for a number of years, and a large audience has built up.

Music with commentary

Having a performer talk about the music he is playing is one of the best kinds of library musical programs. One unusual program involved a pianist who played for silent films; he showed film clips, played the appropriate music, and then discussed his techniques. This kind of program could be interestingly applied to styles of music (ragtime, blues), a particular instrument (lute, sitar), the music of a period (Elizabethan), or the music of a culture or country (American Indian, African, Chinese). A series of programs could be worked out along this line. For example, the

evolution of a type of music from blues through ragtime to
jazz and rock could be followed. Appropriate books, recordings, scores and libretti could be mentioned and/or displayed. There could be exhibits of musical instruments,
pictures portraying music, and other musically related materials.

One library had a series of lectures, with discussion,
of various aspects of rock music. The lecturer used tapes
of current stars such as Bob Dylan and the Rolling Stones,
and tapes of performers of the past, such as Bessie Smith
and the Andrews Sisters, to show the antecedents.

Ethnic music

Numerous programs presenting the music of a particu-
lar culture have been held in libraries. In its "Voices of
Brooklyn" series, the Brooklyn (N.Y.) Public Library had
several programs of this kind. For "An African Musical
Night," there were spirituals, gospel, jazz, soul, African,
Latin and Calypso music. At another program in the series,
"An International Music Festival," there were folk songs
from the Balkans and Eastern Europe, Gaelic ballads, songs
from Norway, and songs--by one versatile performer--in
Yiddish, Hebrew, Arabic, and Greek. Since, probably,
every ethnic group in the world has its own music, the possibilities for this kind of program are, for all practical
purposes, endless.

A program might also focus on the work of a composer. There could be, for example, a performance of the
works of Penderecki or Stockhausen, interspersed with commentary. There could be programs presenting, and about,
the Gregorian Chants, the songs of the troubadors or the
Moog Synthesizer. There are a thousand musical subjects
that could be used.

Library as showcase for new works

An annual musical program of the Dallas Public Library fulfills one important library function; that is, to
make new material available to the public. They call this
program a "Composer's Conference." Composers submit
scores, to them, of new music. This music is played by
professional musicians; it is then discussed by the audience

and a panel of music critics. This program gives the young composers a chance to hear their work performed by professionals. It gives the audience a chance to hear new music played and discussed. To pay for the program, volunteers solicit funds, local colleges supply musicians, and a musicians' union pays part of the musicians' fees. [5]

The audience are the musicians

In some programs, for teenagers, the audience has been indistinguishable from the performers; they have made their own music. One of these programs was called a "Rock Music Festival." Teenagers were encouraged to bring their own instruments, music and recordings. Another program was called "Sing Thing." This library had a fireplace and at Christmas time the teenagers gathered around it to sing folk songs and Christmas carols; some of them brought their own instruments to accompany the singing; cider and cookies were served.

Libraries in the state of Washington have demonstrated that useful, interesting and successful musical programs are possible in even the smallest library. A series of programs, "Behind the Scenes with the Seattle Opera," was presented in libraries in rural communities and small towns around Seattle. Arias are sung, accompanied by commentary on the background and story, and they are followed by an informal discussion with the audience. [6]

DANCE

Involvement is one of the key words of the last decade; we have seen participatory theatre, participatory politics, and people engaged in every kind of craft from making their own bread to making their own bombs. A dance program is one of the easiest ways to get people involved in a program. One teenage dance group, performing in a library, put on a program of dance, drama, and music, and, as a finale, went down among the audience and urged everybody to dance. A Puerto Rican dance group, performing before an audience of adults and children, did the same with conspicuous success. A library in Sweden held a dance as part of a Sunday evening youth program. A German library had "dancing among the bookshelves." And a Danish library had an evening of jazz with dancing.[7]

> O body swayed to music, O brightening glance,
> How can we know the dancer from the dance?

American libraries are also engaging in these (as they still seem to some) unlibrarylike activities. The Plainfield (N.J.) Public Library has held a dance contest for children, and they have had a square dance for children and their parents.

Folk dances

One of the most likely, and most frequent, kind of library dance programs is a program of folk dances. Folk dances, for all practical purposes, offer an endless variety of programs. One might put on a program of the dances of the ethnic groups in one's community, or a program of the dances of some exotic cultures with which most people are not familiar. (In addition to being exotic, folk dances are sometimes erotic, so be forewarned and know your dance and your audience.) Sometimes the dances of several different groups are presented in one program. The Brooklyn (N.Y.) Public Library presented "An International Dance Festival" at which there were Israeli, Scandinavian, Irish, Italian, and American Indian dances. And the Fond du Lac (Wisc.) Public Library recruited local citizens, who dressed in their native costumes, and gave an evening of folk dances and tales from Denmark, Finland, Germany and Iran.

Often dance is used as part of a many-faceted program, including music, poetry and drama, to present the heritage of a culture. Black groups frequently use dance as part of such programs, and traditional African dances are often used. One such group moved away from the traditional to experiment with new forms. They wanted to present a new image of Black dance by "moving away from the purely traditional, and expanding into unexplored and vital dimensions." They tried to unite dance, music, poetry and design, to express more powerfully and dynamically the message of today's Black artist. Chinese dances have also been presented as part of programs on that cultural heritage, in some libraries.

Demonstration and instruction
===

Sometimes the dance program includes commentary and demonstration of the steps. When a Puerto Rican group performed in a library, the leader prefaced each dance with a demonstration, and comments on the symbolism and historical background. The leader of a group of belly dancers opened a program for teenagers with a talk on the history of belly dancing, and gave demonstrations of technique between dances. Going a step further than demonstrations, the Brooklyn (N.Y.) Public Library conducted a class in African dance techniques, for all ages. The public library of Bloomfield, N.J., also gave dancing lessons. Teenagers and children age three and up were taught to dance the hula. They were also given a chance to play Hawaiian musical instruments.

Other possibilities include ballet, modern, jazz and tap dancing. Dancing, which goes naturally with music, can also be combined with other media. In a library program for children, the dancing was done to the recitation of poetry, and sometimes dancers perform in front of projected images, such as slides or a film.

Poetry readings: a summary and checklist of preparations
===

KINDS

Reading of poems in English

Reading with commentary and/or questions

Reading of poems in one or more foreign languages accompanied by English translations

Reading to music

Reading to dance

Reading in combination with music, dance, drama

Film or slides with some of above

MATERIALS

Books, periodicals, pamphlets, recordings for use in program, for display and for borrowing

EQUIPMENT (as required by poet/performers)

Lectern

Chairs or stools

Microphone

Pitcher of water and glasses

Record player

Projector(s) and related equipment

STAFF

One to introduce program and to relate it to library's services

Ushers, ticket takers as needed

AUDIENCE

All ages--often popular with older teenagers and young adults, but don't discount any age

From twenty persons to capacity

SESSIONS

Number--one, a series of several programs, or several times a year as a regular feature of library programs

Length--one to one and a half hours

SPACE

Can be held in small space, from 400 sq. ft. up

Away from public use area

Think freely--library yard or front steps, basement, story hour room, work area

SUBJECTS

Poetry of a culture, country or group (Italian, Hispanic, Zuni Indian)

Work of one poet

Poetry of a historical period

Work of a school of poets (New York School)

Poetry on a theme (love, war)

Humorous poetry

Dramatic monologues

Narrative poems

Parodies

Poems in memory of a person or event

Unpublished poetry

SOURCES

Schools and colleges; unaffiliated poets (especially unknown or unpublished); actors; others who read well, or who have a special knowledge of poetry or the ability to read in a particular language

PLANNING AND PRODUCING

Hear reader first--for content and reading ability

Contact poet/reader and discuss fee (if any), length of performance and his role, library's role, kind of audience, contents of program

Arrange date

Decide on location

Gather library materials appropriate to subject for display or borrowing

Gather materials and equipment needed by performer

Checkup--microphones, record player, projector, lights to read by

Print tickets (if wanted)

PUBLICITY

Get biographical details, poem quotes, picture of poet

Read some of poems in order to better write publicity and make introduction

Publicize in schools and colleges, literary organizations, organizations of college graduates, appropriate ethnic groups, selected individuals

Drama: a summary and checklist of preparations

KINDS

Complete play

Scenes from play/plays--on similar theme

Reading of a complete play, or scenes from plays

Dramatizations of stories

Dramatic reading of other than play (story, poem)

Combination of some of the above (useful when presenting the work of an author, or when program is built around a theme)

Presentation of the works of new or unknown playwrights

Pantomime

MATERIALS

Copies of plays or readings for actors. Books and recordings for display and for borrowing

EQUIPMENT (can run the gamut from one chair or lectern to a full range of theatrical props; much can be improvised)

Lectern

Chairs (a few)

Table(s)

Screens--one or two for entrances, exits, and quick changes

Other--many small props, household items, etc., can be borrowed

STAFF (if outside group performing)

One to make introductions and relate library materials to program

Possible needs--someone to control lights, ushers, ticket takers

STAFF (if group formed by library)

For directing, costuming, staging, etc.

AUDIENCE

All ages--everybody loves the theatre; library programs have been successful with children aged three to five on up

Size--probably not practical for less than twenty, but up to capacity

SESSIONS

Number--one, several performances of same program, or short series; if resident company is formed, have potential for continuity over a period of years

Spacing--if same program, repeated because of popularity, have performances close together; otherwise could be a month apart, or several times a year

Length--one to two hours, but might be longer

SPACE

600 sq. ft. up. A theatre in the library is desirable, but not likely. Next best is a stage or raised platform with side entrances (screens can be substituted for entrances). At worst, an empty space on the floor can be used, or even library yard. Pantomine could be done in public use area

Audience can be facing the performers, around them, or on either side

Dressing room, curtain, spotlights are sometimes useful

SOURCES

Schools and colleges; local theatrical groups; library users; aspiring, unemployed or retired actors

SUBJECTS

Popular plays, little-used plays, short plays, short stories, dramatic poems, original plays

PLANNING AND PRODUCING

See a performance by them before contacting any group (if possible)

Contact performers and discuss fee (if any), contents of program, kind of audience expected, length of program, library's role

Arrange for performers to examine performing space and discuss lighting, dressing rooms, props

Arrange date(s)

Arrange for rehearsals with performers and library staff; plan for delivery and storing of props

Gather library materials for display and borrowing

Check any audiovisual equipment to be used and be sure
it is in place and working on day of program

PUBLICITY

Get biographical details and pictures of previous performances

Possibly use quotes from plays on publicity

Publicize in schools and colleges, among drama groups,
and everywhere, via playbills/oral announcement

Music: a summary and checklist of preparations

KINDS

Concert by small group, or by individual

Group or individual performing and describing or commenting on instruments, style of music, historical
background, etc.

Performers and audience are one--group singing, each
one playing

Performance followed by discussion of music

Presentation of compositions by new or unknown composers

MATERIALS

Scores, song lyrics, books about music, recordings--
for use in program, and for display and borrowing

EQUIPMENT

Piano is highly desirable, because it is useful in many
kinds of programs (if regular musical events are
planned, library should consider buying a secondhand
piano)

Chairs or stools (as needed)

Music stands (as needed)

Microphones (as needed)

STAFF

One to introduce program, and to relate it to library's

services and materials; can also handle discussion, question period

Ushers, ticket takers as necessary

AUDIENCE

All ages--from preschool children to the end

Size--from twenty to capacity

SESSIONS

Number--one, a short series, several times a year, or part of library's regular programming every year

Length--one to two hours

SPACE

600 sq. ft. up; must be removed from public use area, or when public use area is closed; stage or platform desirable

Area should be tested for acoustical properties beforehand

SOURCES

Schools and colleges; local, unaffiliated, musical groups; individual performers, professional or amateur

SUBJECTS

Rock; jazz; chamber music; folk music; blues; gospel; opera; avant garde; electronic; movie music; individual instruments; music of countries, cultures or groups; music of a historical period

PLANNING AND PRODUCING

Listen to performers beforehand--for quality and content

Contact performers--discuss fee (if any), length of performance, their part in program, library's role

Have performers examine performing space

Arrange date

Gather printed materials and equipment

Checkup--have piano tuned, check microphones, see that everything is in place

PUBLICITY

Get biographical information and details of program; also pictures of performers with instruments

Learn something about the music to be played for publicity and introduction

Publicize among library record borrowers, schools and colleges, music stores, music clubs, teachers of music, and on radio stations playing appropriate kind of music.

Dance: a summary and checklist of preparations

KINDS

Straight performance

Performance interspersed with commentary or explanation

Performers involving audience

Performers and audience are one--"a dance"

Dance used with other media--dancing to recitation of poetry; dance and film; dance integrated into program with music, drama, poetry

Dance contest

MATERIALS

Books, periodicals, recordings for display or borrowing

EQUIPMENT

As required by dancers (probably little or nothing)

STAFF

One to introduce program and relate it to library's services

Ushers, ticket takers, someone to operate lights, play records

AUDIENCE

All ages

From twenty persons to capacity

SESSIONS

> One, a series of related programs, or a regular feature of library's programs
>
> Length--one to one and a half hours

SPACE

> 400-500 sq. ft. if a single dancer and a small audience (much depends on kind of dancing)
>
> Floor should be clean, smooth and free from splinters
>
> Location depends on decibels; could even be in public use area if one or two dancers demonstrating without music

SUBJECTS

> Ballet; folk; ballroom; modern; square; dance of a country, culture or group; original dances

SOURCES

> Schools and colleges; aspiring and unaffiliated dancers; members of ethnic and racial groups, local groups concerned with theatrical arts

PLANNING AND PRODUCING

> See a performance by prospective dancer(s) first
>
> Contact performers and discuss any fee, length of performance, their part in program, library's role, content
>
> Have dancers examine space, discuss lighting and other requirements
>
> Arrange date
>
> Arrange for rehearsals with dancers and library staff
>
> Checkup--see that audiovisual equipment is working and everything in place

PUBLICITY

> Get biographical details, pictures of dancers dancing, and contents of program
>
> Learn something about the dances for writing publicity and for introduction

Publicize in schools and colleges, local cultural organizations, among appropriate ethnic group, and in music stores and stores selling dance equipment

NOTES

1. LaFleur, Lydia. "Poetry Evenings in Harlem," Top of the News, Nov. 1967, pp. 44-6; reprinted by permission of the American Library Association.
2. Mitchell, Loften. Black Drama. New York: Hawthorn Books, 1967, p. 106.
3. Foglesong, Marilee. "Between Librarian and Teenager," Wisconsin Library Bulletin, March-April 1971, p. 86.
4. American Libraries, April 1974, p. 178.
5. Bradshaw, Lillian. "Cultural Programs--The Dallas Public Library," Library Trends, July 1968, pp. 62-7.
6. American Libraries, Sept. 1973, p. 467.
7. Renborg, Greta. "Pop in the Library," Top of the News, April 1968, p. 291.

Chapter 4

TALKS, DEMONSTRATIONS, INSTRUCTION

A program in which a talk is the main feature can take many forms. Speakers--sometimes there are several together--can just talk, with no props. They can show objects. They can use slides, films, filmstrips and recordings. Sometimes they demonstrate aspects of their subjects. Often there is room for a question and answer period, or an informal discussion. There are many varieties of talk programs that involve more than one speaker. In a panel discussion, a few (three, four, or five) persons discuss a subject informally and a moderator leads the discussion; this kind of program is useful for controversial subjects. Symposia also involve several speakers; they each give a short talk on some facet or side of a topic; these talks are usually followed by some form of audience participation, and, again, there must be a leader. A dialogue is a discussion between two persons, and an interview is an interview is an interview. Dialogues and interviews are useful for some subjects, kinds of people, or forms of programs. They are often used on radio and television, and they are useful if you have secured an author or other celebrity for your program.

Question period

If questions are to be asked of the speaker, they can either be written questions that are handed in to be read by the speaker or moderator; or they can be asked verbally from the floor. Written questions have several advantages; they avoid long speeches from people who are supposed to be asking questions; they can be put into a sequence that is more useful than random questioning; they avoid repetition (people often ask repetitious questions); rambling questions can be shortened or rephrased; and, if necessary, you can

77

leave, until it is too late, a question that is irrelevant or
in bad taste.

Written questions do involve handing out paper and
pencils, and collecting them again. Such things can be dis-
rupting, but they needn't be. The materials can be handed
out before the program, and they can be quickly collected
by ushers if this detail has been well-planned. Verbal
questions are also useful in some situations; they create an
air of informality, and even excitement, that written questions can kill; they are probably best used with small audiences.

Librarians talk (about books and the library)

Librarians have traditionally given talks both in and
out of the library. Adult librarians have given book talks
on radio and television, and to women's clubs, men's clubs,
garden clubs, parent-teacher associations, church groups,
ethnic and racial groups, and many other kinds of groups
and organizations. For these talks, they frequently go to
the group's meeting place and talk about three or four books
of interest to that group. It is often hoped that members of
that group will then rush to the library. They rarely do.
What many groups want is a program--something to fill the
available time. However, if you can follow Ezra Pound's
advice and "make it new," maybe you can interest them.
Talks of this kind are a lot of work; they are less work if
you give a lot of them, however, since you can repeat them,
or rework them for different groups. In spite of the drawbacks, they can be useful. They are good publicity; they
build good community relations; and they may draw people
to the library indirectly.

It is probably best to talk about books for which
there are several copies available, in case they do come.
Most talks of this kind are chatty and informal; you are
probably not there to give a detailed critical analysis of a
book. Just tell something of the plot or the contents.
Throw in an anecdote or two about the author. Relate it
to other books and, possibly, read a passage or two. This
is also an opportunity to mention the library's many services
and resources; one doesn't do this in great detail, giving
the audience a lot to remember, but merely mentions, or
briefly describes, the salient points.

Adult education (literacy) classes

Adult classes are good groups to give talks to. It is most useful if these groups can come to the library, and the teachers usually agree that it is worthwhile. These classes will usually be in English for the foreign-born, or for the semi-literate native-born. Sometimes citizenship classes are combined with English. The students are often eager to learn, which is a big plus. One difficulty is that there may be many different educational levels, ranging from the semi-literate to the highly educated (in any language); that makes giving a book talk a problem. There will also be different levels of competence in English. It is naturally best if the speaker or another staff member can speak the main language of the group. Often, however, there are several different languages represented within the group. But, their eagerness to learn will overcome most of these obstacles. For such classes, particularly if the group isn't too large, a tour of the library, talking as you go, is most desirable. They can then be registered and handled like any reader. Tours of the library can be made interesting by showing them things which they may never have been aware of; things like your audiovisual gadgetry, your treasured books, or a hundred-year-old newspaper on microfilm.

Book talks to high school classes

Many young adult librarians feel that the most effective way of reaching the largest number of teenagers at one time is by talking to classes of students, either in the school or public library, about books and the library. In this way the librarian is able to get across information on the library's materials, resources and services (many of which teenagers often are not aware exist), as well as tell them about books on a variety of subjects that are of interest to them. The latter is done in the format of a "book talk." This consists of telling about an incident in the book, usually one that comes near the beginning of the book, and telling it so effectively that the students want to read the whole book.

The librarian may work out his own book talk and/or --as is true in some libraries--draw from a pool of book talks that he and his fellow workers have contributed to. He talks about books that he himself enjoyed reading so that he can communicate his enthusiasm to his audience. First and foremost, he talks about books that he knows will be of interest to the majority of his audience. (Later when doing "floor work" in the library he will get to know the teenagers individually and will help find the right books for those who have more unusual or specialized interests.) Emphasis is put on recreational reading and not on curriculum-related materials, since the latter are felt to be the special province of the school library. If this program is well done, the librarian communicates both the pleasure that reading can give and the fact that teenagers are welcome at the library--that librarians are interested in serving them.

The book talk program also gives the library an opportunity to extend amnesty, either complete or partial, to the many teenagers who have kept books out for a long time or who owe fines, often from early childhood, and who, thinking that they now owe a fortune, have stayed away from the library ever since. It is a chance for these teenagers to clear up any such problems with the library; this encourages those who might otherwise never return to start using the library again. For all these reasons, many young adult librarians feel that this program is one of the most valuable the library has to offer. It is also an experience that most of them find enjoyable and even exhilarating.

It is the feeling among many librarians that this program has more successful results if classes go to the library (rather than librarians to the school) because the materials and services they talk about are right there, and the teenagers can take out the books they hear about, or others, immediately, clear up their overdue problems on the spot and register for adult cards. The chances of their coming to the library on their own are greater if they establish or reestablish contact with the library through a class visit.

In the New York Public Library, many eighth grades still come on class visits to their neighborhood branch library. These visits are arranged ahead between the librarian and the teacher or principal. They usually last an hour; if they are any longer, the students, even the brighter ones, begin to get restless. The activities during the visit proceed generally as follows:

For the talk, the class congregates in the library's meeting room. Hopefully this is not in the children's room; teenagers will often resent it. However, if that is the only place available, the librarian explains this fact apologetically.

The talk itself is then given, lasting approximately twenty minutes, about books and the library, during which time the students have a chance to ask questions and make comments. The librarian gives book talks for about ten minutes on three or four books, spending about four or five minutes on the first or main book, two or three minutes on a second and one minute on the other one or two. There is at least one copy of each title he talks about available for circulation. It sometimes happens, however, that some of them may not appeal to anyone in one class, while in another class, half the students want the same book. It is a good idea, therefore, to have other books displayed on a table and a word or two said about them.

The remaining time is devoted to registering or re-registering for adult borrower's cards, clearing up overdue records, possibly a tour of the library, pointing out the reference area, and browsing and checking out books, magazines and recordings. It is a chance for the librarian to help the teenagers find what they want and also to establish contact with the teacher if it is the first time they have met.

However, because of transportation problems, discipline problems and tight class period scheduling, schools in New York City (as well as in other parts of the country) often prefer to have librarians give book talk programs in the schools. Such a program requires more experience and a larger repertory of book talks, because the librarian talks for most of the forty-minute class period on as many as ten books. They always bring either the book itself or the book jacket, although students are often disappointed if they cannot see the book itself. Librarians prefer to speak to individual classes in their English period (or in the school library if there are no distractions) rather than to large numbers in an assembly, because the former allows for better rapport between the librarian and the students. Also, in a classroom the students are able to look at the books; some librarians leave five or ten minutes at the end of the period for this activity. Another advantage is that it gives the students a chance to make comments and for the librarian to find out more about their reading interests. However, the librarian still does most of the talking for the whole period, and this can be quite demanding. Therefore, most of them schedule no more than three classes each visit.

Some things to remember when scheduling book talks in the school are: (1) Make the arrangements with the school librarian whenever possible. In some schools the principal prefers this be done by him, the assistant principal, or the English chairman. It is best to visit the school rather than do it by telephone. (2) If a teacher contacts you directly for book talks, make sure the school librarian knows why and when you are coming. Stop by and see him and let him know ahead of time, if possible, what books you are going to talk about. It is important to get across to the school librarian that you are not trying to usurp any of his province and that you are both working towards a common goal: to get young people to read. (3) Stop by the school office and introduce yourself to the principal. They are usually glad to hear of any outside services being rendered their school, and it will help establish good relations between the school and the public library.

The New York Public's Young Adult Services does high school classes to a certain extent. However, its main emphasis is on working with the eighth and ninth grades because of the feeling that these young people need the help of the young adult librarian the most, now that they are in that transitional stage of going from the children's into the adult department.

Sample list of books

The following are some books which young adult librarians of the New York Public Library have used successfully in book talks. Some titles, such as Clyde, by Walt Frazier, and Secrets of Magic, can be used with classes on more than one grade and reading level.

8th grade--coed--below grade reading level

Little Men in Sports, by Larry Fox
The Dangling Witness, by Jay Bennett
Almost April, by Zoa Sherburne
The Folklore of Love and Courtship, by Duncan Emrich
Best Wishes, Amen, by Lillian Morrison

8th grade--all boys--below grade reading level

Durango Street, by Frank Bonham
Escape! by Ben Bova
From Lew Alcindor to Kareem Abdul Jabbar, by James
   Haskins

How to Draw People, by Arthur Zaidenberg
Bonneville Cars, by Edward Radlauer

8th grade--coed--on grade reading level

Basketball: the American Game, by Joe Jares
Zanballer, by R. R. Knudson
Secrets of Magic, by Walter Gibson
In Search of Ghosts, by Daniel Cohen
Candle in Her Room, by Ruth Arthur
The Girl Who Knew Tomorrow, by Zoa Sherburne
Great Monsters of the Movies, by Edward Edelson
Heads You Lose, by Pamela Hall
Sidney [Poitier], by William Hoffman
Touch of Magic, by Lorena Hickock
The Miracle Worker, by William Gibson
Ask Beth, You Can't Ask Your Mother, by Elizabeth C.
    Winship
The Funny Side of Science, by Melvin Berger and J. B.
    Handelsman
Clyde, by Walt Frazier

8th grade--coed--above grade reading level

Posers, by Philip Kaplan
The Martian Chronicles, by Ray Bradbury
Guinness Book of World Records, by Norris and Ross
    McWhirter
The Pigman, by Paul Zindel
Teacup Full of Roses, by Sharon Bell Mathis
Play the Man, by Brad Park
Clyde, by Walt Frazier
Voodoo, Devils, and the New Invisible World, by Daniel
    Cohen
Science Against Crime, by Stuart Kind and Michael
    Overman
A Long Way Up, by E. G. Walens
Wanna Make Something Out of It?, by Carol Duvall
Through a Brief Darkness, by Richard Peck

9th grade--coed--on grade reading level
but reluctant readers

Houdini, by Melbourne Christopher
The Secrets of Magic, by Walter Gibson
Basketball: the American Game, by Joe Jares
Voodoo, Devils, and the New Invisible World, by Daniel
    Cohen

Posers, by Philip Kaplan
Fitzgo, by Paul Wilkes
Clothing Liberation, by Laura Torbet
Bicycle Repair and Maintenance, by Ben Burstyn
Night Fall, by Joan Aiken
Teacup Full of Roses, by Sharon Bell Mathis
His Own Where, by June Jordan
Young and Female, by Pat Ross

10th grade--coed--on grade reading level

Mother Nature's Beauty Cupboard, by Donna Lawson
Basketball: the American Game, by Joe Jares
The Will to Win, by Willis Reed
Posers, by Philip Kaplan
Somewhere Within This House, by Jean Francis Webb
Smokescreen, by Dick Francis
Stunt, by John Baxter
The Angel Inside Went Sour, by Esther Rothman
Joshua, Son of None, by Nancy Freedman
Woodstock Craftsman's Manual 2, by Jean Young
ESP, Seers and Psychics, by Melbourne Christopher
Bird Lives!, by Ross Russell

10th grade--all boys--on grade reading level
but reluctant readers

Alive!, by Piers Paul Read
Survive the Savage Sea, by Dougal Robertson
Glenn's Complete Bicycle Manual by Clarence W. Coles
    and Harold T. Glenn
Play the Man, by Brad Park
Clyde, by Walt Frazier
Guinness Sports Record Book, by Norris and Ross McWhirter
Witcracks, by Alvin Schwartz
Wisdom of Kung Fu, by Michael Minich
Racing Cars, by Ferruccio Bernabo
Stunt, by John Baxter
Deathwatch, by Robb White

10th grade--coed--below reading level

Basketball; the American Game, by Joe Jares
The Long Black Coat, by Jay Bennett
Guinness Sports Record Book, by Norris and Ross McWhirter
Big Star Falling Mama, by Hettie Jones
Fitzgo, by Paul Wilkes

Black Cop, by Ina R. Friedman
The Bicycle Book, by Godfrey and Lillian Frankel
Witcracks, edited by Alvin Schwartz
Pardon My Fangs, by Elizabeth Starr Hill
Vampires, by Nancy Garden
Great Monsters of the Movies, by Edward Edelson
Young and Female, edited by Pat Ross
Let the Hurricane Roar, by Rose Wilder Lane
Teacup Full of Roses, by Sharon Bell Mathis

Tips for success

One young adult librarian in the New York Public Library offers the following tips on how to do successful book talks:

(1) When choosing a book for a talk before teen-agers, select one that you have enjoyed reading and you feel will be of sure-fire interest. It should lend itself easily to a book talk; many do not. Sometimes it is necessary to go through a half dozen books or more to find one that will make a good book talk.

(2) Select books appropriate to the grade and reading level. Find out in advance from the teacher if the class is below, on, or above grade in their reading.

(3) Prepare by the method that suits you best. Write the whole thing out, write a few notes, or just keep going over it in your mind. Practice is important. When the class appears, all notes should disappear.

(4) If the class is coed, start out with a book that will appeal to the boys such as sports or adventure. Girls are more willing to listen to a book for boys than vice-versa. Once you have the boys' attention, you can then use a book addressed primarily to the girls.

(5) Do not spend more than five minutes on any book, and keep within the time. Your opening statement can be related to the weather, something you have read in the paper, a school happening or even a background comment on the book itself, the time period or the setting. It should not be, "Here's a book you will like," or "This is the funniest book I've ever read." The audience will decide that when they hear the talk.

(6) The closing statement should be prepared; then

you won't ramble. You will want to come to a nice, neat end but not too dramatically. Avoid cliff hangers ("Will Pete get out of the cave? Read this and find out"). Your audience will groan. But do give them a little promise of what they can expect beyond what you have told them.

(7) Give the author and title at the beginning and end.

(8) Choose an episode that occurs early in the book. You don't want to give the story away. Don't tell the whole story unless it is a short story in a collection. Don't tell the only exciting incident in an otherwise unexciting book. They will just feel cheated when they do read the book.

(9) Use a few of the author's own words if you can do it casually, to give the flavor of the book.

(10) It's usually not a good idea to read unless it's a poem or questions and answers such as those in Ask Beth, You Can't Ask Your Mother. Reading from a book tends to separate you from the audience.

(11) Don't gesture wildly or be too theatrical. Your audience will feel uncomfortable and embarrassed for you. Don't tell in the first person.

(12) Be careful of suggestive words or scenes that will upset them.

(13) Limit descriptions and introduce only one to three characters. If they lose track of what you are talking about, they will become bored and stop listening.

(14) Define hard or unusual words by restating them in simpler words--but not in a pedagogical way, naturally. Do it casually. Make sure that they know what you're talking about.

(15) Be sure to get all information correct. Special terms and facts should be accurate.

(16) Keep your feelers out for responses to what you're saying and be responsive in turn.

(17) Ask the teacher to remain in the room. It is hard to be entertaining and play the authority figure at the same time.

(18) Wear attractive but not distracting clothes.

(19) Have a good time and the class will too!

At Prince George County Memorial Library System,

the young adult librarians prefer to work as a book-talk team of two or more people who talk to no more than six classes a day. They, too, prefer, giving talks to individual classes and do not do assemblies. The team works out a list of books that are popular with YA readers, titles that meet as many reading interests as possible and on several reading levels, and books that the librarians enjoy and feel comfortable in presenting. The number of titles varies on the lists, but they try to talk about as many as they can, usually twenty to twenty-five. Copies of this list are given out to the students who can then select the titles they want to hear about. Staff often take along additional books and try to match up titles on the list with those in the collection.

Basically they use the Enoch Pratt Free Library's technique of book talking which Margaret A. Edwards describes so well in her book, The Fair Garden and the Swarm of Beasts (Hawthorne). Their presentation is informal and chatty and they try to get reactions from the young people. They use mostly short talks of under one minute that would answer the question, "What's this book about," and it is not memorized. At least one long book talk is given in every class period; this one is memorized. There is a "pool" of long talks available for staff to use. One of the lists which they have used consisted of the following titles:

Across the Barricades, by Joan Lindgren
Admission to the Feast, by Gunnel Beckman
All Creatures Great and Small, by James Herriot
Ammie Come Home, by Barbara Michaels
Bankshot, by Donald E. Westlake
Bonecrack, by Dick Francis
Cages, by Paul Covert
Claudia, Where Are You?, by Hila Colman
A Cluster of Separate Sparks, by Joan Aiken
Crack in the Sidewalk, by Ruth Wolff
Deathwatch, by Robb White
Dog Who Wouldn't Be, by Farley Mowat
Dove, by Robert Lee Graham
Duelling Machine, by Ben Bova
Fortune Hunter, by Ira J. Morris
Friends, by Rosa Guy
Haunted Summer, by Hope Jordan
Hog Butcher, by Ronald J. Fair
I Never Had It Made, by Jackie Robinson
Jade, by Sally Watson
Johnny Got His Gun, by Dalton Trumbo

Maggie Now, by Betty Smith
Miracle at Carville, by Betty Martin
P.S. Your Not Listening, by Eleanor Craig
Pstalemate, by Lester del Rey
Report from Engine Co. 82, by Dennis Smith
Runaway's Diary, by Marilyn Harris
Soul Catcher, by Frank Herbert
Survivor, by Robb White
Tales from the Crypt, by Jack Oleck
Wilt, by Wilt Chamberlain
Why Not Join the Giraffes?, by Hope Campbell
Year of the Intern, by Robin Cook

Both the New York Public Library and the Prince George County Memorial Library Systems concentrate on the book in their presentations. On occasion both have used short films. The former has used them with non-English speaking classes and the slower classes. Also they have at times played records, especially at the beginning while the class is settling down in the library. The feeling in both library systems is that books can stand on their own.

On the other hand the young adult librarians at the Free Library of Philadelphia have presented successful multi-media programs in which books are highlighted to assemblies of as many as one thousand students. From their experience they found that traditional book talks require a great deal of staff time, that some librarians feel uncomfortable speaking for such a long time, and that many high school students will "turn off" a twenty-minute talk by one person. Therefore, they devised a multi-media program called "On Your Own" which includes short films, slides, a tape recording of music and narration and three librarians on stage who present five one-minute bookspots in between.

They may start with a film such as Ashes of Doom, an anti-smoking commercial starring Dracula which has proved to be a good attention getter. The introductory part of the slide/tape show deals with being "on your own" after school. The main sections are usually on movies, sports, problems, arts and crafts, the occult and love and sex, with career information sometimes added; in one case science fiction was substituted for love and sex upon the teacher's request. Appropriate books are highlighted after each section.

Then they may end with a movie such as <u>Vicious Cycles</u>, a satire on a cycle gang minus their motorcycles.

The whole program runs about thirty minutes. Their objectives are twofold: to encourage reading and to entertain the students at the same time. The same tape is used in each program; the ninety basic slides are the same although sometimes they have substituted some slides of the school's students. However, the books highlighted are chosen specifically for each school. There are approximately three hundred book slides on file, but they continue to add new books to the file. In addition to seeing the slide of the book cover, the student also has a program flyer, listing the featured books. This assembly package, the second one prepared as of this writing, was planned by a committee that worked for about four months writing the script, selecting magazine illustrations and photographing them for slides. The script was recorded in a professional sound studio by a friend, who also selected the music used to introduce each section. The slides include pictures of people teenagers may be interested in such as Mark Spitz, Diana Ross, Joe Frazier and Al Pacino, and the music includes the lively theme from <u>Shaft</u>. They have presented this program to individual classes in school libraries and in branch libraries as well.

One such program that was presented at an assembly at an all-boy's Catholic high school included talks on the following books:

Books Made into Movies

Serpico, by Peter Maas
The Andromeda Strain, by Michael Crichton
Deliverance, by James Dickey
Dove, by Robin Graham
Bless the Beast and Children, by Glendon Swarthout

Sports

Bobby Clarke and the Ferocious Flyers, by Stan Fischler
I'll Always Get Up, by Larry Brown
Clyde, by Walt Frazier

People with Problems

The Contender, by Robert Lipsyte
A Hero Ain't Nothin' but a Sandwich, by Alice Childress
Alive, by Piers Paul Read

Report from Engine Co. 82, by Dennis Smith
Down These Mean Streets, by Piri Thomas

Occult

Sun Signs, by Linda Goodman
Chariots of the Gods, by Erich von Däniken

Do-It-Yourself

How to Service and Repair Your Own Car, by Richard
Day
Anybody's Bike Book, by Tom Cuthbertson

Science Fiction

Stranger in a Strange Land, by Robert Heinlein
The Gods Themselves, by Isaac Asimov
The Doomsday Gene, by John Boyd
I Sing the Body Electric, by Ray Bradbury
The Immortals, by Rene Barjavel

Non-librarians talk (about a lot of things)

Absorbing and even exciting programs can come from
talks by experts on various subjects. There are almost as
many possibilities as there are subjects in the book collection. Such talks can be combined with displays of books and
other library materials that relate to the subject. Objects
that relate to the talk can also be displayed. This is also a
good opportunity to describe library resources in the subject
area, and to distribute booklists on that subject.

Authors

Authors often make good programs, and one can
usually get local authors to talk at the library. One library
invited a herpetologist to speak when his first book was published. They displayed copies of the book, the manuscript,
galley proofs, photographs and snake collecting equipment.
The author arrived complete with a boa constrictor that
crawled around his neck when he talked and a rattlesnake
that did not. The large audience of all ages was charmed.
Another author, of a book about caring for hurt, wild birds,
has described her experiences to library audiences, in successful programs.

Subject experts

When interest in a subject swells, experts often surface like flotsam on the rising tide.   This concurrence of
events makes such subjects good material for library programs.   Taking advantage of the opening provided by the
recent surge of interest in chess, a library checked on experts in its area.   They found one who talked about openings,
end games, and other knighttime activities.   Another library
used the current interest in China to sponsor a series of
lectures, illustrated with slides, on several aspects of
Chinese culture, including acupuncture and herbal medicine,
the liberation of Chinese women, and education in China.
(Not unexpectedly, the acupuncture lecture was by far the
most popular.)

Slides and lectures, of course, go well together.
The public library of Elyria, Ohio, developed a unique
slide/lecture program, which was prepared and produced
entirely by staff members.   They wrote scripts and prepared slides relating to local history and culture.   They
then took this program out into the community, presenting
it at the meetings of various organizations.[1]   Talks on
many subjects--all art, for example--work well with slides.
The Brooklyn (N.Y.) Public Library has illustrated lectures
on the sculpture of Black Africa and on an archeological
field trip to Puerto Rico.

Arts and crafts

The arts and crafts provide many possibilities for
lectures.   A program on egg decorating, that lovely art that
is so common in Eastern European countries, has been successful in libraries.   So have programs on macramé, Christmas decorations, furniture finishing, automobile repair and
sewing.   A sculptor and instructor at a local college spoke
and demonstrated his art at a library.   A demonstration of
how to make mobiles was given at another.   Maybe you have
a cartoonist living in the neighborhood.   They can, and do,
give chalk talks in libraries.   A Chinese-American artist has
given a lecture-demonstration, combined with an exhibit, in
some New York state libraries.   The president of the Feder-
ated Garden Clubs of New York State talked about all aspects
of growing house plants to a group of apartment dwellers.
Gardening generally has many program possibilities.   A

representative of the United States Department of Agriculture, using slides, spoke on the subject of organic gardening and on its logical concomitant, the canning of the produce. An observer at this program pointed out that the speaker talked too much about large-scale farming, whereas the audience was made up of people with small yards. The speaker should have been told about his potential audience.

Hobbies

Programs can be centered around all kinds of hobbies. The president of a coin club set up a display of coins in a library, and talked about the history of American coins, how to start a collection, how to acquire coins and how to evaluate them. An expert on stamp collecting should be as easy to find. Antique collecting is of great interest in some areas. An expert on antiques brought to a library some silver, porcelain, and cut-glass objects, such as bowls and candlesticks. She talked about judging antiques, described her collecting experiences, and suggested books for an enthusiastic audience of about forty-five persons. This program was held in a library with a very small circulation, and for that library it was an important and successful program.

Geologists can show and talk about rocks and minerals, and describe identification techniques for amateur rockhounds. A photographer introduced his library audience to the intricacies of the camera; his work was on display, at the library, at the same time. A library found a staff member who could give a cookery demonstration for teenagers. A young batik craftswoman gave an informal talk and demonstration to an audience of thirty to forty, mostly teenagers (there was one 65-year-old man in the audience). She demonstrated the process from beginning to end, answering questions as she went along. A comment--to be remembered--was that this program of an hour and forty minutes was too long even though the audience was interested and knowledgeable. In related events, the room had been decorated with examples of batik done by teenagers, and the entire program was video-taped by a group of teenagers from another library (a good example of interlibrary cooperation).

Careers

Talks about many careers could make good programs

for teenagers. An article in the Wisconsin Library Bulletin described a program for teenagers entitled "Learn to Earn." Four speakers talked about ways teenagers could prepare for jobs. Representatives of the state employment service and private business described such things as how to apply, being interviewed, and what businesses expect of an applicant. There was a talk on etiquette and appearance and another on the value of volunteer work in gaining experience for a job. [2]

In another program for teenage girls, a representative of a school for models spoke in a New York City library. She discussed modeling as a career, gave tips on how to dress, and demonstrated makeup on two girls, one black and one white.

A librarian in a vocational high school in Brooklyn, N.Y., aroused interest in the theatre among her teenage patrons by inviting an actress, who had appeared on Broadway, to speak at her library (without pay). The high school had a large percentage of black and Puerto Rican students, and this black actress evoked an enthusiastic response from the teenagers. She spoke about her experiences and her career, read a scene from a play, and answered many questions. The good behavior of the students, and their obvious interest, came as a great surprise to the teachers.

Sex, drugs and other matters

Teenagers have many other problems and interests that would make useful and interesting programs. A library presented a program on venereal disease for teenagers; a doctor from the local department of health spoke, and the film, A Quarter Million Teenagers, was shown. The same library is, at this writing, planning a program that will bring to teenagers the facts on abortion and contraception. Many adults would also benefit from programs on these subjects, both as parents and as consumers. At one library program, some teachers and five teenagers from an alternative school spoke to the local teenagers about educational alternatives, drugs, alcohol and other problems. Representatives of the Peace Corps have talked to teenagers on library programs.

Religion

Many young people, and older people as well, have

become interested in religions from other parts of the world, and in alternative ways of life. Voodoo is a subject that fascinates many people, and facts about it are little known-- a combination that makes it an ideal library program. The New York Public Library's Countee Cullen Branch arranged for a Haitian artist to display his work in the library and to talk about voodoo and its connection with Haitian art. He gave two lectures; one was entitled "The Origin and Significance of Taino, American Indian and African Symbols in Haitian Voodoo," and the other was "How the Modern School of Haitian Art Utilizes the Haitian-African Experience in Its Symbols." Talks on Buddhism, Hinduism, the religious beliefs of the American Indians and other religious orientations suggest themselves as library programs.

Yoga

Another subject that is very popular, and one that has a religious orientation, is yoga. A library found a yoga instructor living in the neighborhood, and persuaded him to appear on a program. He discussed and demonstrated "the relation between yoga and the emotions," "the relation between breathing and thinking," and "the creation of different states of consciousness through yoga." The audience was mostly young, but there always seem to be some older adults who are interested in anything--fortunately.

Consumer affairs

There are many social, legal, and economic problems that can be, and have been, used as the bases for library programs. Among these, the problems of consumers are important. In one library, the Consumer Protection Specialist of the Federal Trade Commission told an audience how to guard against mail-order frauds, about truth-in-packaging legislation, and other aspects of consumer protection. At another library, a representative of the Better Business Bureau described some frauds that have been practiced on the consumer, and demonstrated some useless items that had been purchased. One gas company sends out people to speak on various consumer problems; one of their representatives gave a talk entitled "Your Food Dollar" in which she described shopping techniques and how to save money. A library in a Spanish-speaking neighborhood of New York City conducted a seminar on unit pricing. Representatives from the education department of a social service center appeared in the library to talk on the subject and to answer questions. Naturally, they spoke in both English and Spanish. A talk that magnified the fine print on insurance policies, and that told the audience how to get its money's worth, was given in a library.

Investments

Interest in investments has risen greatly in recent years, and useful talks, or series of talks, that discuss investment problems can be arranged. The New York Stock Exchange provides three series of lectures, with a film, for libraries in parts of New York, New Jersey and Connecticut. It seems likely that similar programs could be arranged in other parts of the country. Their complete program is listed in an appendix.

Social security, tenants' rights and other legal problems

It is one thing to have rights, and another to know about them and how to get them. The Social Security Administration, for example, will send out speakers to inform the public, since many people are unaware of the benefits due them. Similarly, many people are unaware of the benefits to which they are entitled under various welfare programs. One library, in cooperation with the National Welfare Rights Organization, conducted a forum on the subject. The rights of tenants are important to large groups of urban citizens. Related to tenants' rights is the subject of rent control. Both subjects are worthy of library programs. One library ran a series of lectures by lawyers on subjects that many citizens need to be familiar with. The problems of wills, serving on a jury, buying a house or other property, the legal rights involved in buying or selling anything, patents, insurance, divorce, and other subjects were covered. Many young people need to know about legal problems today, also. Such subjects as the laws covering demonstrations and picket lines, drug laws, what to do when arrested, laws on marriage, abortion and related subjects, are all possible program topics.

Aspects of mental and physical health make subjects for lectures. Child care, nutrition for the elderly, diet in disease and mental health have all been parts of library programs. There is a whole range of social problems about which information is needed. "What Does Women's Liberation Mean to the Black Woman?" is the title of a presently planned library program. It will use the panel format, since there will undoubtedly be a variety of opinions.

Retirement

Old age brings with it many problems. A series of programs on retirement was held in a New York City church. It consisted of six sessions with a speaker and a question and answer period for each. The following subjects were covered:

1st session: Self image of the elderly
Social security benefits

2nd session: Financial planning for retirement
Taxes and legal aspects of retirement

3rd session: Maintaining health and nutrition
Medical needs: medicare, medicaid and
hospital care

4th session: Supportive services and recreation
Employment and volunteer opportunities

5th session: Housing
Nursing homes and alternative planning

6th session: Retirement associations
Political considerations

If this series had been held in a library, much material to support each session could have been supplied. The participants could have been made aware of the informational resources that were available in the libraries to help them with their problems. And they could have been made aware of the recreational resources, film programs, large print books, service to the homebound, that libraries offer to the elderly.

Community issues

Sometimes issues become a big problem in a community; in such cases, much light is needed and the library can supply it through programs. When a highway is planned to be built through a city, or public housing is projected, there are many problems that citizens should be able to get information about, and should be able to discuss. Libraries can supply printed information and arrange for speakers. Such subjects as urban planning generally and the preservation of landmarks need to be talked about. It is likely that libraries could find architects and others who would be willing to talk about them. Problems of conservation and the environment need to be discussed, particularly when it is a local issue that may effect jobs or other personal matters. Prison reform is a problem that has been debated in libraries.

Intergroup relations

People need to know about each other. This has always been true, but now more than ever antagonistic groups need to know about each other's feelings and attitudes. A library titled one program, "What Older People Would Like Young People to Know." This idea opens a wide range of possibilities. Certainly the reverse of such a program would be valid; young people also want old people to know their needs and desires. There are many such groups that need to be enlightened about each other: black and white, Indian and non-Indian, the many ethnic groups about each other.

The American Indian Movement will hold an informal discussion to enlighten others about their aims. How about a program in which the governors and the governed could learn about each other's problems (city, county, state and federal officials and their constituents)? Patients need to know what they can expect from doctors and doctors need to find out what the patients would like to know. All of these programs could be conducted with a panel of speakers--most of whom would probably be eager to present their views-- possibly a film, and a period for discussion or questions and answers. Speakers could recommend readings, of library materials, that they thought would be useful for further information.

Sometimes libraries have even given full-fledged courses in topics of special importance to their patrons. One library has conducted a course in Spanish-American literature. This series of lectures was given in either Spanish or English according to the preference of the audience. It was conducted by a Spanish-American poet. It covered such little known (to most Americans) literatures as

Cuban, Puerto Rican, Mexican and that of the Dominican Republic. There were separate lectures on such outstanding poets as Gabriela Mistral, Pablo Neruda and Jorge Borges.

Tours of the library and its environs

Some libraries conduct tours of the library. This kind of walking lecture might be useful if you have some interesting behind-the-scenes work, such as an audiovisual department, some rare books, or other unusual features that would attract a public. Other ambulatory lectures can take place outside the library. This kind of program would only accommodate a small group, and would require good weather. Walks could be taken to spots of local historical interest, or to places connected with literary or other artistic figures. A library in lower Manhattan sponsored a walk to find out why the streets meandered in all directions, and how they got their names.

A potpourrí of programs

Here are a variety of programs that have been successful in libraries around the country:

Book Reviews. In addition to librarians giving book talks, libraries often bring in guest experts to review books. The East Meadow (N.Y.) Public Library has had both an evening series, and a "Lunch'n'Books" series; in the latter, the audience brings their lunches and the library provides coffee. The Bloomfield (N.J.) Public Library has also had a noontime (12:30 p.m.) series with appropriate specialists reviewing a variety of books, including Politics of Lying by David Wise, Seduction of the Spirit by Harvey Cox, The Summer Before the Dark by Doris Lessing, and News from Nowhere by Edward J. Epstein. In what might be considered an extension of book reviewing, the public library of Livingston, New Jersey, offered a complete course on the novel.

Income Tax. At the East Meadow (N.Y.) Public Library, a representative of the Internal Revenue Service, using chalk and a blackboard, told an audience how to prepare their income tax forms. His special emphasis, because of his audience, was on senior citizens' and homeowners' problems, casualty losses and medical expenses, and contributions. He also answered questions.

Government. The Bloomfield (N.J.) Public Library offered a five-part evening series on the workings of the government.

Cooking. The East Meadow (N.Y.) Public Library gave a program on organic cooking. The author of an organic cookbook talked, and staff members baked bread, cookies and cakes. They also provided a health punch made of grape juice, apple juice, lemon juice and honey. A branch of the New York Public Library gave a program for teenagers on cookless cooking, featuring what they described as "no-bake recipes."

Radio. The Minot Air Force Base Library had a demonstration of citizen's band radio.

Real Estate. The Everett (Washington) Public Library cosponsored, with a local savings and loan company, a series of talks on real estate. It was entitled "Lunch Hour Learning," and the savings and loan company provided the speaker and coffee and doughnuts.[3] They plan future programs on "Retirement and Women," "Interior Decorating," and "Transactional Analysis."

Budgeting. A library near Seattle presented, in that depressed area, a series on consumer education, the most popular of which was a program on stretching the food dollar. There were other programs on clothing and home furnishings. They also had sessions for training leaders in consumer education; these programs were videotaped for more widespread distribution.[4]

Crafts. The East Meadow (N.Y.) Public Library used a Sunday afternoon, when library users wouldn't be disturbed, to present an arts and crafts festival. The craftsmen demonstrated and the public had a chance to ask questions. Included were watercolor painting, acrylic flower painting, wire sculpture, silver jewelry making, metal flower crafting, pottery, silk-screen printing, linocuts, woodcuts, batik, hand weaving and leather craft. Refreshments were served and a good time was had by all. In another library, similar demonstrations were given in public use areas, while the library was open, every day for a week. In the teenage room, there were demonstrations of string art, crocheting, knitting and silk-screen techniques. And in the adult department, passers-by watched craftsmen making jewelry, enameling, doing macramé, ceramics and batik. Piles of paperback

books on the subjects circulated "like mad," and there were
no objections from the public about the noise, which was
minimal.

Circus. Ringling Brothers and Barnum and Bailey
Circus has a goodwill ambassador; he is a clown, and he
has presented slide shows, in libraries, on the history of
the American circus.

Landscaping. Representatives of the Department of
Agriculture have given talks on landscape design, including
the selection of materials, and where and how to place them.

Dog Shows. This is a kind of demonstration and is
suitable for a library with a yard. One library presented a
show given by the Lhasa Apso Club of Greater New York.
This is, admittedly, somewhat special, but any breed, or
breeds, will do.

Football. The New Orleans Public Library has had
a smash (appropriate word) hit on its hands, in the form of
a football demonstration.[5] Four members of the New
Orleans Saints have provided these demonstrations (free) at
eight branches. The five-day clinics were divided into two
parts; morning sessions were devoted to films of football
highlights, with the players making comments on the action
and answering questions; afternoons were devoted to demonstrations of passing, tackling, blocking and running on library lawns.

Skydiving. The public library of Montgomery County,
Maryland, has had a skydiving training session.[6] A college
student, who was part of a skydiving group, spoke, without
fee. A film, Sky Capers (Pyramid), was shown and the
speaker explained the moves the skydivers were making. He
then demonstrated the packing and unpacking of a parachute,
answered questions about costs and other things, and provided a list of local instructors. More than forty people,
ranging in age from teenage to over forty, attended. The
audience was mostly male but a few young women attended.
The library suggests that one can write to the U.S. Parachute Association (P.O. Box 109, Monterey, Cal.) for brochures about the sport and for posters.

The very active public library of Rockville, Md., also
has presented--among others--the following unusual programs:
Aquaria--how to set them up; Architecture--of Old Rockville;

Astrology--a sample horoscope; Calligraphy--a slide talk and demonstration; Caving, Rock climbing and White-water rafting--slides and information; Gliding and soaring--slide talk on where and how to do it; Mime--a demonstration.

Health fair. The New York Public Library's Wakefield Branch conducted a health fair for teenagers, although adults attended, on two days from 10 a.m. to 4 p.m. There were free and confidential tests for blood pressure, diabetes, tuberculosis and venereal disease and there were examinations of eyes and teeth. Health counseling information booths were also provided and there was entertainment, including music, and light refreshments.

Mountain Climbing. In Minnesota, at the Southdale-Hennepin Area Library, a demonstration of mountain climbing techniques was presented. Among other things, the demonstrator scaled the west wall of the building. [7]

Sexuality and the Law. The Clark County (Nevada) Library District is centered in Las Vegas. They have held a series of panel discussions on this unusual subject, with panel members including teachers, lawyers, doctors and others. A discussion of prostitution included an ex-prostitute and a local madam. [8] Some of the other subjects discussed were:

The Sexual Revolution--Myth or Reality?
Sex in Marriage and Otherwise (including the film, "A Very Special Day")
Sex and the Media (including the film, "The Love Goddesses")
Sexual Learning (including the film, "Sugar and Spice")
Pornography: Raging Menace or Paper Tiger?
Sexual Deviance

Bibliographies on all these subjects were compiled and were printed on a very attractive flyer.

Mayan Culture. At the Rosenberg Library in Galveston, Texas, the Friends of the Library planned and carried out a most unusual year-long program. Through films, speakers, reading and studying, the group learned about Guatemala and Mayan culture. The series culminated in a trip to Guatemala and Yucatan. The library compiled a bibliography of its holdings and presented the following programs:

Film--"The Lost World of the Mayas" (Time-Life)
Speaker (University of Texas)--"The Mayas' Religion, and the Spanish Conquest"
Speaker (anthropologist, University of Texas)--"The Archaeology and Anthropology of the Mayas"
Speaker (natural science museum director)--Discussed Maya explorations based on Stevens and Catherwood's Incidents of Travel in Guatemala and the Yucatan
Speaker (fine arts museum curator)--"The Arts and Crafts of the Mayas"
Speaker--On how to travel in Mexico and Central America

More ideas

Here are some further programs. We have never heard of any library having programs on most of these subjects, but they could. Many are suitable for teenagers, but adults would be interested in some.

Horseback Riding. If the library has a suitable yard, persuade somebody from a local stable to come and bring a horse. He could demonstrate the techniques of riding and the care of horses. (In the process, the library's lawn might acquire some much-needed fertilizer.) One library did so with success, partially because, being held outside near a busy street, the horse attracted many passers-by who had not heard about the program.

Winter Sports. A local expert could be found to demonstrate the techniques of skiing, skating, snowshoeing, bobsledding or hockey. How about curling? We bet that hasn't been a library program. Again a yard, or a patch of ice, would be desirable, but some things could be demonstrated indoors. Films could also be used with this kind of program.

Model Building. This could be a workshop, and/or a contest. Ships and planes could be built, and there could even be variations such as World War I planes, clipper ships or junks and sampans.

Motorcycles. The care, repair and riding could be demonstrated. Certainly outside the library, if the engine is going to be started. Otherwise it would probably be indoors, if you can get the motorcycle in.

Antique Cars. They could be assembled in the library's parking lot, if there is one, or at the curb outside the library. Maybe the police department would arrange to keep a space clear for an hour or two. Owners would discuss their care and maintenance.

Weightlifting. This is an activity beloved by younger teenagers, and undoubtedly a weightlifter could be found who would demonstrate, describe techniques and discuss hazards.

Canoeing. Especially good if there is a nearby waterway. The audience could assemble there, and then go back to the library for printed materials and/or a film.

Camping. What to take, how to pack, health and safety, where to go, laws and regulations. One expert offered libraries a talk on camping in Europe.

Personal safety and home protection. Police departments offer speakers on these subjects.

Insurance. The Life Underwriters Association of New York City, and doubtless other such organizations, offer speakers on any aspect of health and life insurance, including pension plans and retirement benefits.

Book, magazine and newspaper collecting. As one example, a collector of historical newspapers offered to talk in libraries.

Cooking. Have cooked, by staff, friends, professional cooks and others, all kinds of unusual foods. Have them displayed for the audience to sample, and have as many cooks as possible on hand to discuss their preparation. Use recipes from cookbooks in the library's collection.

Talks: a summary and checklist of preparation

KINDS

Panel--several speakers and moderator informally discussing subject

Symposium--several speakers and moderator; short speeches; audience takes part

Single speaker

Speaker using audiovisual aids (films, slides, charts, blackboard)

Speaker giving demonstration (of an art or craft)

Speaker displaying objects connected with subject (snakes, antiques, a horse)

Dialogue

Interview

Ambulatory talk (tour of library; historical, architectural or literary walk in community)

MATERIALS

Books, pamphlets, periodicals, recordings on subject are very desirable for display or for borrowing by public; library may supply films or slides for speaker

EQUIPMENT (as needed by speaker)

Lectern

Microphone(s)

Pitcher of water and glasses

Chair(s)

Table(s)--for speakers to sit at, for demonstration, for display of objects

Blackboard, pointer and chalk

Flashlight

Record player

Projector(s) and related equipment

EQUIPMENT (as needed by audience)

Chairs--have extras to bring out, in case audience larger than anticipated

Microphone(s)--if large room

Paper and pencils--for submitting written questions

STAFF

One to introduce speaker, talk about library's services and materials related to subject, and to close program

Projectionist--may be same as introducer

Ushers, ticket takers, clerk to charge out books--depends on size of audience

AUDIENCE

All ages; any number (small audience of twenty or thirty is best for demonstration)

SESSIONS

Number--one, a series of several, a series for a season, or a continuing part of library's programming

Spacing--if related subjects, a week or two apart; if long, unrelated series, once a month or several times a year

Length--each session from one to one and a half hours

SPACE

Size--can range from about 400 sq. ft. up

Location--depending on subject, can utilize public use area (for demonstration), auditorium, story hour room, library yard, work room, or parking lot

SUBJECTS

Almost any subject is suitable; for example: acupuncture, astrology, Africa, the aged, aquariums, architecture, astronomy, automobile repair, basketball, Buddhism, birth control, cats, chess, China, cinematography, conservation, consumer protection, death, dogs, existentialism, geology, gift making, glaucoma, golf, investments, law, mental health, motorcycle repair, painting, plant diseases, pollution, pottery, religion, sculpture, sewing, snakes, taste, tea ceremony, venereal disease, vocational guidance, wills, Xosa literature, Yaqui Indians, zoning laws, Zuni poetry

SOURCES (of speakers)

Schools and colleges (both faculties and students), museums, aquariums, zoos, scientific associations, businesses, athletic organizations, religious organizations, health agencies and organizations, consumer protection agencies, conservation organizations, clubs, artists, representatives of foreign governments, lawyers, ethnic groups, hobbyists, other individuals with special skills or backgrounds

PLANNING AND PRODUCING

Select subject and find speaker (sometimes one finds a speaker first)

Contact speaker--discuss fee, purpose of program, equipment he or she needs, kind of audience expected, length of speech and other parts of program, question period, role of library in program; arrange date

Publicity--get biographical details and possibly a picture of speaker (also useful for introduction); learn something about the subject for writing publicity and for introduction; think of potential audience and places they will gather, for distributing publicity

Checking up--make sure microphones and audiovisual equipment are working at least several hours before program (in time to replace); see that enough chairs are in place or are available and that the room is well ventilated (important for large crowds); check off list of other equipment; remind speaker a day or two before program

Before the program--be there in plenty of time to greet speaker, offer him coffee, the use of a rest room, and a place to store his equipment and hang his coat; arrange with speaker and staff the handling of questions; discuss with ushers the seating of latecomers and other problems

NOTES

1. Library Journal, April 15, 1969, p. 1570.
2. Foglesong, Marilee. "Between Librarian and Teenager," Wisconsin Library Bulletin, March-April 1971, p. 86.
3. American Libraries, June 1974, p. 489.
4. Library Journal, Oct. 15, 1971, p. 3291.
5. American Libraries, Oct. 1974, p. 468.
6. Library Journal, March 15, 1975, p. 549.
7. Library Journal, Sept. 1, 1975, p. 1468.
8. Ibid.

Chapter 5

WORKSHOPS

With people becoming increasingly interested in participation rather than mere observation--witness the rise in
crafts, audience participation in the theatre and in sports--
workshops have become popular as library programs. There
have been workshops in film, drama, poetry, many kinds of
crafts, and the big new fad that everybody talks about, videotape (for which, see Chapter 6).

Workshops need experts; at least one person to teach
whatever is being workshopped. Some workshops need a lot
of space and some need expensive equipment. They must
also cater to small groups, since they rely on individual attention and on every participant's making or doing something; from five to fifteen members is the range for most
workshops. Some of them extend over a period of months.
Some require a great deal of staff time. Other kinds of
workshops, particularly some crafts, can be held in a few
hours, require little staff time, and require little, or at
least inexpensive, equipment and/or material.

The library programs that are expensive in terms of
staff time, space, equipment, materials and publicity, especially considering the small number of people involved, can
nevertheless be of great value to the participants. Since
something usually results from a workshop, they can also be
of further value to the library; videotapes can be shown many
times, plays can be presented, poetry can be read and published, and crafts can be displayed. In short, the results of
workshops spread like ripples, and maybe like waves if you
are lucky.

Rapping, writing, music--for teenagers

An unusual workshop for teenagers that was given in

107

one library combined the subjects of several workshops in one. It was called "Rap and Rite" and it was held during the summer. In the spring, the librarians--the children's and young adult librarians were both involved--gave an interest flyer to teenagers, asking them to comment on the themes and to return the form. This is the way the flyer was worded:

"We are planning a series of Summer Workshops for teens. The sessions will give YOU a chance to 'Rap' on various themes, ideas, subjects, etc. that interest YOU, and will give you the opportunity, if so moved, to contribute by writing, reading, and creating your own work.

"To help us: Please comment on the themes below; what books, records, art, advertisements, or personal ideas do they call to mind? Also include your own suggestions on the back; they will be most helpful. If you would like to join us for the workshops this summer, include your name, etc. below."

"Love is all you need.
The me nobody knows.
I never promised you a
    rose garden
Peace, where are you?
The times they are a
    changin'.

Said computer to com-
    puter...
Who is free?
What have you done to
    my song?
Who is my brother?
Johnny got his gun."

This flyer had been subjected to considerable experimentation, because the librarians wanted to find out what wording or ideas would draw the teenagers. (The themes listed here were au courant when they were written. Anyone planning such a workshop would have to find out what was of current interest at that time.) The results of this experimentation showed more than sixty teenagers responding during a three-month period. Names and addresses were collected, and a series of three sessions was planned.

For the first session, a theme was supplied: "Everything is beautiful in its own way." A variety of materials were supplied that would be used as a springboard for discussion. Included were I Heard a Scream in the Streets, edited by Nancy Larrick, The Whole Earth Catalog, pop and rock lyrics, excerpts from the Concert for Bangladesh, and the African Mass. Each person was encouraged to participate by contributing something creative such as poetry, prose,

music, art or handicraft. Several teenagers brought in
items for the first session; they were a poem, a guitar,
drawings and a piece of sculpture. They then talked about
the suggested theme, and about group-suggested themes
such as politics, family problems, school and movies.

For the second session, no theme was suggested; the
group provided the direction. They brought, among other
things, a tape recording of several dramatized stories, a
poem, puppets, and parts of a play. Sharing was the theme
provided for the third session. The librarians presented a
variety of poetry, prose and song lyrics written by or about
teenagers which were used as jumping-off points.

The emphasis in this workshop was on flexibility and
informality. It was a chance for the teenagers to express
themselves in an unstructured situation; the community of
which this library is a part is highly organized, and one of
the librarians said, "We were more interested in authentic
sharing, and in giving teens a chance to express themselves
than in producing a school-structured 'A' poem." More than
half the teenagers who participated came back later to ask
for another workshop; as has happened on other occasions, a
follow-up workshop failed to materialize because one of the
librarians moved to another job and no one else had the time
or inclination to do it.

Journalism

Another workshop for teenagers that involved writing
was a journalism workshop. This group meets on Saturdays
from 10 to 4. Professional reporters work with the teenagers and they produce a community newspaper every three
weeks.

Exploring another culture

Several libraries and museums have conducted workshops that have explored the culture of a country or an area.
An African workshop was conducted for teenagers. They
learned African dances, made music with African instruments and tried out hairstyles and clothes from Africa. A
similar program was an "Arts Workshop in Puerto Rican
Culture." The participants danced, and engaged in painting,
woodcarving and various art forms in order to explore the

cultural tradition and heritage of Puerto Rico. A third program of this type was a piñata workshop, which was followed by a piñata party.

Arts and crafts

There have been many kinds of workshops in the arts and crafts for people of all ages. For one workshop, those interested were asked to bring some of their clothes; they learned how to decorate them with appliqué and embroidery. Each week there was a different theme: dream images, independence, beaches, feet, and clowns. A similar workshop was held using silk-screen printing. Teenagers were asked to bring t-shirts on which they would learn to print. A macramé workshop was also held for teenagers. Forty-one attended, many of them from a drug rehabilitation center, and their response was very enthusiastic. They made belts and plant hangings. At another library, 55 teenagers attended a needlepoint and weaving workshop where they learned the basic stitches on small canvas samples. There have been library-run workshops in sewing, knitting, crocheting, batik, mobiles, sculpture, pottery, painting, drawing and kite-making.

One program that could be called a workshop was a demonstration of yoga techniques. Participants brought blankets or mats and tried to follow the leader. Some of these craft workshops have lasted an hour or two, some have had two sessions, and some have lasted over a period of weeks or months. In many cases, staff members were found who were able to conduct the workshop. Otherwise, community residents were often willing to perform for nothing. The owners of crafts shops have frequently conducted workshops. In one case, the staff provided a babysitter for the demonstrator. In most cases, the library supplied some or all of the materials. When participants are asked to bring materials, they often bring the wrong thing; they are also often inhibited from coming at all. A library that conducted eight such workshops found that none of them cost more than ten dollars and some were much less. Books such as The Illustrated Hassle-Free Make Your Own Clothes Book, by Sharon Rosenberg, or The Macramé Book, by Helene Bress, are usually made available to the participants by the library. One young and talented librarian--and many of the librarians who are conducting these programs are young--has conducted many arts and crafts workshops. She makes do with materials available in the library or with materials she can find or pick up. For an origami workshop, she used plain, brown wrapping paper from the library's shipping room. She cut it into the appropriate sizes and taught the teenagers how to make simple figures--a seal, a penguin and a Chinese fortune teller. She has also conducted a papier mâché workshop; they made Easter eggs (balloons covered with papier mâché) and a variety of animals.

Bicycling

Several libraries have conducted bicycle workshops. At one, held on a Saturday morning for about fifty teenagers, the author of a book on bicycles worked with a group on care and repair. He also discussed safety and legislation for bicycles and he showed the teenagers how to work for better legislation. Teenagers themselves conducted another workshop, covering care and repair, safety, racing and patrols.

Film

Film workshops can be very effective and useful programs. They are of particular interest to the young, up through college age. The Queens Borough (N.Y.) Public Library conducted a three-session Saturday morning series. They obtained the services of a professional filmmaker. Two sessions were devoted to the theory and aesthetics of film and the third was a practical hands-on demonstration. The filmmaker used 8mm equipment, since it was felt that that was what teenagers could most likely afford. There were about thirty teenagers in the group, and they ranged in age from 11 to 20; most of them were high-school seniors. Some had made films but most were beginners.

At the practical session, some of the films that had already been made by members of the group were screened. That was followed by a discussion and a critique of the techniques. Then the filmmaker demonstrated the use of the camera and light meter, and the process of editing, and he described ways of achieving various effects. He then gave individual instruction for those who had questions and problems, and the group talked with him and with each other about filmmaking problems.

A high-school class in Sandy, Utah, went further and made a complete movie from start to finish.[1] They selected a 32-page short story by John D. Swain and turned it into a 58-page, 105-scene scenario. This writing of the script took most of three six-week mini courses. An original musical score for a 14-piece orchestra was also produced. The students made the properties including a shrunken head and a sword to do the beheading. The scriptwriters did the casting. Since there was no money for sets, they shot on location around town. They had the cooperation of the police, the airport, a local mortuary and a church. Initial contacts were made by the teacher and the students did the rest. Technical assistance was provided by a group called Filmakers, Inc. Although this was a class project, it could well have been done by a library and libraries have several advantages over schools: they can be more flexible and they can provide a freer atmosphere for those to whom the structured school has become anathema.

This was the case in one area of Boston, Massachusetts, and a branch of the Boston Public Library conducted a successful film workshop, made a movie, and inspired some bored teenagers.[2] Because teenagers used the branch library very little, and because they showed little interest in the other formal organizations in the community (there were no informal organizations), it was decided to try a filmmaking project combined with a series of semimonthly film programs. The film showings, it was hoped, would enhance the young filmmakers' appreciation of film. The program was planned neither to increase circulation nor to turn nonreaders into readers. Stimulating the thinking and imagination of the teenagers was considered goal enough.

As with many library programs, the money came from a variety of sources. An anonymous donation started the project, and the library provided a $100 charge account at a photographic laboratory. A young, professional filmmaker loaned his equipment and provided technical assistance. The project was publicized through school announcements, posters and talking to teenagers. The last method was the most successful. About twenty teenagers participated and most of them had not been in the library for years. Meetings were held twice a week. Wednesday afternoons were for planning in the library, and Saturday afternoons for shooting the film out in the community. The teenagers wrote the script, acted, directed, shot and edited the film. At first, jobs were rotated but later each settled into the kind of job

he preferred. Shotting on location incurred some suspicion
from local people but they became impressed by the hard
work and seriousness of the teenagers, which is an added
benefit. 16mm film was used, presumably because it was
available. The film cost about $180. As is usual in film-
making only about one-fifth of the film that was shot could
be used. Some of the films shown in the other half of the
program were "An Occurrence at Owl Creek Bridge," "Two
Men and a Wardrobe," "Neighbors," "Night and Fog" and
"On the Bowery."

The results of the project were obvious and gratifying.
One 15-year-old boy spent every afternoon for a month
editing film at the height of the softball season. An "un-
disciplined, bored" 14-year-old boy spent half of his weekends earning money to buy film so he could spend the
other half of the weekends shooting it. And a usually in-
articulate school dropout was heard to talk excitedly about
the technical qualities of a shot. No librarian could ask for
more.

Clubs

Sometimes libraries form clubs of various kinds that
are akin to workshops, because members are often given
instruction at meetings and they are involved in doing whatever it is that interests the club. Libraries have run
camera clubs, stamp clubs, film clubs and chess clubs.
The season of one library-run chess club ends each year in
a tournament.

Chess tournaments

Another library decided to have a chess tournament,
following a successful lecture/demonstration on chess. Although such a tournament is not a workshop in the usual
sense, since there are no instructors, the participants certainly worked at their subject and they probably learned
something. For this workshop (tournament), registration
was required, since the number of players had to be limited.
A simple registration form was used. (It was adapted from
one used by a local chess club.) Players were asked to
bring chessmen and boards, a notation pad, and a tournament clock if they had one. The tournament was open to
all, but they were required to know chess notation. It was

run according to the rules of the United States Chess Federation, and was divided into two parts, one for members of the United States Chess Federation and one for non-members.

The tournament was held on three consecutive evenings, with each participant playing 2 games per evening. Fifty players registered and the ages ranged from eight to about sixty; many of the players were teenagers. It is believed that many more persons would have registered if the publicity had been more widespread; because of space limitations, however, they held the publicity down. The event itself generated much publicity; the local newspaper printed several news stories, mentioned it in their weekly chess article, and printed a photograph of the players in action. (If action is the word to describe chess players.) No fee was required, and no prizes were given.

Quite a lot of space was needed for the tournament, although it might have been held in a smaller space if the right kind of furniture had been available; round library tables had to be used in some cases. It was held in a large children's room, little used during the evening hours, which opened off the adult reading room. Library users could, thus, wander through and watch the play. It was, needless to say, a fairly quiet kind of program and thus ideally suited for a public area--although, occasionally, the hum from either army stilly sounded.

Poetry

Libraries have conducted poetry workshops with varying degrees of success. One of the most successful, in a branch of the New York Public Library, is now in its third year. There are 16 sessions every year, running from October through May. The sessions are on Saturday afternoons and they last for about two hours. Since this workshop is for teenagers, it is held in the browsing room of the Nathan Straus Young Adult Library; this is a quiet area set slightly apart from the rest of the library.

These young people come, of their own accord, from all over New York City and they are seriously interested in writing poetry. They read their own poetry aloud and comment on each other's work. The poet-in-charge does not criticize, but merely guides the teenagers; sometimes he gives them subjects to write about, and sometimes they write a group poem, each one contributing a line.

The attendance varies, but averages about twenty, and the ages range from 13 to 18. There is no registration or other formality. Recently some middle-aged men and women attended. At first the teenagers were not happy about having an older audience to read their poems to, but as the afternoon wore on they became used to it, and in the end everyone enjoyed themselves.

Et cetera workshops

Libraries have conducted several other kinds of very useful workshops. The Port Washington (N.Y.) Public Library has conducted a résumé-writing workshop, which should be very popular when jobs are scarce. (This is a good example of how to provide programs to meet special situations.) There were two sessions of two hours each, including instruction in how to gather the information, how to present it selectively, and how to write the accompanying letter. Each participant prepared a résumé which was then criticized by a guidance counselor. Participants were expected to register, and to pick up forms before the first session.

Port Washington has run other helpful workshops for difficult times. Volunteers trained by the Internal Revenue Service and the New York State Department of Taxation helped retired persons with their income tax problems by answering questions and assisting them in preparing their returns. As part of a program described as a "Food Day," the same library held workshops on nutrition, home gardens, food stamps, the food dollar and consumer-interest legislation.

Workshops: a summary and checklist of preparations

KINDS

Film

Videotape

Arts and crafts

Poetry, short story, journalism

Drama

Dance

Music

Citizen action

Culture of an area or group--usually combines some of above

MATERIALS

Books, pamphlets, periodicals, films, recordings on subject--for consultation during workshop sessions, for borrowing during workshop, and for follow-up by those wishing to go further

EQUIPMENT

Leader/expert will designate equipment needed; varies tremendously

Dance--music (i.e. record player, recordings)

Writing--paper, pencils and possibly some books and records

Arts and crafts--often inexpensive materials, sometimes supplied by library, sometimes by leader, sometimes by participants

Film and videotape--expensive, delicate and intricate equipment (see appropriate section)

General--work tables, chairs

STAFF

One, or sometimes two, to work with expert and with group in conducting the workshop in accordance with the library's policies and goals (staff member may receive enough training to conduct future workshops); many workshops conducted initially by librarian experts

AUDIENCE

All ages--most are of interest to teenagers, many to adults and some to children depending on level; suitable for small groups, five to ten for film or videotape, and up to fifteen or twenty for others

SESSIONS

Number--one (for some crafts) to ten or twenty depending on scope

Spacing--at regular intervals, once or twice a week

Length--from one hour (for some crafts) to several hours for film or videotape (travel is often involved)

SPACE

Probably small (400 sq. ft.)

Might require--electrical outlets, sink, dressing room, good lighting, dark room

SUBJECTS

Drama--could be as simple as play reading, or could encompass the whole range of theatrical activities

Dance--square, folk, modern, etc.

Arts and crafts--macramé, photography, kite making, sewing, clothing design, pottery, knitting, yoga, batik, automobile repair, egg decorating, poodle clipping

Film and videotape--record library activities, community events, create original film

Citizen action--learn how to protect environment, protect tenant's rights, lobby effectively

Writing--produce book, pamphlet, newspaper

Culture of area or group--learn about, create, and perform music, dance, drama, arts and crafts (Chinese, American Indian, Israeli, Mexican, etc.)

PURPOSES AND USES

Film and videotape--show library events, community events, on television, in the library, or elsewhere in the community; spread knowledge of the techniques and uses of videotape

Drama, dance, music--groups can perform in library

Arts and crafts--objects can be displayed in library

Poetry--can result in further library programs

Culture of area or group--further library programs (All these results can be used for further library publicity)

SOURCES

> Schools and colleges, independent artists and craftsmen, poets, theatrical, musical and dance groups, newspapers, businesses

SELECTION

> Since some of these workshops require large investments in time and money for small groups, it is wise to predetermine interest by formally or informally polling the community; it would also be wise to register participants

PLANNING AND PRODUCING

> Find the expert or technician

> Be sure there is a suitable space

> Obtain equipment--if it is one time only, or an experiment, and expensive equipment is needed, rent it; if workshops are to continue, it is cheaper to buy

> Gather printed or recorded materials on subject--on the advice of an expert

> Schedule--arrange with leader/expert, and, if it is a small group meeting over long period of time, with participants

> With leader/expert--plan workshop's goals, discuss what library can and cannot do, what money can be spent, and what is to be done with products of workshop

> Before first session--be sure equipment arrives on time and is working; remind participants, if small group

PUBLICITY

> Describe goals of workshop

> Describe what, if anything, participants need to know beforehand

> Indicate what they should bring to first session

> Publicize in schools and colleges, stores selling related material or equipment, clubs and organizations likely to have interested members, selected individuals

NOTES

1. Boberg, Lowell. "One Head Well Done--It's the 'Reel' Thing," Top of the News, June 1973, pp. 351-6.
2. Brooks, Andrea. "Filmmaking with Young Adults," The Bookmark, Oct. 1969, pp. 14-5.

Chapter 6

VIDEOTAPE,* MULTIMEDIA, AUTOMATED PROGRAMS

No one doubts that videotape can be important in the future of libraries. It presents a whole range of possibilities. With the development of inexpensive, portable videotape recorders, it is possible for libraries to make and store recordings of a wide variety of activities, people and places that would otherwise have been lost. Exciting things have already been done in the New York Public Library and in the Port Washington (N.Y.) Public Library.[1]

One way that libraries can engage in the production of videotapes is to have a workshop. In spite of the relatively low cost of such a project, this may seem like an expensive program. It can, however, be an investment for the future. If the library purchases the equipment, successive workshops can train more and more people (previous participants can train others) so that a large body of community residents may become expert; thus the library has a ready supply of people who can make tapes. The Port Washington Public Library, as of the summer of 1972, had trained 450 people to videotape, and about fifty people were trained to edit tapes.[2] Of course, the products of these workshops have become useful as well as the experience; the same library had, as of 1972, collected more than 380 hours of tapes made by local residents. These tapes covered such subjects as town planning board meetings, interviews with older residents, local football games, interviews on the street with people who talked about drugs and youth, young people talking about drugs and themselves, volunteer firemen, interviews with local mayors and many others. More than 7500 people had, at that time, viewed those tapes--an indication of the need and interest.

---

*The checklist of preparations for videotape programs is included in the summary at the end of Chapter 5.

If two or three thousand dollars can be found, then the purchase of videotape equipment seems like a good investment. Equipment can also be rented but the cost is such that buying it seems more economical. Sometimes equipment, or part of it, can be borrowed. Colleges and other institutions have videotape equipment, and they might be persuaded to share it with you. A psychiatric research center, for example, has offered to share all its equipment and tapes with one library. Even if you can get to use some editing equipment until you can get your own, or you can get technical advice, you can save a lot of money.

It seems useful to describe a particular videotape workshop in some detail. This one took place at, or at least originated from, the Port Richmond Branch of the New York Public Library. This branch is on Staten Island in a decaying suburban neighborhood; the population ranges from lower middle class to very poor and is racially mixed; it is also apathetic. The branch has been the recipient of a small L.S.C.A. grant and has one extra staff member as a result. The money for the videotape workshop came from a private foundation. It provided for equipment, the salary of a part-time technician, and other expenses such as publicity and carfare. The technician who was hired was a student who worked in the media center of a local college. Flyers and newspaper publicity were prepared and faculty at the local high school were contacted in an attempt to interest teenagers in the workshop.

To the great surprise of the staff, the nucleus of the group came, not from those sources, but from the local troublemakers; this group had hung around the entrance to the children's room blocking the steps, breaking bottles and creating a variety of disturbances; they had been particularly annoying during library programs which they had attempted to disrupt from both inside and outside the library. This group was transformed during the course of the workshop into interested and helpful teenagers; they no longer caused trouble, presumably because they had found something engaging and worth doing instead; they also learned to handle delicate and expensive equipment and to have respect for it, as well as for other people.

Eleven teenagers gathered for the first session; they gathered very slowly, delaying the start for an hour. The technician first explained the equipment, with many questions being asked. Then she videotaped the group, with various

members taking turns with the camera. She immediately
showed those tapes which "were viewed with glee." The
group then moved outside the library; there some local
children, a woman in a car, and a young girl who was
leaving the library were all stopped, interviewed and taped.
The young adult librarian, who was in charge of the project,
reported that there was much laughter, fun and wisecracking
among the group because most of them were friends.

They all went back inside the library and watched
the tapes they had made, with much interest and pleasure.
So much, in fact, that it was hard to get the group to dis-
perse. They were forced to disband at 5 p.m., because
some plays were being presented in the library that evening
and the cast had begun to arrive. Three of the group and
the technician returned for the first play, they taped it and
interviewed the audience as it was leaving.

Five or six eager group members began knocking on
the door of the library a full hour before the second session
was to begin. They waited patiently on the steps until the
staff was ready. The technician, a young woman, refreshed
the memories of the group by going over the use of the
equipment again. Staff members and the teenagers discussed
ways of approaching people and techniques of interviewing.
A trip had been planned to the local business district and
subjects for the proposed interviews were discussed. That
was the time of the meat boycott and it was a natural for
discussion with shoppers and businessmen. It was a beautiful, warm and sunny day; it was Easter vacation and the
shoppers were out in force. The bakery window had been
decorated for Easter, and that was the first thing they taped.
They went to a shoe store, a grocery store and a men's
clothing store; the proprietors were very friendly and co-
operative, and were glad to be interviewed. They discovered,
however, that the shoppers were wary of them and declined
to be interviewed. So they returned to the library through a
park, where they taped "some very interesting people."

It was next decided to visit an area where garbage
was being used for landfill. They interviewed the workers,
shot pictures of the scale weighing the garbage trucks, a
bulldozer mixing garbage and dirt, piles of garbage and individual citizens who had come to dump their trash. On returning to the library, they viewed the tapes and they all
became quite excited when their taping came into view. This
time there was notable improvement in the tapes.

The next session illustrated a number of programming problems. A visit to the zoo had been planned. One boy had to deliver papers but he made such an "impassioned plea" for the group to wait for him that another member went to help him with his route. Two other boys phoned their mother to see if she could give them a ride and avoid further delays with the bus. Meanwhile, the equipment had been taken to another library for the taping of a program; that meant an extra trip to pick it up. When they got to the zoo, they found, to their disappointment, that the animals were all in interior cages; the inside lighting turned out to be adequate. They shot a tiger, hyena, wolverine, monkeys and otter; the birds were particularly attractive and they shot hornbills, vultures, cranes and a large display of exotic birds. The zoo attendant roused the sleepy alligators for them, and their annoyance and unusual and eerie sounds made an excellent segment of tape. Two zoo attendants were interviewed, but the visitors to the zoo (like the shoppers) were shy. The next disappointment came when they discovered that the zoo closed at 5 p.m. and that the children's zoo was closed; the moral of this story should be clear to all. They did manage to shoot, through the wire fence, some portions of the children's zoo, including a flower cart, rabbits, ducks and a peacock.

The Staten Island Ferry and its environs was to be the scene of the next taping. Again, problems of transporting equipment (because equipment was being shared by a number of branch libraries) caused delays. They taped the ferry leaving the dock, and then they got permission to visit the engine room and to interview the captain. During the ferry's return trip, they were in the midst of the rush hour. This part of the trip produced an interesting segment; one person photographed the New York City skyline, the Statue of Liberty, Brooklyn Bridge, Governor's Island and other harbor scenes; another member of the group, meanwhile, was a few feet away interviewing; this gave the tape a nice combination of scenes, interviews, and a natural background of conversation and noise. On the Staten Island side again, they gathered in the terminal and shot the crowd rushing onto the ferry. They then went to the attic of a nearby branch library, which is high on a hill, and shot a panoramic view of the bay.

Islands naturally abound in marine activities, so for the next session they were also drawn to the water. This time they found a company that had a fleet of tugboats. They again asked, and received permission to shoot on the company's property. Going to the end of a long pier, they got some fine shots of tugboats, the water, and the nearby New Jersey shore. They had started off again, when the equipment began giving them trouble (another aspect of working with videotape, and one which emphasizes the need for a technician). On returning to the library, however, it was discovered that only a minor adjustment was necessary. There the group clamored to put on and tape an original play. Two short plays were taped.

High Rock Park is a hilly, wooded wildlife refuge on Staten Island and it was chosen for the next session. A group of sixth-grade children and their teacher, who were visiting the park, were interviewed and taped first. Then they went, with a guide who had been assigned to them, to a lab where he (the guide) talked and showed the plants and animals, indigenous to the park, that were on display; the snake that he draped around his arm as he talked fascinated them. Some beehives were taped as the guide talked about the bees. Some park workers (other than the drones) were interviewed, and then they went along the swamp trail with the guide; there they videotaped skunk cabbages, sassafras trees, blueberry bushes, ferns and other inhabitants. As with most sessions, this one lasted longer than they thought it would and their return to the library was late.

At this point, a public showing of the videotape equipment was arranged. Fliers were made and distributed, a poster placed in the library, an article put in the local newspaper and an announcement made on a morning radio program. The day's demonstration began with a showing to about fifty adults and pre-school children of a tape of the last meeting of that group. Then the equipment was moved to the library's main reading room. There many people stopped to be shown the equipment, to be taped, and to see themselves on television. The newspaper photographer, whose visit had been arranged, did not appear. So it goes.

A trip to Manhattan was arranged for a few days later. They visited a batik demonstration at another branch library, taped people in a small park, taped St. Thomas's Church, the Museum of Modern Art, the Creative Playthings store and other Manhattan scenes. The group also visited Richmondtown, Staten Island, an area where historic buildings were being restored, and other local points of interest.

There are many other kinds of activities and places that might be videotaped in such a program and the tapes would be useful to keep in the library for showing in library programs. One might visit one of the many kinds of experimental schools that are springing up. Tapes could be made of barbers, dentists, and doctors working; they could be used to prepare a child for his first visit. Tapes of unique community cultural events could be made for if such a record is not made, these activities are lost forever. Interviews with political candidates, town council meetings, and hearings on new highways, housing developments and sewers are all good subjects for videotaping; they would then be available to any citizen who had been unable to attend, or was unaware of, the original meeting. The value of these activities to the library and to the community is clear. The value to this particular library, of the workshop described, is also clear, when one considers the transformation of a group of troublemakers into helpful teenagers. One can also see the value to the teenagers in their excitement and enthusiasm; in a follow-up workshop, for example, it was planned to use some of the original group as teachers. Obviously, in spite of the cost, this program paid off in many ways. The following is a sample list of costs for equipment. After the equipment is purchased and the people are trained the costs become minimal. Not included are: staff time, which is expensive; transportation and other miscellaneous costs, which vary greatly; and the cost of somebody to do the training, which might be about $200.

Portapak system--Sony Rover II	$1875.00	
Editing Deck--Sony 3650	1369.00	
Videotape	11.00	each $\frac{1}{2}$ hour
Service contract	225.00	
9" Monitor/TV--Sony	275.00	
Microphone	75.00	
1 can head cleaner	5.00	
Floodlight-Colortron 1000w	68.00	
1 bulb	15.25	
Gaffer's tape	8.50	
2 grease pencils & 5 yellow dots (for cataloging and editing)	1.16	
32'-camera extension cable	77.00	
Carrying Case	115.00	
Tripod	75.00	
Headphones	20.00	
3-hour battery pack	118.00	
Total (incl. 2 hrs videotape)	$4365.91	

The following is the format of a videotape workshop that was prepared for the Public Library of Bridgeport, Conn., by Video Life Associates* of N.Y.C.

1st session. "Introduction to 1/2-inch Equipment": cables, cameras, decks, porta-pak, editing deck, monitors, TV, RF, power sources, what to do and what to avoid, threading, video modes, cleaning, off-the-air recording, wrapping cables

2nd session. "The Tape, the Camera, and the Crew": video tape, synchronization; the camera--frame, focus, composition, f/stops, types of shots; taping under a director, functioning as a crew, definition of jobs, interviewing, tape roll, audio dubs, multi-camera concepts

3rd session. "An Introduction to Audio": cycle, frequency, volume, clarity, perspective, types of microphones, the audio mixer, mixing sound, setting up a multi-microphone system, signal-to-noise ratio

4th session. "Editing/Lighting and Staging (I)": editing-- set-up of equipment, cleaning aesthetics, backtiming, assembly editing, insert editing, butt editing, AU meter, video meter; lighting and staging--components of picture making, center of interest, how the picture communicates, communications gray scale and contrast ratios, depth of field, the camera, lighting equipment

5th session. "Editing/Lighting and Staging (II)": editing-- editing workshop; lighting and staging--objectives, color temperature, placement of lights and the camera, three-point lighting, lighting stills, graphics

6th session. "Video Technology": the vidicon camera, the plumbicon camera, synchronization, servomechanisms, resolution, distortion, frequency, interlacing, trouble-shooting

7th session. "Audio Visual Communications and Education":

---

*Video Life Associates specializes in video systems and their applications; among their services are the design and installation of video systems, program design, production and post-production services, sales, rental, and servicing of equipment.

audiovisual programming, internal uses of video, an overview of educational uses, undergraduate and graduate programs in communications

8th session. "Film and Video--A Comparison": economics, aesthetics, applications, opportunities

9th session. "A Group Production": editing to be done during the week

10th session. "Critique and Discussion" of the program produced the previous week; summary and evaluation

Combinations, mixed media, multimedia

Whatever you call them, these are programs that use two or more elements or media either serially or simultaneously. Some kinds have been mentioned in other chapters, including lectures with slides, discussion groups with books and records, and discussion groups using films and books. Such programs could include some or all of the following: lectures, poetry, drama, dance, music, films. They have several uses, and they have advantages and disadvantages. Much more work is required to put together a program containing disparate elements, but it is often worth it. There is one very practical reason for having a program of this kind. If one part fails, or more than one, you still have some kind of program left. This important lesson was drummed into the authors in a very dramatic way. They were conducting a program on African culture that consisted of several films and an African percussionist. Fifteen minutes before the start of the program, one of the authors was waiting for the performer at a bus terminal, with the car engine running, when a staff member came racing up the ramp to say that the drummer wasn't coming. The films were shown anyway, and the audience, although disappointed in the non-appearance of the musician, enjoyed the program.

Programs of this kind are useful for presenting the culture of a group, a country or an area, since no culture can be shown through one medium. A program we called "In the Black Fashion" was made up of many diverse elements; it included a fashion show, poetry, music and dance. The Salt Lake City Public Library, in an attempt to reach the Spanish-speaking community, presented a week of activities, including guitarists, a folk-ballet, poetry and dramatic

readings in Spanish, bilingual story hours, a film, an art
exhibit and artifact displays. (If the elements take place at
different times, it is still essentially the same program.)

This presentation of a series of connected programs
in a short period of time--a day, a few days, or a week--
is an economical way of reaching large numbers of people.
The festival nature of a group of programs presented in
this way is likely to attract more publicity and more people.
Also the publicity you put out will be good for the whole
series. If the programs are to be held outside the library,
the materials and equipment need only be transported once.
There is also an excitement about such programs that in-
fects the staff with enthusiasm.

When a neighborhood center opened a few years ago,
a branch library in Staten Island, New York arranged with
them to produce six programs during Negro History Week.
A large exhibit of books and recordings was prepared; this
was accompanied by a borrowed exhibit on Black inventors
and discoverers. Library staff members were on hand
during the week to accept applications for borrowers' cards,
to accept reservations for books, to distribute booklists,
and to talk informally about the library's services. Films
were provided by the library, as were the projector and
projectionist. Performances were given by both staff members and community residents. The program follows:

Monday evening

Film--"Black History: Lost, Stolen or Strayed" (BFA
color, 54 min.)

Performance--music and dance (neighborhood residents)

Tuesday evening

Poetry--a staff member talked about and read from
some black poets and a community resident read
some poems (Robert Hayden, LeRoi Jones, Langston
Hughes, Countee Cullen and others)

Wednesday afternoon

Film--"Body (BFA color, 25 min.) a film about black
athletes

"Soul" (BFA color, 25 min.) a film about Afro-
American music and musicians

"The Black Soldier" (BFA color, 25 min.), about

black soldiers in the U.S. from the Revolution to
Vietnam

Book talk--young adult librarian talking about black
literature

Wednesday evening

Discussion--analysis and discussion of the various phi-
losophies of black leaders (led by community residents)

Talk--the role of the black artist in America (visiting
teacher)

Thursday evening

Performance--dance, music and drama depicting black
heritage (performed by a local drama group)

Friday evening

Film--"New Mood" (Indiana University, 30 min.), the
story of the civil rights movement

Talks--"The African-American," "Black Treasures,"
and "The Black Man in Medicine" (given by a local
teacher, a black Army officer, and a black medical
doctor)

Branch libraries in the area encompassed by the New
York Public Library's South Bronx Project have produced
many programs, with several media, that portray the culture of an area or a country. One of these was devoted to
the folklore of the Caribbean countries; it utilized a film,
and the dances, music, arts and crafts of those countries.
Another one was devoted to Puerto Rican culture; it combined music, dances, poetry and an informal discussion.
Similar programs explored the cultural experiences of Colom-
bia and El Salvador. A whole week of programs was presented to show facets of Spanish culture; included were
dances, a puppet show, storytelling, and the presentation of
various dramatic works. One program was held in honor of
Eugenio María de Hostos and José Martí, the Puerto Rican
and Cuban patriots; there were poetry and music from those
two countries, and there was a dramatization of an imaginary
dialogue between the two men. Programs were also given in
memory of particular events; two of these were a celebration
of Colombian independence and a celebration of the centennial of the freeing of Puerto Rican slaves. This kind of
program can be approached in many ways and can be given
many forms; the scope for the planner is great.

The recent upsurge of interest in China has provided another opportunity. Several programs in Chinese culture have been popular. One branch library in Staten Island presented a two-part program: a series of films at noon, and a group of live performers during the evening. The films were borrowed from the Chinese consulate, and the performers were found through a staff member. Neither films nor performers cost the library anything. The evening program was followed by a reception at which authentic Chinese delicacies were served. The food, and some decorations, cost less than $25. The program follows:

Film program:
"A Night at the Peking Opera"--Chinese opera; includes dance, mime, opera, comedy and tragedy, played by the famous Peking troupe in a performance of great humor and virtuosity
"T'ai Chi Ch'uan"--one of the ancient Chinese martial arts, a means of self-defense; it is also a spiritual as well as a physical exercise
"A City of Cathay"--a famous large painting from the Ch'ing Dynasty; the film shows part of the painting intercut with scenes of people performing the tasks represented in the painting

Live program:
Reading of poetry in Chinese and English, with a commentary on Chinese poetry
Singing of the Lao-Sheng (old man) parts from Chinese operas, accompanied by the hu-chin (two-string violin)
Demonstration of t'ai chi (Chinese classical exercises)

The Brooklyn (N.Y.) Public Library came up with an interesting variation on the idea of a program about a particular culture; they have presented the cultures of a number of diverse countries, or groups, on a single program or series of programs. Brooklyn has large numbers of people whose ancestry is Jewish, Italian, Irish, black or Puerto Rican, and in lesser numbers, German, Polish, Scandinavian, Russian, Arabic or Mohawk Indian. Consequently, the library decided to show the community they wanted to serve all the people; they also hoped to promote understanding among these groups. They gave thirty presentations in three locations. In addition to the performances at each program, there was commentary by a folklore expert that gave added depth.

One event, entitled "A Festival of Poetry and Song,"

presented a reading from a book about the experiences of
Jews in America, the singing of English and Appalachian
ballads, the presentation of a mixed media event, titled
"Poland 1931, " and various readings by poets. Another program, entitled "Ellis Island Elegy, " presented a collage of
drama, song, dance, and folklore celebrating Irish, Italian,
Jewish, Scandinavian, and Middle Eastern contributions to
America.[3] At "An African People Theatre Experience, "
there were scenes from the plays of Langston Hughes and
LeRoi Jones, drummers from Africa, and a Haitian folklore
group.

Combination programs are useful when presenting the
work of an artist (poet, painter, novelist) particularly one
who has worked in several media. The centennial of Dickens'
death provided one such opportunity; an expert on Dickens
talked about his illustrators and showed slides and an actor
read selections from the novels and stories; a Pickwickian
reception, with appropriate food, followed the program. Recently, the poet Countee Cullen was being honored with a
series of programs. The Countee Cullen Branch of the New
York Public Library, in Harlem, conducted a black poetry
festival (at which poets read their own works), a lecture
series, a series called "Writer Meets Reader, " films for
children and teenagers, a children's art workshop (based on
one of Countee Cullen's books), and a very unusual program
in which a librarian conducted a literary walk to places
associated with Countee Cullen, Langston Hughes and others.
All of this culminated in an open house.

One might use a variety of media to present the art
and the attitudes of a period. Programs on classicism, ro-
manticism, the baroque, Elizabethan and modern periods
could be presented in this way. They could utilize readings
from poetry, plays, novels and other writings; they could
contain live or recorded music of the period; they could display works of art, or show those works through slides or
films; there could be talks on the philosophy, science or
social life of the period, which could also utilize slides,
films, filmstrips or other audiovisual aids.

A program on the eighteenth century could include an
essay or two from The Spectator by Joseph Addison, Alex-
ander Pope's "The Rape of the Lock, " some of Jonathan
Swift's poems (those not used in college anthologies), Mozart's
"Quintet for Clarinet and Strings in A, " some songs from
John Gay's The Beggar's Opera, "The London of William

Hogarth" (a 28-minute film from Contemporary /McGraw-
Hill), reproductions of some of Joshua Reynold's paintings,
and pictures of some examples of eighteenth-century architecture. Before the program, as the audience assembles,
the Mercury recording (Sr 90458) of "18th Century French
Flute Concertos" could be played.

A program on the nineteenth century would be started
with passages from the Preface to the Lyrical Ballads and "I
Wandered Lonely as a Cloud" by Wordsworth, and could continue with passages from Byron, Baudelaire, and Heine; the
songs of Schubert and Schumann could be used (possibly,
"Du bist wie eine Blume" thus combining Heine and Schumann).

The twentieth century has many possibilities. Films
like "The Reality of Karel Appel" (13-minute color film,
Contemporary /McGraw-Hill) and "Jackson Pollock" (10-
minute color film, Radim), could be used. There could be
readings from Kafka, Joyce and Beckett, and the music of
Béla Bartók and Arnold Schoenberg could be used. For the
twentieth century, particularly, there are films on all kinds
of artists and you could have an all-film program. However, live is better.

Some combination programs have contained segments
that drew the audience into the action. One such program in
Spanish, which drew on the cultures of several Spanish-
speaking countries, started with two plays: Grillos y Ranas
by Gabriela Mistral, and La Fiercilla by Luz Castano; they
were followed by a puppet show, and finally, the performers
joined the audience in some Mexican dances.

A teenage group that has performed in some New
York City libraries brings the audience into the action twice
during the program. They perform skits, songs and dances,
and read poems; in the middle of the program they urge the
audience to join them in singing, and at the end, they go
down among the audience and join them in dancing.

Another reason for having a program that combines
a variety of media is to present the services of the library
to a group. At a drug rehabilitation center, for example,
the authors gave two book talks, played a recording of
poetry and jazz, and showed a film; descriptions of the library's multiplicity of services were interspersed throughout
the program.

Having an open house is a way of presenting the library's services to the public in the library itself. An open house often consists of a variety of activities throughout the day and evening. Or, it can be held during a specified time, with several activities taking place at once. Sometimes these activities can be repeated several times for different groups. Often there are tours of the library, films, storytelling, puppet shows, displays or exhibits; sometimes there are refreshments. As with any other program, one must do things that will attract the public's attention and make them want to go to the library.

The Countee Cullen Branch of the New York Public Library had an open house which presented a great variety of activities that would appeal to people of all ages and interests. This is what they did, starting in the morning:

10:30 - 12:30	Reading-aloud workshop for parents and adults working with children ages 3-6 years
11:00 - 12:00	Cable television program for adults only
12:00 - 1:00	Demonstration of library services for the blind and physically handicapped
1:00 - 2:00	History of Afro-Americans and their cultural library centers in Harlem-- a talk, a film and a tour of the library
2:00 - 3:00	Library skills and information resources workshop
3:30 - 5:30	Art workshop for children age 7 to 10
3:30 - 5:00	Demonstration of cornrowing hair styles for teenagers
5:00 - 6:00	Chess workshop
6:00 - 7:00	Black music of two worlds--recordings
7:00 - 8:00	Steel band concert
Continuous throughout the day	Haitian photography exhibit; African art objects; Videotape demonstration; Art works from a junior high school

Many of these programs were run by staff members or by librarians from other libraries. The rest were conducted by community residents. The exhibits were borrowed from museums and from the artists.

The anniversary of the founding of a library is a good excuse for an open house, and the public library of East Meadow, N.Y., had one which they called a "Sweet Sixteen Birthday Party." There were games for people of all ages, there were madrigal singers, there were never-before-shown films (a good public relations device), and there were refreshments (another good drawing card).

The public library of Bloomfield, N.J., runs a program that seems to be unique among libraries, and it is put here because we don't know where else to put it. They sponsor day and overnight bus trips to interesting places. Participants sign up and pay the cost, and the library makes the arrangements. Trips have been taken to such places as Newport, R.I., and New Hope, Penn., and to the American Shakespeare Festival in Stratford, Conn.

When a program does contain several elements, some thought must be given to the order in which they are presented. A t'ai chi demonstration, with its slow and stately movements, could be followed by a lively dance or music. A tragic scene from a play might be followed by a comic scene or by some light verse. In other words, vary the length, the tone, or the style. Try also to plan the sequence so that there is a smooth transition from one event to another; there should be a minimum of furniture moving, people going in and out, changing of film reels, and other disruptions. You don't want to have people waiting for long periods of time between parts of the program, although some intermissions may be desirable, and you want to have a program that seems to run smoothly or you may turn people away instead of attracting them.

Somewhat trickier than running parts of a program serially is running two or more media simultaneously. Such a presentation can be useful, however. Media can be used to complement each other, or they can be used to present a sharp contrast. (Irony is often brought out in this way, such as playing "America the Beautiful" while showing scenes of pollution.) It is important, though, to use works of art that enhance each other in some way and not to use them simultaneously merely as a gimmicky idea. Jazz and poetry, a film and a dancer, slides and actors are all media that have been used in this way. In one library program for children, some college students danced to the rhythm and meter of poetry; sometimes they recited as they danced, and at other times some read while others danced.

Automated programs

Technology has provided a great deal of gadgetry that can be used for what might be called automated programs; that is, ones that don't require the active presence of a staff member once the switch has been turned on. Video cassettes, slide projectors, film loop and filmstrip projectors allow visual presentations to be made in lighted, public areas with little or no staffing needs. Thus staff can carry on their regular functions and still be around to service the projector or talk to the public about the program.

For one such program, repeated several times during various Earth Weeks, slides were taken of local polluted areas. Two slide projectors were then hooked up to run sequentially and continuously, and the pictures were then flashed onto a screen that greeted people as they approached the charging desk from the front door.

In another program, films made by teenagers were put onto video cassettes. The cassettes were then run continuously, during specified hours, in the young adult room. The main beneficiaries were a group of hardcore truants (who had something to do and who may have learned something) and the staff of the library (who had relief from the troublemaking of the truants). As more material becomes available, this kind of programming will offer a great deal of flexibility and will enable librarians to respond to events quickly with a program.

The Brooklyn (N.Y.) Public Library has dreamed up a psychedelic slide show.

> We procured two automatic slide projectors, a makeshift screen larger than the conventional one used in libraries, a tape recorder, two 'spinners' which contained a polarized material and two sets of transparencies (100 per carousel).... Briefly, the slides themselves were a combination of commercial reproductions of famous works of art (Rembrandt, Picasso, etc.), parts of photographs taken of friends (an eye here, an ear there), and the handmade transparencies constructed basically of Scotch tape and cellophane. The result was a mad collection of wild colors in motion in an unusual juxtaposition to ordinary or familiar objects against a background of blues rock.[4]

This program was run whenever the staff felt like turning it on and they ran it anywhere from fifteen minutes to two hours. It was watched with fascination by children, teenagers and adults. One young man, who was writing an important paper, worked every day facing the screen. The staff believe that because of this show, and probably because of other programs that were making the library seem like a good place to be, teenagers who had formerly dashed in to get a book and then dashed out again were tending to linger more; they were also spending more time picking out their books, and some of them were even beginning to browse.

A high school senior in New York City developed a slide show entitled "A Trip to Mars," with synchronous sound. It was described by a librarian as "an ingenious simulation of space travel, precisely crafted." It too was used in young adult rooms.

A kind of automated outreach program has been conducted by libraries in Pittsburgh and in Cedar Rapids, Iowa. In both cities, stories were recorded and the recordings were connected to telephone numbers so that children could "dial-a-story." The response was so overwhelming in Pittsburgh that they had to stop. In Cedar Rapids, possibly because it is smaller, the program has worked. They too were overwhelmed at first, but the calls later stabilized at 2000 to 2500 a week. The stories were changed every other day. [5]

The Mead Public Library of Sheboygan, Wis., has developed a talking kangaroo that could be used for automated programming. It was built by staff members and relatives and cost approximately $500. A wooden frame was constructed. Then a casing was made and stuffed with plastic foam. In the meantime, the outside coat had been sewn together. (It was made from a tan fur-like material purchased from a local clothing manufacturer.) The coat was drawn over the casing and stitched together. Then eyes, tongue, arms, etc., were sewn on. A pouch is included to house the library materials the kangaroo talks about. A 5" by 8" opening in the top of the head and an opening in the neck house the recording mechanism, including a cassette tape player. A mat switch (available commercially) in front of the kangaroo activates the voice. The message is a one-minute continuous loop cassette tape, with pauses between messages. All parts are available commercially except the control timing device which was made to order locally. The tapes are made for special occasions and on specific subjects and are changed frequently. The kangaroo is in the lobby of the library and acts as a magnet drawing patrons in, and, the staff feels, causing them to stay for other things the library has to offer.

One sees a variety of possibilities for such a device. Tapes would have to be very short, a minute or two, since a child couldn't be kept standing there very long. However, there are some very short stories, and a lot of poems and songs that could be used. One might even use jokes or riddles. Riddles would certainly be a great come-on.

NOTES

1. Film Library Quarterly, Summer 1972.
2. Dale, Walter A. "The Port Washington Experiment," Film Library Quarterly, Summer 1972, p. 25.
3. Nyren, Dorothy. "Voices of Brooklyn: Report on a Project Funded by the National Endowment for the Humanities," Wilson Library Bulletin, Jan. 1972, pp. 443-5.
4. Quimby, Harriet. "Brooklyn Grooves," Top of the News, April 1970, p. 289.
5. American Libraries, June 1970, p. 289.

Chapter 7

CHILDREN'S PROGRAMS

Perhaps because children are more flexible, mentally
as well as physically, or because they are interested in more
things than adults, programming for children tends to be
more varied than programming for adults; it also seems to
involve audience participation more. Whatever the reasons,
there are some children's librarians who are leaving no programming avenue unexplored.

An article in Illinois Libraries about the Chicago Public Library, shows something of the range of programs being
tried; it also expresses the idea that the library has no
walls--it can go anywhere--and that any medium or device
might be used to serve the library's purposes. Each center,
the article says, carries on a "full program of creative
drama, writing workshops, musical choruses, camera clubs,
reading clubs, tutoring, and whatever else seems to be worth
trying." They also have rock festivals, magic shows, puppet shows, games and crafts, not to mention the traditional
activities of story hours and films. They work in the library
or anywhere in the community and they use the full range of
audiovisual equipment and other devices.[1]

Children's librarians in Wisconsin have had many unusual activities. The Grafton Public Library had a kite
flying contest. Another Wisconsin library, working with retarded children, borrowed from a pet store some rabbits and
a kinkajou, which they let the children handle. A librarian
in New York City tried something that Wisconsin, with its
wide open spaces, might not need; she got a local hardware
store to give her one hundred packets of seeds; using a
walled-in, unused roof area that abutted the children's room,
she had a plant-in; now she and the children have a roof
garden with boxes of tiny marigolds, long-legged sunflowers,
and even some lettuce. A New York City librarian also had

a kite program; the owner of a store that sold unusual kites demonstrated kite building; during the program the children made their own kites, and then went to Central Park to fly them.

In Brooklyn (N.Y.) they had a top spinning contest, and something called a footsie[2] contest, with prizes for the winners and consolation lollipops for the losers. A librarian in the New York Public Library's Central Children's Room conceived an unusual program, a tongue-twister contest. Using a book from the library's collection, and an overhead projector, she flashed the tongue twisters onto a screen. The children, who were all of approximately the same age, were divided into teams of boys and girls, and the contest was run like a spelling bee. (If the ages varied significantly, one could run several contests.) As an added bonus, the author of the book acted as judge.

Some libraries have had another kind of contest, a pet show. The children would probably be asked to register so that enough space could be allotted and so that any necessary arrangements could be made or problems foreseen. This would be a good kind of program for the library's yard, if there is one. Outdoor programs provide added publicity by attracting passers-by. Prizes are often given in this kind of program and it is usual to be sure there are prizes for everyone. There might be prizes for the biggest, smallest, most unusual, etc. Judges might be a librarian, somebody from a pet store or the zoo, a veterinarian, or a farmer.

Games were the focus of a different kind of program in one library. First a large exhibit of antique and modern games was arranged in the library, through the cooperation of the Toy Manufacturers of America. (An individual manufacturer or a toy store might serve this purpose.) Many kinds of games were used including Scrabble and Monopoly in five languages. Then the children, age seven and up, who had registered for the program, were shown the games and heard a discussion of them. Finally they designed their own games using cardboard, various kinds of paper and fabrics, and some miscellaneous items, all supplied by the library at a cost of about $20. About forty children attended the program which lasted four afternoons. Two afternoons were devoted to designing the games and two afternoons to teaching them to other children and to playing them.

Programs for pre-school children present great opportunities for imaginative programs. Since these children are usually brought to the library by parents, programs for the parents can be arranged at the same time. One library that regularly produces these doubleheaders considers them to be one of their most effective programs. For the parents, they showed films on education and child development; among these were "Kindergarten" (McGraw-Hill), a 22-minute film that shows a kindergarten class in action and in which the cinematographers become part of the classroom experience of the children; and "Four Families" (McGraw-Hill), a 58-minute film that looks at the child-raising customs of India, Japan, France and Canada. At another program, a librarian and an educator spoke on the importance of reading to children. To vary this fare, at other sessions, a librarian gave a talk on some books of general interest to adults, and the staff showed some films of Chaplin, Keaton and other silent comedians. A recent suggestion, as yet untried, is to talk to mothers on dangerous toys.

For the children, a wide variety of activities was offered. They even formed a band. The children were asked to bring in coffee cans, pie plates and cereal boxes. The library supplied some bells, string, rice (for rattles) and other small materials. They made some simple instruments and played them. At another time, the staff taped two sheets of brown paper (the length of the room) to the floor. Then they read Little Blue and Little Yellow by Leo Lionni and Colors by John Reiss to the children. The children were then invited to color the strips of paper while the staff played records with colors as themes. During the program, the children grew tired of coloring; they were urged to dance to the records, and later they returned to their coloring. During other mornings, the children fingerpainted, listened to picture books being read, and watched films and filmstrips. One session was devoted to an Easter party, complete with baskets. This library had a videotape workshop for teenagers going on during this period. The teenagers taped the last pre-school session and showed the tape to the parents and the children. The children's librarian also displayed, for the following month, the long sheets of paper that the children had colored.

Another library had a party during Easter vacation. It started with an Easter egg hunt on the front lawn, using balloons for eggs. An Easter egg piñata was made of papier mâché by one of the staff members. It was filled with candy,

balloons and confetti and then smashed amid much excitement. Then films were shown, followed by refreshments.

A "Summer Reading Club" run by the public library
of Plainfield, N.J., presented many kinds of activities for
children. It was built around a theme: "See the U.S.A."
During the summer, there were three film programs on
various aspects of life in the United States. There was a
puppet show, a sing-in, and square dancing for the children
and their parents. There were numerous craft activities;
the children could make candles, do knitting or crocheting,
and engage in several other crafts. And there were discussion groups for various age levels. The children were also
asked to read one book of fiction and two non-fiction books,
show how they used the library to get information for an
activity, and also engage in four activities. They were then
awarded certificates. In addition to the activities described
above, they could write annotations that would be kept on
file in the library; make a scrapbook of the places they
visited during the summer; read a story to a friend; choose
a folk hero from the folklore map and read a story about
him (her?).

Storytelling

Although another field of human endeavor is usually
said to be the oldest profession, storytelling may be the
oldest of the arts, and it is certainly the oldest kind of library program. The Carnegie Library of Pittsburgh has had
storytelling as a regular part of programming since 1899
and the New York Public Library dates regular storytelling
from 1908. Not only is it the oldest kind of library program, but it is undoubtedly the most widespread. Storytelling is done in bare library basements and luxurious
story-hour pits, in parks and on the front steps of city
houses. Stories are told in different languages, to all kinds
of children, in all parts of the country (see the section on
outreach in Chapter 10).

Storytelling is also one of the most rewarding of library activities, both to the children and to the teller. The
New York Public Library in a policy statement says:

> Stories are one of the most effective methods of
> introducing children to their literature, and of
> building through the folklore of the world, a

universal basis of understanding between people. The storyteller sees storytelling as an opportunity for boys and girls to hear the spoken word, develop their powers of listening, and share an experience with a living personality. Storytelling has grown out of the relationship between children and books that has developed within the Library walls. Great emphasis is placed on the use of the best literary versions of stories. The story hour assumes a dignity through the kind of stories told, and the manner in which the story hour is conducted. [3]

Because it is not advisable to tell stories to children of widely different ages, this activity usually divides into three main categories: a pre-school group, kindergarten through second grade (ages five to seven), and third grade and up (age eight and up). Picture books are usually used with the first two groups, so that children can see the pictures as they are hearing the story. With the older children, the longer stories are told without the book.

The length of the program varies with the age group. For the pre-school children, this may be their first social encounter. In any case they, unlike the older children, are not used to school with its more-or-less orderly ways. So one must start slowly, gradually increasing the length and complexity of the program. This is, of course, only possible if approximately the same group attends each time. The first session might run from twenty to thirty minutes, with succeeding sessions building up to about forty-five minutes. Individual stories for this group usually range from three or four minutes to about ten.

With the five-to-seven age group, a storytelling session might last about thirty minutes and each story run from eight to ten minutes. For the older group (ages eight to ten or eleven, usually) the program can last from thirty to forty minutes, and the stories run up to twenty minutes in length. These time limits are all, of course, approximations and will vary with the sophistication of the children, the experience of the storyteller, and other factors.

The scheduling pattern is important. As indicated above, it is useful if the same group of pre-school children attend each time. Some libraries run a cycle of storytelling sessions of from six to eight weeks for pre-school children.

One might have a series in the fall and another in the spring. It is useful, in such programs, to have the children register. Registration helps to insure regularity of attendance, and one can find out their ages and bar children who are too young. Young children have been known to ruin an otherwise good program, and unfortunately some mothers will even lie about their children's ages to get them into a program. Name tags are also a good idea. The tags can be simply made by a staff member out of construction paper of two or three different colors--perhaps in a simplified animal outline-- with the child's first and last name lettered on them, and they are left in the library between sessions. Tags enable the librarian to call a disruptive child by name, and the children enjoy having them and picking them out each time they come to the library. Programs for parents can be scheduled at the same time as the pre-school story hours, and they have been discussed elsewhere. A regular schedule for the older children is also important. Such scheduling has publicity value; in time it will become known that the library has a story hour on Thursday afternoons at 4 or on Saturday mornings at 10, and the audience will be gradually built up. Story hours can be scheduled weekly, bi-weekly or monthly, depending on the number of storytellers available, the number of children likely to attend, and the space available. Storytelling can also be tied in with Black History Week, Puerto Rican Discovery Day, Christmas, Halloween and other holidays.

The first thing a storyteller must do is select the stories to be told or read. Variety is important, particularly with the younger children. Since a diet of straight stories would probably be too much for very young children, one might intersperse story books with game books, for example. Ellin Greene suggests the kinds of books to use with pre-school children. One should, she says, choose

"books that represent a variety of art styles and literary forms;

books that employ word play, sounds and rhythms;

books with pleasing repetition;

books that encourage imaginative play;

books that present a positive self-image;

books that recognize feelings and deal with them sympathetically."

With the increasing age of the children, the stories chosen will become more complex: there will be more characters, a more involved plot, etc. The most important point, all storytellers agree, is to choose a story you like; if you like it, you will communicate that feeling to the children. Eulalie Steinmetz Ross, in The Lost Half-Hour, [5] mentions some other points to consider. It is often a good idea, she says, to choose stories from one's own background. She mentions several literary qualities to look for: straightforward story lines, brisk dialogue, economy of words with emphasis on nouns and verbs, and characterization that comes from action rather than description.

Ross says folk tales will often be the easiest for the beginning storyteller because they usually contain these elements. When looking for folk tales to read, Ross suggests reading them very slowly--and possibly aloud--to make yourself aware of the fine points, since such stories move very rapidly and much happens in them. It is best, she says, to choose versions of folk tales that have been told by other storytellers, or by authors "with an instinct for oral interpretation." She particularly recommends versions of folk tales by the following authors:

Joseph Jacobs
Wanda Gag
Seumas MacManus
Gudrun Thorne-Thomsen
Parker Fillmore

Howard Pyle
Richard Chase
Walter de la Mare
Ruth Sawyer

No one should need to be told that in the decade since Mrs. Ross's book was published, tremendous changes have taken place. Among these has been an increased awareness of different cultures and there has been a trend in storytelling, at least in urban areas, to include folk tales from the many ethnic collections now being published. Pura Belpré White's Puerto Rican collections, the two volumes of folk tales, of many countries edited by Augusta Baker, and the several collections of African folk tales by Harold Courlander and others are some that are being used. China, Mexico, the American Indian and the Eskimos are among the other cultures represented in this trend.

The second necessity for a storyteller is to learn the story. Stories fall into two broad categories; original stories by creative writers and folk and fairy tales. Stories by creative writers (since style is important) must be learned word for word. Some believe folk tales need not be learned word for word, and, of course, it is in the nature of folk tales that they have changed as they have been passed down from generation to generation. Folk tales, however, that have been retold by a creative writer should be told word for word, since presumably they are stylistically better than the storyteller can do. And Ross believes that, at least for the beginner, all stories should be so learned; she says that changes tend to lose the flavor of the story and may violate its spirit. [6] In the end, the decision probably depends on the taste, skill and experience of the storyteller.

Ross says that, in learning the story, one should read it over and over again, preferably aloud, until one has a feeling for the style. Then, she says, put the book aside and get the story into your mind. She does that by seeing the story as a series of "colored moving-picture frames." Others type out the entire story and learn it in that way. Some make notes to refer to until they have the story memorized. When the story has been memorized, practice it by telling it aloud to a mirror or to anybody who will listen.

After the story has been selected and learned, and the time has come to tell it, the children must be prepared for listening. As indicated earlier, stories are being told in all kinds of places, and under all kinds of conditions. If the program is to take place in the library, it should be held in an area that is free from noise and interruptions, and, as in all programs, the audience should be comfortable and able to concentrate on the story. Ross, who likes chairs better than stools, suggests placing them in short

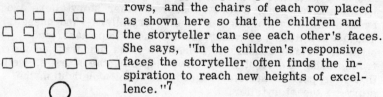

rows, and the chairs of each row placed as shown here so that the children and the storyteller can see each other's faces. She says, "In the children's responsive faces the storyteller often finds the inspiration to reach new heights of excellence." [7]

The children who have assembled for a storytelling session have to be made quiet and must have their attention focused on the storyteller. Various devices are used. If they assemble in the children's room and must go to the storytelling area, it seems to be a good idea to form them into a line and have them process--this helps to quiet them. Some libraries use a "wishing candle." The candle is lit after the children have been seated, and the children are told they cannot talk once this has been done. When the story is over, the children make wishes and someone blows out the candle; one may select a birthday child, or, if it is a small group, they can all gather around to blow it out. At Halloween, a candle inside a jack-o-lantern serves the same purpose, and also, when the lights are out, provides the right atmosphere.

Ellin Greene suggests setting up a table with fresh or dried flowers, the books to be used in the program, and any objects that might complement the stories. One need not buy expensive flowers, for as Greene points out, "weeds are pretty, too!"[8] Many librarians could find some goldenrod, chicory or Queen Anne's Lace along a roadside, and every lawn has its dandelions (which last, however, only a short time once picked). Greene also suggests the possibility of using a puppet to introduce the stories.

The last thing the storyteller must do is tell the story; Ross gives some hints.[9] Start slowly, she says, and she gives several reasons; the ears of the audience can then adjust to your voice, you can raise the volume if your voice is not carrying to the back (watch for restlessness) a beginning storyteller is likely to be nervous and speak too rapidly, and since much happens in the opening sentences of a folk tale the listeners need time to assimilate it. She feels that the beginner need not be much concerned with techniques and should not strive for dramatic effects. These things will come in time, and one will learn when to vary the pitch of his voice and the pace of the story, and when and how long pauses should be to be effective. (Two ways of learning these things are by observing other storytellers and by listening to recordings of other storytellers--and oneself.) The quality Ross believes to be the most important, and other librarians concur, is sincerity. And sincerity comes from finding the right story, from learning the story so well that it is part of the storyteller, and from a delight in the story by the storyteller.

Given the changes that have taken place in recent years, and the expansion of library services into a number of previously unserved or poorly served areas, some librarians are exploring variations on the traditional story hour. One children's librarian acquired some coloring books of fictional and historical characters; she gave them to the children who worked while she was reading, and the results were very satisfactory; restless children were settled down and, as one of them said to her, "I never knew what to do with my hands while I was being read to." In the Woodbridge (N.J.) Public Library they have a variation in their storytelling program called "Lunch with the Librarian." During vacation periods, children take their lunches to the library and eat them with the librarian. After lunch she tells them stories, and they find the program very useful in helping the children to get to know the librarian. A branch of the New York Public Library has a pajama story hour for pre-school children. It is held in the early evening and children arrive dressed in their pajamas, and carrying teddy bears and blankets.

An article in Library Journal[10] suggests among other things, ways in which the overhead projector can be used to create an environment that is compatible with the story being read. As a setting for A Tree Is Nice by Janice Udry, the author suggests using a green transparency in an overhead projector; it will, she says, "flood the children in an environment of green." For And it Rained by Ellen Raskin, she suggests a blue transparency with a sound effect recording of rain. When The Great Blueness by Arnold Lobel was being read, she used a water-filled ash tray; each time the wizard changed the world's color, she added a different food coloring. An entirely different approach was used with The Small One by Zhenya Gay; a fifty-foot strip of black paper was spread out and an artist chalk-sketched the story as it was being read.

The proliferation and improvement of audiovisual devices in recent years, and the resultant awareness of the possibilities for combining two or more media in a program, have resulted in multimedia story hours as well as other kinds of programs. The section at the end of this chapter on multimedia programs for children describes some methods and materials that can be used in this area.

Retarded children

Telling stories to retarded children involves some special problems. One librarian found that repeating the story was effective, and she has read the same story as many as fifteen times to a group. When she did that, she was rewarded when one of the children jumped up and told the story, even imitating her manner. Another librarian found that those stories which have repetition and rhythm are

most successful and that simple story lines are usually best.
Books with large pictures are useful for reading aloud, she
says, and many resources can be used successfully if they
are adapted to the particular group. Because of the very
short attention span of most of these children, these materials must be scaled down and broken down into simplified
parts. She found that records and sound filmstrips were
especially enjoyed.

Retarded children often have other disabilities, such
as poor sight or lack of coordination, which add to the difficulties of using ordinary materials. There are also a
great variety of intelligence and age levels in most groups.
Both these librarians suggest the need for experimentation
when working with retarded children. One recommends
getting into, and getting to know, the group first. The
most important attributes she feels are lots of patience and
love and an open and flexible attitude. She warns against
looking for quick results or, in some cases, even any results, or one is bound to be discouraged. In spite of the
difficulties, the benefits can be great, for the librarian as
well as the children. As one librarian put it, "Working
with the retarded ... does a world of good in ways that
you can't possibly measure."

Puppet shows

One of the most popular kinds of programs for children is the puppet show. Sometimes it is a show presented
to the children by librarians or others, and sometimes the
children make the puppets, scenery and stage, and present
the show themselves. Either way, puppet shows are usually
howling successes. Some librarians have successfully made
puppet theatres and puppets themselves, and have put on
very professional performances. One children's librarian
has made two puppet theatres. One of them folds into a
compact box and can be made from materials costing (in
1973) about $25. The other does not fold and cost $10.
Plans for making the theatres were found in The Puppet
Theatre Handbook by Marjorie Batchelder (New York: Harper,
1947). Instructions for making puppets can be found in a
number of books, listed in the Bibliography at the back of
this book.

Puppet workshops might not produce productions as
finished as those put on by adults, but they are undoubtedly

more engrossing and of more value for the children. A typical puppet workshop is described in the following excerpt from an annual report.

"A three-week puppet workshop drew 142 children and many spectators. Session I was devoted to demonstrating a variety of easy puppets; papier mâché, sock, finger puppets, stick, paper bag, and paper plate puppets. Children were encouraged to create their own characters using paper bags, plates and socks. We provided basic materials, while the children provided material for special effects, i.e. sequins, special bits of ribbon or buttons, fur etc. Children tried making favorite fairy tale and TV characters. I suggested a variety of characters from books that might make for good puppet plays later on.

"Session II was a group effort, resulting in a stick puppet presentation of Lionni's Swimmy. I began by explaining the technique of stick puppets. I read the story aloud to the group and invited children to choose the character from the book they would like to make. The choice of a neutral story (sans prince, or 'sissy stuff') made it easy to involve boys as well as girls in the production. There is nothing sissy about a six-foot electric eel, or an enormous tuna with tin foil teeth.

"Younger children helped to decorate 'the sea,' a yard long roll of tissue paper which, with a collage of yarn, paper, and magic marker sea creatures, was used in the auditorium to hide from view our young puppeteers when on the stage. Children were given about forty minutes to construct their puppets, then all the characters were taken downstairs to our auditorium for a dress rehearsal. The sea was attached to the auditorium wall, a volunteer 'bubble blower' was recruited from the audience for atmosphere, and with me reading the book out loud, the puppets told the story on stage for parents and assembled friends. Two days later a second performance was scheduled. We asked for children to volunteer in assisting to manipulate the puppets. They seemed particularly elated to oblige. All together 25 children manipulated puppets on stage, quite a feat on our small stage.

"Session III emphasized relating puppet characters

to stories for plays with puppets. I demonstrated
simple finger puppets and showed how cardboard boxes
in varying sizes could be decorated for puppet stages.
Shoe boxes made good finger puppet stages; cardboard
boxes were used for hand puppets, the boxes varying
in size from table top variety to a huge refrigerator
packing crate. Working in groups, children chose a
story to dramatize, worked on stages, and dialogue,
and prepared for a formal puppet show. Finger puppet
plays were given of: Whistle for Willie, The Three
Bears, nursery rhymes, and an original fantasy called:
The Indian Family. Using an exhibit case as a stage,
hand puppet performances included: Cinderella, Red
Riding Hood, and an original story, The Cat Lover.
A repeat performance was scheduled for two days
later, this time using our auditorium and our full
sized puppet stage. Audience and performers were
enthusiastic, and several asked if the workshop could
be repeated in the Fall. "[11]

Dramatic programs

From Finland (the Youth Theatre of the Tampere
Public Library) to Seattle (Let's Pretend with Fours and
Fives) libraries have long had active dramatic programs for
children and young adults. Boston, with creative drama
classes, Providence, with improvisational theatre, New York
City and Philadelphia, mentioned later in this section, and
various libraries in Westchester County, N.Y., are committed to some form of drama in the library. Sometimes
outside theatre groups of adults bring programs to the library. Sometimes librarians themselves form groups of
children to perform. There are classes and workshops.
There are structured plays. And there is improvisational
drama. But, whatever forms they take, librarians in all
these places agree that dramatic programs are valuable and
that they serve a variety of functions.

The Free Library of Philadelphia has a long history
of working with children and drama. They have conducted,
for a number of years, classes for children in creative
drama and workshops for adults who teach those classes.
With funds from the library, a foundation, and the Library
Services and Construction Act, such classes expanded from
a modest beginning of three in 1961 to 36 classes in 1968.
The purpose and justification for this program are well presented in the program's brochure:

Creative Dramatics offers participants the immediate experience of 'doing drama.' Unhampered by
scripts and memorized lines, children explore the
essentials of drama--action, plot, character, dia-
logue--and use these as the building blocks for
their creating. The value to the individual child
evolves from his extemporaneous doing of drama
rather than from any attempt to prepare a polished
production for audience enjoyment.

... the purpose of the Creative Dramatics project
is to develop in youngsters an awareness of themselves as individuals and of the world around them
through experience in improvised drama. Its in-
tent is to foster an appreciation of literature and
interest in books while encouraging creativity, im-
proving the self-image of the child, and helping
him relate to others.... The Free Library Program generates in the child a curiosity and desire
to explore the world of literature through the art
of drama. Literary appreciation grows as children 'try on' characters from familiar as well as
unfamiliar tales and respond to poetry with its
range of expression and mood. Art, music,
history, science, current events--any of the Library resources--can provide a starting point for
dramatization. [12]

A librarian in New York City who was conducting a
drama workshop expressed some similar ideas. She said,
in conversation, that these workshops helped the child to
use his imagination, to gain confidence, and to get into the
story. She also said that they helped the child's reading
and awakened him to other areas of reading, especially plays.
She also stressed the lack of solemnity in her workshops.
She, above all, wanted the children to take pleasure in what
they were doing. She had had the experience of reading
funny stories to children who weren't sure they were allowed
to laugh, and of seeing children, in and out of school, whose
whole lives were structured and formal. "Children," she
said, "should be able to laugh."

The flyer for this workshop says, "These workshops
are designed to help your child improve his listening skills,
utilize his imagination, and improve his skill at self-expression. Week to week, we move from familiar concrete situations and characters (family members, dinner time, farm

animals) to more abstract, less familiar concepts (imaginary animals, inanimate objects, sounds)."

This particular workshop was created for children from five to seven years old. The librarian would usually read the story and the children would be asked to act along as the story was being read (they would all roar like lions or swim like fish); or she would read the story first, and then they would act different parts. At the conclusion of the workshop there would be a recital which might take various forms, depending on how the workshop developed.

TUESDAY, JULY 10, 10:30-11:30 a.m.

Mexicali soup--Hitte
When mother goes to make her famous Mexicali soup, everyone in the family has a suggestion about what to leave OUT. Join the family ... be mother, father.

Terrible roar--Pinkwater
A little lion discovers he has a terrible roar. Every time he opens his mouth a terrible roar comes out, and every time he roars, SOMETHING VANISHES.... Be a lion, an elephant, a mountain, a star....

TUESDAY, JULY 17, 10:30-11:30 a.m.

The turnip--Donamaska
Grandpa planted one little seed. He never expected such an enormous turnip. It got so large he had to call the whole family and the farm animals to help pull it up. Be grandpa, boy, dog, gaggle of geese, a turnip.

I wish that I had duck feet--Geisel
Just suppose you suddenly grew duck feet, an elephant's trunk, a deer's antlers....

TUESDAY, JULY 24, 10:30-11:30 a.m.

Where the wild things are--Sendak
When Max was bad he got sent to his room, but instead he went to where the wild things are.... Make a mask and be a wild thing too....

TUESDAY, JULY 30, 10:30-11:30 a.m.

Magic Michael--Slobodkin
Michael was always being something or other. Can you be a stork, a light bulb, a book?

TUESDAY, AUGUST 7, 10:30-11:30 a.m.

What kind of sounds can you make?
Mr. Brown can moo! Can you?--Geisel
    Can you be a hippo chewing gum? A goldfish kiss?
    A base drum? A fife?

TUESDAY, AUGUST 14, 10:30-11:30 a.m.

The buried moon--Jacobs
    Once in the long ago, when the world was filled with
    bogs and such, the moon came down from the sky
    and was trapped in the swamp by the ghouls and
    mooly things. Be a mooly creature....

TUESDAY, AUGUST 21, 10:30-11:30 a.m.

Conclusion and recital.

    At the same time, this librarian conducted a work-
shop for children age nine and older. This group started
with skits taken from books in the library. They then went
on to plays of one or two pages which they used as starting
points for improvisation. Still later they did dramatizations
from things like Alice in Wonderland and Stone Soup.

    This librarian has done dramatics in two libraries in
widely different communities, and she has seen dramatic
differences in the children of the two areas. In the community with a preponderance of children from low-income
families, there were many poor readers and the children
had difficulty learning their lines; however, they were much
less inhibited and got into their parts much more than the
children from the more affluent families. The more affluent,
however, read very well and learned their lines more easily.
She concluded that the children from the higher income
families led much more structured lives, and needed an unstructured workshop.

    In an article in Top of the News, Irene Cullinane and
Theresa Brettschneider list the activities for a ten-session
program in creative dramatics that was given at Poughkeep-
sie, New York.[13] This program was for children up to 13.

Sessions 1 and 2. RECREATING FAMILIAR PHYSICAL
    ACTIVITIES (throwing a ball, jumping rope, running in
    the wind) to activate the imagination, develop the powers
    of concentration, and to relax the body by encouraging a

natural response. Charade games (guess what I'm doing?)
are popular and effective.

Session 3. EXERCISES INVOLVING PHYSICAL SENSES
(eating sour pickles, listening to the grating sound of
fingernails on a blackboard).

Session 4. RANDOM WALK. Group walks in a circle and
reacts to words called at random by a leader (sticky,
afraid, ocean).

Session 5. ADDING EMOTIONAL REACTION TO AN AC-
TIVITY (looking at a report card, an automobile accident,
a banana split).

Session 6. CHANGE-OF-MOOD PANTOMINE. In small
groups of two or three, children act scenes with a
definite transition of mood (walking proudly in new
clothes and being caught in the rain, being afraid of approaching footsteps on a dark night only to discover it
is a favorite uncle).
    From this point on children are encouraged to think
as someone other than themselves. They are eager to do
this from the beginning but they need the discipline and
stimulation of formal exercises in sensory perception and
emotional responses.

Sessions 7 and 8. CHARACTER IMPERSONATIONS. Each
child is handed a card (king, clown, detective) and walks
as that character. Action cards (crossing a brook,
riding a bicycle) are then distributed and each child am-
plifies the given character.

Sessions 9 and 10. FORMING SKITS. Small groups are given
character and action cards and told to make up a story
using all of the cards. Speech is a natural addition at
this point. Each skit is presented to the group for ap-
proval and analysis. Some skits are expanded to include
more characters and repeated with other members of the
group.

    Cullinane and Brettschneider say, "the group is now
ready for full-scale dramatization of their own plays or
familiar folk stories such as Stone Soup, Three Billy Goats
Gruff, Rumpelstiltskin." These techniques can be adapted
for all upper elementary age levels. For those younger
children who are not ready for interpretive dramatics, they

suggest the imitation of animals, imitating characters in a story, simple games, pantomines, finger plays and other such activities.

In another kind of program, students of a graduate course in children's literature presented dramatized versions of fairy tales and picture books. Their purpose was to "entertain the children and to encourage them to listen, and to read on their own."[14] One of the plays was a version of The Giving Tree by Silverstein, complete with a seven-foot cardboard tree that had real branches and a smiling human face. The audience had to be restricted to ages seven to eleven, because of the overwhelming response to similar programs--an indication of the popularity of this kind of program. The children's librarian believed that these programs "served a special role in linking the community, the library and the children." This was partly so because the performers were parents of the area, teachers in the local schools and volunteer workers in neighborhood service groups; thus they were linked to community, library and children in several ways.

Librarians have gathered children together to put on traditional, structured plays. One librarian has been over (almost)whelmed with the response to her idea. She wanted to form a theatre group for children in the fourth through the eighth grades. One hundred and fifty children responded to her initial request. She selected the plays to be presented and, with the help of volunteer directors, held auditions, selected the cast, rehearsed the actors, prepared the publicity and presented the plays. Up to fifty or sixty children were auditioned for each play. Those that were not given speaking parts were asked to work on other important aspects of play production, such as publicity, props, costumes, stage crew, and ushering. No money was spent on costumes or props, both for the sake of the children and because the library (so, what else is new?) had no money.

One extra benefit to the staff was that the children became very excited about the plays; they made suggestions about what plays should be produced and they continually asked when the next production would be. It is times like these that make programming seem very worthwhile. If the response of children who wanted to be in the play was greatly enthusiastic, the response from those who wanted to attend was David Merrick's dream. One hundred tickets were prepared for the first performance of Sleeping Beauty,

and they disappeared on the first day. At a second performance, after all the seats were filled, one hundred additional children wanted standing room. Performances were
later given at other libraries and, in additional spin-off, a
neighborhood group was formed to give backyard plays.

Chamber theatre

A different kind of drama program is "chamber
theater." It is described in another article in Top of the
News[15] (a gold mine of information on dramatic programs).
The advantages of chamber theatre are that it is easily
produced, you can be flexible, and it costs very little in
terms of both money and staff time. It is described as
"an oral interpretation by two or more voices of a story
or poem. It is not an adaptation of any sort, but rather a
word-for-word presentation with all the 'he said's and 'she
answered's left in."[16] The material, the author suggests,
should be carefully selected to suit the age group and it
should have a lot of dialogue. Thurber's "The Unicorn in
the Garden" and "The Secret Life of Walter Mitty" are suggested as sure-fire stories. She says that if you have
enough talented readers, you can choose works that are
basically narrative and that don't have much dialogue.
Henry James's "Beast in the Jungle" and chapters from
Ray Bradbury's Dandelion Wine are possibilities. They
should be carefully divided to take advantage of the variations in prose and the talents of the readers. For poetry,
she suggests as examples, Eliot's "The Hollow Men,"
Frost's "The Death of the Hired Man," and Benét's "John
Brown's Body."

The properties, sets and costumes are kept very
simple. One device she considers effective is to have all
the readers dress alike. Certainly libraries will want to
make adaptations depending on their circumstances and
other work they are presenting. This seems like an important program for libraries, because of its effectiveness
and simplicity. It will certainly be important for the performers, for many reasons--not the least of which is that
it will make them pay close attention to the words on the
page, a consummation of the reading act "devoutly to be
wished."

For those who want help with dramatic programs, the
Children's Theatre Conference is available. This organization,

with headquarters in Washington, D.C., was formed in 1944
to "promote work in children's theatre and creative drama;
to raise standards of productions and of informal dramatic
work with children and to encourage excellence in training
for workers in the field."[17] It is divided into 15 geographi-
cal regions that sponsor local workshops, festivals and
other projects. Children's Services Division of the American
Library Association has set up a committee to work with
them. CTC can hold workshops for librarians to teach them
the techniques of creative drama. They can also provide an
annotated bibliography of books on creative drama and children's theatre, and will suggest children's plays. If they
are already producing plays in the community, you can invite them to perform in the library.

Radio and television

As with adults and teenagers, there are good opportunities for library radio and television programs for children, and some libraries have been doing this kind of programming for many years. Such programs have frequently
been aired on Saturday and Sunday mornings, no doubt on
the theory that young children need to be entertained at those
times while their parents sleep, and quite likely because no
one else wants to produce programs at those times. At any
rate, they probably are good times for both those reasons;
parents are often asleep, and there is no competition from
commercial programs.

Storytelling is particularly suitable for radio, and the
Dayton and Montgomery County (Ohio) Public Library has had
a particularly successful radio program of storytelling.[18]
The 15-minute program is aired on Sunday mornings at 7:45
and is designed as a breakfast-time program for the whole
family. The program is taped during the week, and the
theme song, "Frère Jacques," and the standard opening and
closing announcements are added on. Stories are chosen for
their broad appeal, for literary quality, for fast action and
minimum of detail. Folk tales often fit these criteria.
Stories about such characters as Paul Bunyan and Pecos Bill,
because they are fast-moving and also because of their humor,
have been found to be good choices. Animal stories and
stories about things in everyday life are also used.

It is often necessary to get the permission of the publisher to use the stories. Permission is usually granted, but

if there is a fee the story is not used. Timing is an important consideration in radio and television so stories must be chosen for length. Sometimes details, and even complete passages can be left out, if the stories are too long. If the stories are up to one minute too short, they sometimes compensate by playing more of the theme song. If the story is less than 12 minutes long (13-1/2 minutes is the maximum length) some other item, such as a poem appropriate to the story, is also read. For example, for a Japanese folk tale, some haiku were read. Announcements of other library programs for children are sometimes made.

The article's author goes on to give some hints about storytelling on the air. The microphone, she points out, is a delicate instrument and it picks up all noises made in its presence. So one should be careful not to rustle papers or move chairs about. Enunciation should be clear, and the story must not be read too fast. One should learn the value of dramatic pauses, but not pause too long or the radio listeners may think you have finished and turn the dial. And the stories should be read in a natural, conversational manner.

Taping, of course, allows a program to be redone. If there are too many extraneous noises, if the program is too long or too short, or if the reading needs to be improved, one can simply retape. But one can't go on retaping indefinitely--tape and time are expensive--so one should practice reading the script aloud several times. And one needn't worry about all extraneous noises. If the tape is edited, they can sometimes be cut out. Some noises, such as a cough, may even add to the naturalness and can be left in. If the program is being done live, this writer has found that the program's director or the floor manager will lead you through. They will tell you when to speed up or slow down, and when the end of the program is approaching.

Deaf and hearing children are told stories simultaneously on a television program run by a library in Columbus, Indiana.[19] The camera shows, at the same time, the pictures in the book, the lips of the librarian who is reading, and a young girl seated next to her who is telling the story with sign language. The librarian reads slowly, tries to read in phrases or thoughts, and watches the girl to make sure she isn't getting ahead of the signs.

Arts and crafts

Some imaginative programs for children have been developed in this area by some unbound children's librarians. These activities can easily be related to books (both imaginative and informative) and other materials. And there are many art forms, art materials and formats around which programs can be built.

One children's librarian planned a "Summer Arts Festival." It was entitled "Pictures with Imagination." Children were invited to "explore a variety of materials, textures, and ideas as they make a different picture each week." It was a series of six programs, for children five years and older. The first session was a chalk-in, and it was loosely based on The Tale of Peter Rabbit. The children were asked to draw a chalk picture of Mr. McGregor's garden, or to make up a garden of their own. If the sun was shining they were to draw outside on paper or on sidewalks. Rain would send them inside to draw in the library to music. It did rain, but it was a very festive festival. The brightly lit children's room with children all over it drawing on large pieces of paper with colored chalk and music in the background was a happy place to be.

For the second session, drawings and paper cut-outs were used; children were asked to make pictures of their favorite fruits. Suggested were an apple tree with cut-outs of red apples, pumpkins and scarecrow, or berry patch and cut-out birds. Felt was used for the third program. They were asked to make felt cut-outs of characters from their favorite story or fairy tale, and to use them in making a story picture. A nature collage was the next art form used. Children brought in dried grass, leaves, feathers, twigs, hemlock cones and small stones and combined them with drawings that made pictures to express their feelings about nature.

The next picture was determined by a treasure hunt. Children were given instructions for the hunt; they hunted for objects, inside and outside the library, that had been hidden by the staff; then they made pictures using the objects they had found, so that no one knew in advance what kinds of pictures would develop.

An illustrator of children's books attended the last

session. She talked, informally, about her work and about drawing, about how a drawing is made, and she answered questions from the children. Her books were exhibited during the program. The theme of the session was the sea. Children brought in shells, starfish, sand and pebbles; from these they made drawings and collages about the sea.

Materials for these program were supplied by the library at the cost of a few dollars. The attractive flyers used for publicity included very simple line drawings of flowers, birds, shells, etc. which were done by a staff member; they also featured quotations, appropriate to each session and adding much to the charm, from The Tale of Peter Rabbit, The House at Pooh Corner, Wind in the Willows and others. Most of the musical selections that were played during the indoor parts of the program were those that were familiar to the children, so that they would feel at home. The children's librarian did say, however, that she was experimenting to find out what kinds of music would best enhance the program for the children. In any case, the use of books, art work, and music in great variety, the visit of the illustrator as a culmination of the festival, and the interaction among children, librarians and materials provided an enriching experience for all concerned.

At another "Summer Arts Festival" the librarian described her goals in this way. "We wanted," she said, "an informal, relaxed atmosphere; activities that would lend themselves to broad themes and simple materials; an emphasis on the individual response. We also wanted books, the feeling of books, to be a real part of every program. Even if they might not be at the center of the activity they should at least be around--in exhibits relating to the week's activity, or on hand for the child needing help with ideas or in shaping the details of an idea." She went on to say that the word festival was the key to the tone and spirit of these programs: "we wanted most of all that everyone have a good time, that some good spirit be around, that everything that was to happen should spring from that."

The response to this festival was great. Children were waiting outside the library in the early morning before the first program. There were so many that they forced the library to open an hour ahead of schedule. Throughout the summer this response continued; they filled the children's room bringing to it "life and enthusiasm." Many arts were encompassed in this festival. The children drew murals,

made nature collages, and made things from clay. There
was a three-week creative writing session; during this activity, they sewed simple books, wrote stories and poems,
and decorated them with pictures done in watercolors and
pastels. There were also two storytelling festivals, American and European, featuring stories, folk songs and poetry.

Children came in bathing suits, on their way to a
local swimming pool. Friends came in groups, brothers
and sisters came together, and some children came alone.
Some children had traveled widely. Others had never been
as far as the local beach. But, during the summer, these
children from a variety of backgrounds, shared their work,
their experiences and their ideas. For various parts of
this festival the following books and music were used:

American Folklore Festival

Macmillan, Cyrus. "Glooskap's Country" and "The
Indian Cinderella," Glooskap's Country and Other
Indian Tales, Oxford, 1956.
McCormick, Dell J. "Paul Bunyan and the Giant Mos-
quito Bees," Tall Timber Tales, Caxton, 1939.
Songs--group sing: "Clementine," "I've Been Working
on the Railroad," "She'll Be Coming 'Round the
Mountain," and "Swing Low, Sweet Chariot."
Recording--"Pete Seeger Sings America's Favorite
Ballads."

Making a Book and Original Writing

(these books were used to show examples of children's
writing, poets writing for children, imaginative kinds
of books, unusual shapes of books, etc.)

Lewis, Richard, comp. Miracles, Simon & Schuster,
1966; and Journeys, Simon & Schuster, 1969.
Behn, Harry. The Golden Hive, Harcourt, 1966.
Mizimura, Kazue. I See the Wind, Crowell, 1966.
Hoffman, Felix. A Boy Went Out to Gather Pears,
Harcourt, 1966.
Sendak, Maurice. Chicken Soup with Rice, Harper,
1962.
Morrison, Lillian. Sprints and Distances, Crowell,
1965.
Larrick, Nancy, ed. On City Streets, Evans, 1968.

European Folklore Festival--The British Isles

Alger, Leclaire. "The Lass Who Went Out at the Cry
of Dawn" Thistle and Thyme, Holt, 1962.
Jacobs, Joseph. "The Rose-Tree," English Folk and
Fairy Tales, Putnam, n.d.; and "The King o' the
Cats," More English Folk and Fairy Tales, Putnam,
n.d.
Folksongs with guitar: "Fox Went Out on a Chilly
Night," "Cockles and Mussels," "Frog Went A-
Courtin'," "Down in the Valley."

Make Your Favorite Character in Clay

Some that were chosen were: the turtle in Voyages of
Doctor Dolittle, the rabbit in Rabbit Hill, the bear from
Helpful Mr. Bear, and Gollum from The Hobbit.

Still another "Summer Arts Festival" was centered
around a theme--"Celebrate the Earth." The series began
with a session on the creation myths. The following programs corresponded to the Biblical sequence of the creation
of the world. The second program, "Sun-Light-Awakening:
Moon-Stars-Darkness," tried to relate the growth and sleep
processes of nature. The titles of the other programs were
"The Ocean," "The Green Earth," "Creatures of the Earth,"
and "People." Simple techniques and materials were used:
colored paper, chalk, oil pastels, clay, collage, leaf-prints,
scratch-drawings.

At the beginning of each session in this series, the
children's librarian met with the children to talk about the
morning's theme. There were books on exhibit, and there
were objects from nature for children to see and feel.
"Foreign language poetry and picture books were especially
helpful in conveying a deep feeling for the earth." The
simple objects--leaves, shells, seeds--created a sense of
wonder. They were passed around; the children held them,
examined them, felt them. Many of the children had never
before seen, or looked closely at a milkweed. Its beauty
surprised them. Sometimes the children spoke of their own
experiences; they told about making a garden, taking care of
a pet, or vacationing at the beach. After they exchanged
ideas, the children spent the rest of the time putting their
images on paper.

For the "Celebrate the Earth" festival, the following
books were used:

Creation Myths

Belting, Natalia M. The Sun Is a Golden Earring, Holt, 1962.
Leach, Maria. "Why the Birds Are Different Colors," How the People Sang the Mountains Up, Viking, 1967; and "Raven Finds a Clam," The Beginning; Creation Myths Around the World, Funk, 1956.
World Council of Christian Education and Sunday School Association. In the Beginning; Paintings of the Creation by Boys and Girls Around the World, Nelson, 1965.

Sun-Light-Awakening; Moon-Stars-Darkness

Selsam, Millicent. Play with Seeds, Morrow, 1957.
Webber, Irma E. Travelers All, Addison-Wesley, n. d.
Darby, Gene. What Is a Season?, Benefic Press, 1960.
Hugelshofer, Alice. Kuckuck, Kuckuck, Rufts aus dem Wald; and Wollt ihr Wissen, Wie der Bauer
Oberlander, Gerhard. Das Marchen von den drei Apfelbaumen

The Ocean

Lionni, Leo. Swimmy, Pantheon, 1963.
Lionni, Leo. Fish Is Fish, Pantheon, 1970.
McCloskey, Robert. Time of Wonder, Viking, 1957.
Huntington, Harriet E. Let's Go to the Seashore, Doubleday, 1941.
Engel, Leonard. The Sea, Time-Life, 1967.
Meyer, Jerome S. Picture Book of the Sea, Lothrop, 1956.
Abbott, Robert T. Sea Shells of the World, Golden Press, 1962.
Bevans, Michael H. Book of Sea Shells, Doubleday, 1961

The Green Earth

Andersen, Hans Christian. The Fir Tree, Harper, 1970.
Topelius, Zakarias. "The Birch and the Star," Canute Whistlewinks, Longmans, 1927.
Carlson, Bernice. Make It and Use It, Abingdon, 1958 (used for tracing method).

Creatures of the Earth

White, E. B. Charlotte's Web, Harper, 1952.
The Golden Goose Book, Warne, n.d.
Flack, Marjorie. The Story About Ping, Viking, 1933.
Grzimek, Bernhard. Rhinos Belong to Everybody, Hill
   & Wang, 1965.
Schulthess, Emil. Africa, Simon & Schuster, 1969.
Periodicals: National Wildlife, Ranger Rick, Natural
   History

People

Lewis, Richard, comp. Miracles; Poems by Children
   of the English-Speaking World, Simon & Schuster,
   1966.

Another similar series of programs was based on
stories from around the world in honor of International Book
Year. The first session was a Winnie-the-Pooh Birthday
Party. The children made birthday books, ate cakes and
punch, and blew soap bubbles. (There was only one disappointed child who kept looking for Winnie.) The series
ended with a Topsy-Turvy Nonsense Party. This series, in
addition to the older children, was opened to pre-school
children. The mothers assisted the staff in helping and encouraging the children. In one case, an infant slept in a
portable crib in the midst of all the activity. A simplified
rendering of the way the programs were described on flyers
appears on the following page.

A number of children's librarians have conducted
workshops in which the children made their own books,
writing, illustrating and binding them. A librarian, who
obviously feels the importance of atmosphere in these programs, has described, the scene in this way:

> Tuesday mornings, a little before 10:30, the
> children arrive to work on making their own books.
> It is good to go down into Stapleton's cool base-
> ment meeting room, a pleasant place graced by
> cut-out paper designs made by artist Paul A.
> Lobel for a Paperteer workshop program earlier
> this year. Near the round tables where the chil-
> dren work are a few pictures done in bright, clear
> colors, of animals, of a knightly figure, and of
> children's book illustrator Elsa Beskow's unspoiled

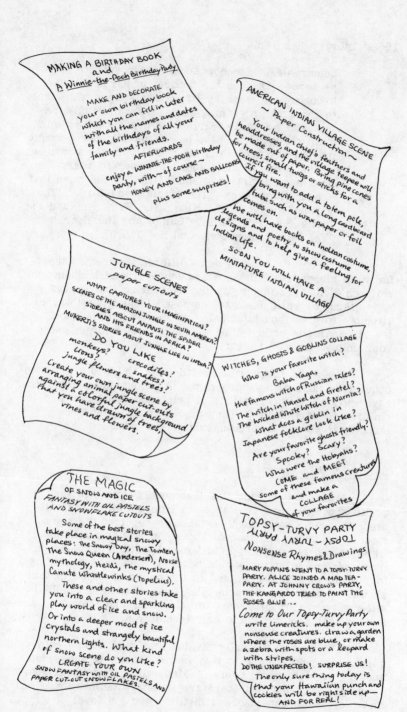

MAKING A BIRTHDAY BOOK
and
A Winnie-the-Pooh Birthday Party

MAKE AND DECORATE your own birthday book which you can fill in later with all the names and dates of the birthdays of all your family and friends.

AFTERWARDS enjoy a WINNIE-THE-POOH birthday party, with—of course—HONEY AND CAKE AND BALLOONS

plus some surprises!

AMERICAN INDIAN VILLAGE SCENE
~ Paper Construction ~

Your Indian chief's feathers and headdresses, and the village teepee will be made out of paper. Bring pine cones for trees, small twigs or sticks for a council fire.

If you want to add a totem pole, bring with you a long cardboard tube such as wax paper or foil comes on.

We will have books on Indian costume, legends and poetry to show designs and to help give a feeling for Indian life.

SOON YOU WILL HAVE A MINIATURE INDIAN VILLAGE

JUNGLE SCENES
paper cut-outs

WHAT CAPTURES YOUR IMAGINATION? SCENES OF THE AMAZON JUNGLE IN SOUTH AMERICA? STORIES ABOUT ANANSI THE SPIDER AND HIS FRIENDS IN AFRICA? MUKERJI'S STORIES ABOUT JUNGLE LIFE IN INDIA?

DO YOU LIKE monkeys? crocodiles? lions? snakes? jungle flowers and trees?

Create your own jungle scene by arranging animal paper cut-outs against a colorful jungle background that you have drawn of trees, vines and flowers.

WITCHES, GHOSTS & GOBLINS COLLAGE

Who is your favorite witch?

Baba Yaga, the famous witch of Russian tales? The witch in Hansel and Gretel? The wicked White Witch of Narnia? What does a goblin in Japanese folklore look like?

Are your favorite ghosts friendly? Spooky? Scary? Who were the Hobyahs?

COME and MEET some of these famous creatures and make a COLLAGE of your favorites

---

THE MAGIC
OF SNOW AND ICE
FANTASY WITH OIL PASTELS AND SNOWFLAKE CUTOUTS

Some of the best stories take place in magical snowy places: The Snowy Day, The Tomten, The Snow Queen (Andersen), Norse mythology, Heidi, the mystical Canute Whistlewinks (Topelius).

These and other stories take you into a clear and sparkling play world of ice and snow. Or into a deeper mood of ice crystals and strangely beautiful northern lights. What kind of snow scene do you like?

CREATE YOUR OWN SNOW FANTASY WITH OIL PASTELS AND PAPER CUT-OUT SNOWFLAKES.

TOPSY-TURVY PARTY
TOPSY-TURVY PARTY
Nonsense Rhymes & Drawings

MARY POPPINS WENT TO A TOPSY-TURVY PARTY. ALICE JOINED A MAD TEA-PARTY. AT JOHNNY CROW'S PARTY, THE KANGAROO TRIED TO PAINT THE ROSES BLUE...

Come to Our Topsy-Turvy Party
write limericks. make up your own nonsense creatures. draw a garden where the roses are blue, or make a zebra with spots or a leopard with stripes.

DO THE UNEXPECTED! SURPRISE US!

The only sure thing today is that your Hawaiian punch and cookies will be right side up—AND FOR REAL!

countryside, somehow adding their special
presence, as does the bouquet of garden flowers
brought each week by two young sisters who come
to the arts program. Soon each child finds the
material he needs (earlier he has chosen to work
with watercolors, pastels, oil pastels, or a magic
marker pen set), and after a look at the previous
weeks' work in his folder, is ready to carry his
book a step further. Some titles of the tales that
are unfolding are: 'The Magic Dodo Bird,' 'The
Flying Dragon,' 'The King, The Princess, and the
Little Boy,' 'Wildlife,' 'Bambi and the Bear,'
'The Mouse, the Owl, and the THING.'

Each child's book is quite different from the others,
for it is his own. With each session everyone including the
children's librarian seems to be discovering that it is a
happy thing to work this way, imposed ideas giving way to
attempts to give thoughtful help, as needed. It is good,
too, to hear one child telling another, "Don't forget, keep
your colors clean and clear."

The Free Library of Philadelphia obtained a grant to
conduct an unusual arts program. At bookmobile stops, they
gave sidewalk demonstrations of printmaking, and invited the
children to participate. They also gave an eight week in-
structional course in printmaking at six branches.[20]

Children's film program

Many of the principles that govern showings for
adults and teenagers also apply to film showings for children; the same care must be taken to see that the equipment is in order and that backup equipment is available; the
films should be previewed, and they benefit from being introduced; and attention should be paid when selecting films
to the intended audience, and to the order in which they are
shown. Some of these principles are, of course, applied
differently to film programs for children, and there are some
factors that are applicable only to children.

Children are usually divided into several age categories: pre-school (up to five years), ages six and seven,
and age eight to about twelve. Many children's librarians,
however, point out that there are no sharp delineations, and
that the child's experience with films and his level of

sophistication also influence the choice of films. Furthermore, age, intelligence and experience are likely to vary
widely within any audience. Ultimately, experience is the
best guide and even then the results are not predictable.
One children's librarian believes that "all you can do is aim
for a good film program" and the experience of the Children's
Film Theater was that they "couldn't always predict what kids
will like."[21] Other librarians have found children attending,
and enjoying, film programs planned for teenagers and for
adults. "One clear thing about planning a film program,"
said a children's librarian, "is that it is a creative process."
Another said, "What you put together will depend on your
own taste and your instincts which will grow surer as you
gain in experience."

When one is dealing with young children, there are
several things to watch out for. Safety is an important
factor. Children are likely to want to explore the screen
and the projector and to knock them over if one is not careful. Or they might grab the film or pull on a cord, etc.,
etc., etc. They may also need to use lavatories and get
drinks of water. For these reasons an extra staff member
to watch the children is essential. Sometimes young children are afraid of a dark room so it is wise to have them
enter when the lights are on, and become familiar with the
surroundings. Chairs are sometimes a problem in programs; one must have enough, they must be set up and taken
down. But with children, particularly young children, it
might be better to let them sit on the floor; they like to do
it and it creates an informal, cozy feeling. When seating
children, it is best to seat those that are there on time at
the front; that way latecomers can be seated without dis-
turbing the others.

Unlike programs for adults, talking at children's film
showings is not looked on with disfavor. One children's
librarian even says that "Talking is an integral part of the
child's enjoyment of the film. It is a sharing and learning
process."[22] And the Children's Film Theater has a similar
experience.[23] They found that some problems in the films--
"scary parts, plot resolutions, questions of reality"--were
resolved by the children's talking among themselves. They
also found that too much or too loud talking was resolved by
the children, and that they didn't need to interfere. ("The
kids are also very adept at quieting their vociferous peers.")
Another children's librarian points out that the film program
may be the child's first social activity. She says, "They may

spend considerable time looking around at the other children
instead of at the screen. They may even walk around and
visit between films." A child, of course, shouldn't be
allowed to disrupt the program, and sometimes the librarian
must step in. One commonly used technique is to let the
troublemakers help you. They can be used to turn lights on
and off, for example, or to hand out materials.

When the New York Public Library trains its children's
librarians, it offers the following guidelines for evaluating
films:

> The film must show respect for the child's intelligence.
> It should not be coy, patronizing or have forced
> humor.

> It should have originality and beauty, both in language
> and visually.

> The subjects and style should appeal to children.

> It should be technically good.

> It should avoid stereotypes.

> Although some educational films are used, the didactic
> is generally avoided.

Within those guidelines there are many possibilities.
One can build a program around a theme or subject. For
example, there are some fine films that are appropriate to
seasons such as winter or spring or to holidays such as
Halloween or Christmas. If animals were to be the subject,
one could have programs about pets or about wild animals.
Places or peoples--Africa, American Indians, Eskimos--
might be the subjects, or one might choose to feature individuals, such as Harriet Tubman or Frederick Douglass.
Or films could be shown about a variety of other subjects
such as circuses, cities, trains, comedy, myths and legends.

If a theme or subject doesn't seem appropriate because of differences in age and experience or because you
can't get the films you want have a variety program. One
can not only vary the subjects, but also the style, technique
and mood of the films. Balance such qualities as realism
and imagination, and comedy and drama, or have animated
and live-action films, or films with and without narration.

The order in which films are shown is important.
A short lively film could open the program and be followed

by a longer, more serious or slow-moving film. Or a scary
film might be followed by a funny one. Some librarians like
to end with a relaxing film, to prepare the children for the
close of the program. In any case, think about the relation-
ships among the films and change the pace and mood.

It is important to introduce the films. For one thing,
an introduction gives the children time to settle down. One
can also explain parts of the film that might be puzzling,
suggest things they might watch for, and introduce to the
children some books that are related to the films. Thalia
Mannon-Tissot of the Brooklyn (N.Y.) Public Library described an incident that showed the importance of an introduction.[24] She showed a sing-along film, Frog Went A-
Courtin' (Weston Woods) to two groups of children on the
same afternoon. For the first showing, she suggested that
the children might like to sing along. Few did. At the
second showing, the children were "specifically told that the
fun of the film was their singing along and the results made
the library resound." One can also use such things as
poetry, finger plays, a puppet, a short story or music to
set the mood for the films. Such things are useful between
films too, especially if there is any trouble with the projector or other equipment. The children could sing a song
or merely listen to a recording.

Programs can be scheduled in a number of different
ways. Showings can be designed for special occasions such
as Book Week, Black History Week, National Library Week,
Christmas or Halloween. There could be seasonal showings
such as a spring or fall series or there could be series related to a day and time such as Saturday morning or Sunday
afternoon. Vacation series such as summer films or
Christmas or Easter vacation showings are often used.
Some libraries have monthly, biweekly or weekly showings
during a school year or they have shorter series such as
six-week or four-week series.

The length of a film showing for children must be
carefully considered. For pre-school children, librarians
have suggested 20 to 30 minutes, and 30 to 40 minutes.
Doubtless this would vary with the experience of the children.
One librarian suggests a "lights on" break every twenty
minutes. Another librarian conducting a pre-school series
starts with showings of 25 to 30 minutes and increases the
length to about 45 minutes as the series progresses. She
also increases the length of the films (to no more than 15

to 18 minutes), and uses more abstract films. But short films are the general rule with this age and there are many good films of six, seven, eight and ten minutes. Other estimates of program lengths are: for six- and seven-year olds, 30 to 40 minutes; for age eight and up, 30 to 60 minutes; and a program for all ages, 30 to 40 minutes. Sometimes--and the possibilities will have to be determined by previewing--a film can be cut short if it seems too long and/or the children are bored or restless.

Since children in groups usually present more problems than adults in groups, the size of the audience is a factor. From 20 to 40 children seems to be an ideal size. Films have been shown to children in groups up to 70 and even 100, but one must be especially sure the program runs smoothly, and that everybody can see and is comfortable.

There are subjects, kinds and styles of films that appeal to children. They like animated films, films about animals and about other children, fairy tales, films with puppets and comedy with slapstick. They like straightforward stories with realism more than abstraction, but sometimes they will respond to some element in the film. (Dance Squared, in which geometric shapes divide and gyrate to the rhythm of a square dance, is such a film and children respond to its rhythm.)

For pre-school children, one librarian suggests using one or two story films (based on picture books they know or can borrow from the library), and possibly a short abstract film showing colors changing to music, or a documentary on zoo animals. Story films can either be the iconographic films, of the kind produced by Weston Woods, or the animated type. Bright colors are important and are to be preferred to black and white unless the film is exceptional. (An exception, it has been pointed out, are the Lotte Reiniger silhouette fairy tale films.)

For school-age children, one might show a feature-length film one time and two or three shorter films the next. Programs might consist of films showing a variety of subjects and techniques or they might be built around a subject or be all of one type.

In addition to merely showing the films, one can do a number of other things that will enhance the value of the showing. Children are likely to be interested in how things

work; younger children can be allowed to watch the projectionist thread the film, and older children might be taught
how to do it.   Thalia Mannon-Tissot has described the ways
in which she encouraged children to learn about the techniques of filmmaking. [25]   Between films she would ask the
children questions about the theme of the film, what scenes
accomplished the theme, what role the music or background
noises played, and what parts they liked and why.   Sometimes they ran parts of the film without the sound, or the
sound without the picture, to help the children see the
functions of each.   At other times, they used stories that
appeared in both books and films (Whistle for Willie, Five
Chinese Brothers) and compared the two media.   When a
Marcel Marceau film was shown, the children mimed various
actions between films.   Sometimes stories were used to provide background.

Those engaged in the Children's Film Theater have
used stories in several ways. [26]   They had "great success"
with reading the stories on which the films were based.
They also had success in getting the children to spontane-
ously make their own sound tracks; a film would be shown
without sound while a tape recorder was left running; the
children unknowingly provided a sound track and the film
was then rerun with that recording.

An interesting variation that was enjoyed by the children was to run a film, without sound, backward.   Films
with a lot of live action and no narration (Jet Car, Young
Directors' Center) worked best.

Painting, drawing and various kinds of artwork can
be related to films, and are stimulated by films.   The
Children's Film Theater had the children make transparen-
cies for the overhead projector; they showed Glittering
Song (Contemporary/McGraw-Hill), an animated film using
a collage of broken glass, and afterward the children made
their own collages of colored pieces of plastic/acetate gels
which they projected; they also wrote their names on the
collages with grease pencils and enjoyed seeing them projected.   Having children mark blank film à la Norman
McLaren is an activity that has been described by several
librarians and others.   Magic markers, felt-tip pens,
crayons and even pins have been used.   A recording can be
used for the sound track, and the children have then made
their own movie.

Multimedia programs

As with adult and young adult programs, there are
many opportunities to produce multimedia programs, or
variety programs that are festival in nature. One can celebrate holidays, special events, special subjects and themes.
The Houston Public Library celebrated National Children's
Book Week with a variety of programs. [27] A new central
library was being built and like all such construction it was
surrounded by a wooden fence. Children were invited to a
paint-in, during which they painted their favorite storybook
characters, cartoon characters and graffiti on the fence.
A hundred children, three to 13, participated and the event
was covered by three television stations. For the adults
there was a Meet-the-Author reception, with about twenty
authors and illustrators of children's books, and luncheon
program during which the book editor of a local newspaper
discussed new directions in writing for children.

In Portland, Oregon, they held a folklore festival for
National Children's Book Week. There were programs in
the central library and in the city's 18 branches. Children's
librarians told folk tales before each program. There were
two puppet shows dramatizing a Slavic folk tale. There
were African, Norwegian, Irish, Balkan, Mexican, Maori
and Scottish dances. There were Swiss songs and yodeling,
Chinese music and a bagpiper. And there was an origami
demonstration and displays of German toys, Russian games
and Indian artifacts. There were also talks about the customs of various countries. [28]

The Greenwich (Conn.) Public Library held a multimedia festival with the ambitious title, "All the Arts for
Kids." Certainly many arts were included and the title was
nearly realized. The whole library was utilized for the purpose. Throughout the library there were art slides flashing
and there were banners made by Greenwich school children.
Events were held in several parts of the library. One program, an electronic concert by local high school students,
was a multimedia event in itself; the musicians were accompanied by films, slides and dancers. Other events during
the four week festival were: a showing of the Beatles' film,
Yellow Submarine; a marionette production of Gilbert and
Sullivan's Pirates of Penzance; a lecture on "Golden Days of
Greek Gods"; a demonstration of various art techniques; and
a sculptor who demonstrated the two-hour inflating technique
for a piece of vinyl sculpture. The opening event, entitled

"See, Touch, Discover and Create," allowed children to touch and play with various pieces of sculpture and other works of art, after which they were invited to create their own art objects from business and industry discards. [29]

In the public library of Westport, Conn., a series of summer programs concentrated on Africa. There was story-telling for all ages, featuring folk stories, animal stories, fairy tales and stories of children in contemporary Africa. A film series, also for all ages, covered similar ground. There were also reading clubs for grades one and two, and for grades three and up.

The Bloomfield (N.J.) Public Library created its own holiday, "Children's Day," and held a party to celebrate it. The party was held on the Town Green, opposite the library, and included a folk singer, free soda (the children brought picnic lunches) and a "Things Not to Do" contest.

A Scandinavian holiday program was presented by a library on Staten Island. It was a morning program for ages six and up, and it was held during the Christmas vacation. Two films were shown: "Ashlad and His Good Helpers" (Modern Learning Aids) and "The Seventh Master of the House" (Modern Learning Aids); Scandinavian folk tales were told; Scandinavian food was served; and there was a drawing session for the children.

One children's librarian took advantage of a current interest to have a multimedia program. She read to the children the sections of the Laura Ingalls Wilder books that deal with wolves (A Little House on the Prairie was then being shown on television), and then she played the recording, "Language and Music of the Wolves" (Columbia C-30769).

There need be no special occasion for multimedia programs; they can be built around themes, subjects or moods. There are hundreds of possible subjects, and materials for children abound in all media. Often a story will be available in a book, film, filmstrip and recording. The point to remember is that material should be selected to supplement and enhance the other material and not used simply because it is there. One librarian has said, "Adding imagination to the use of an audiovisual item may add more than another switch or plug. You don't need to be plugged in to tell a story which will make a film more meaningful." One must also keep in mind that every additional mechanical device

multiplies the complications. It is best to start modestly
with two or three items until one is at home with the
workings of all the equipment, with the transitions from
one medium to another and the other problems of running
a complicated program, and until one sees the ways that
one medium works on another. It is better to have a
limited well-run, well-integrated program than a grand
failure.

The New York Public Library's Office for Children's
Services suggests to its children's librarians that they keep
notes on any ideas for the juxtaposition of materials that
occur to them when they are reading, viewing or listening
to books, films or recordings. They further suggest using
things that feel right. Putting together a multimedia program is, after all, largely subjective and experimental and
one doesn't know in advance what items will work together
for a particular audience. (And what will work with some
members of an audience won't work with others.)

In its training sessions for children's librarians, the
New York Public Library offers the following three programming suggestions:

1. Sample program themes and materials for media programs
   (Symbols indicate forms in which material is available:
   B Book; F Film; FS Filmstrip; R Recording)

   NAMES
   Caterpillar and the Wild Animals (Perennial)   F
   Farjeon. "The Flower Without a Name," from
   The Little Bookroom. Walck. B
   Flora. Leopold the See-Through Crumbpicker.
   Harcourt Brace. B F
   Grimm. "Rumplestiltskin." B R
   Mosel. Tikki Tikki Tembo. Holt, Rinehart &
   Winston. B F FS R

   ART
   colors
   Lionni. Little Blue and Little Yellow. Astor
   Honor. B F
   O'Neill. Hailstones and Halibut Bones. Doubleday.
   B F

   drawings come to life
   Crayon (ACI) F

Emberley. Ed Emberley's Drawing Book of Ani-
mals. Little Brown. B
Hearn. "The Boy Who Drew Cats," from Japanese
Fairy Tales. Liveright. B
Lathrop. Dog in the Tapestry Garden. Macmillan.
B
Leisk. Harold and the Purple Crayon. Harper.
B F FS R
Leisk. A Picture for Harold's Room. Harper.
B F
Zemach. Awake and Dreaming. Farrar Straus. B

A HUNTING WE SHALL GO
Milne. "In Which Pooh and Piglet Go Hunting and
Nearly Catch a Woozle," from Winnie-The-Pooh.
Dutton. B
Moonbird (Radim) F

VALENTINE'S DAY
Belpré. Perez and Martina. Warne. B R
Cooney. Cock Robin. Scribner. B
Fillmore. "Forest Bride," from Shepherd's
Nosegay. Harcourt. B
Langstaff. Frog Went A-Courtin'. Harcourt. B R
Various romantic folk songs available in our record
collections: "Fiddle Dee Dee," "Riddle Song" (I Gave
My Love a Cherry), "New River Train" (Honey, You
Can't Love One)

CHICKENS
Boiled Egg (Cont. /McGraw) F
The Chicken (Cont. /McGraw) F B
Sandburg. "Shush, Shush, the Big Banty Hen,"
from Rootabaga Stories. Harcourt. B

KITES
Kite Story (Churchill) F
Yolen. The Seventh Mandarin. Seabury. B

2. Multi-media programming

BLACK MUSIC IN AMERICA
Film: excerpt from Black Music in America from
Then till Now (Learning Corporation)
Filmstrip: Black Folk Music in America (SVE)

Recordings:
  Theme from Shaft, Hayes (Enterprise 5002)
  Zungo! Olatunji Afro Percussion (Columbia CS
    8434)
  Fisk Jubilee Singers (Scholastic 2372) and
    selections by the Jackson Five, Aretha Franklin,
    James Brown
Books:
  Hughes, Famous Negro Music Makers, Dodd, 1955
  Hughes, First Book of Jazz, Watts, 1955
  Locke, The Negro and His Music, Kennikat Press,
    1968
  Moore, Somebody's Angel Child: Bessie Smith,
    Crowell, 1969
  Southern, The Music of Black Americans, Norton
    1971

MAGIC PROGRAM: TRANSFORMATIONS
  Theme Music: Magical Mystery Tour, Beatles
    (Capitol SMAL-2835)
  Film: People Soup (Learning Corporation)
  Storytelling: "Don't Blame Me" from Don't Blame
    Me by Richard Hughes, Harper, 1940
  Performance of Magic Tricks
  Related books:
    Leeming, Fun with Magic, Lippincott, 1943
    Rawson, The Golden Book of Magic, Golden
      Press, 1964
    Severn, Magic Shows You Can Give, McKay, 1965
    Wyer and Ames, Magic Secrets, Harper, 1967

3. Other sample programs

Friendship program for picture book age:

  Recording: "My Little Rooster," from American Folk
    Songs for Children (Atlantic 1350)
  Filmstrip: Corduroy
  Film: Queer Birds
  Introduction of related picture books

Whale program for story hour age:

  Poem from Beyond the High Hills by Guy Mary-
    Rousselière
  Recording: Songs of the Humpbacked Whale (Capitol
    ST 626)

Storytelling: "Living in W'ales," from The Spider's
Palace by Richard Hughes
Recording: "The Whale" from Burl Ives Sings the
Little White Duck (Columbia HL 9507)

"Shape-changing" program for story hour age:

Storytelling: "Telephone Travel" from The Spider's
Palace by Richard Hughes
Film: The Windy Day
Poem: "The Twins" by Henry Sambrooke Leigh in
Poems for Pleasure edited by Herman Ward

NOTES

1. Vanko, Lillian. "A Metropolitan Library Reaches Out,"
   Illinois Libraries, Sept. 1971, pp. 462-6.
2. A footsie "consists of a hoop to which a length of cord,
   weighted at the end is attached. The hoop is placed
   around one ankle and the idea is to swing the
   weight around with one foot while jumping over the
   revolving cord with the other foot!" For further
   information on the footsie contest and other programs see: Quimby, Harriet, "Brooklyn Grooves,"
   Top of the News, April 1970, pp. 283-9.
3. New York Public Library. Circulation Department Memo.
   No. 21, pt. II, p. 20.
4. Greene, Ellin. "The Preschool Story Hour Today," Top
   of the News, Nov. 1974, p. 83.
5. Ross, Eulalie Steinmetz. The Lost-Half Hour; A
   Collection of Stories, New York: Harcourt, Brace &
   World, 1963; pp. 183-4.
6. Ross, p. 186.
7. Ross, p. 188.
8. Greene, p. 83.
9. Ross, p. 189.
10. Stroner, Sandra. "Media Programming for Children,"
    Library Journal, Nov. 15, 1971, p. 3812.
11. Goldfarb, Elizabeth. Children's Room Summer Report.
    Great Kills Branch, New York Public Library; pp.
    2-3 (unpublished).
12. Fertik, Marian I. "A Crescendo: Creative Dramatics
    in Philadelphia," Wilson Library Bulletin, Oct. 1968,
    pp. 160-4.
13. Cullinane, Irene and Theresa Brettschneider. "Creative
    Dramatics in the Public Library," Top of the News,
    Nov. 1969, pp. 57-61.

14. Goldfarb, Elizabeth. Children's Room 1971 Summer Report. New York Public Library, West New Brighton Branch; p. 3 (unpublished).

15. McChesney, Kathryn. "Chamber Theatre; An Exciting New Tool to Stimulate Young Readers," Top of the News, April 1970, pp. 292-3.

16. McChesney, p. 292.

17. Elgood, Ann. "The Children's Theatre Conference," Top of the News, Nov. 1970, p. 66.

18. Mathy, Margaret. "Folklore and Flapjacks," Top of the News, Jan. 1972, pp. 199-201.

19. American Libraries, Dec. 1974, p. 597.

20. "Roundup of Art Action in Libraryland," Wilson Library Bulletin, April 1971, p. 758.

21. Rice, Susan, comp. and ed. Films Kids Like. Chicago: American Library Association, 1973, p. 15.

22. Mannon-Tissot, Thalia. "Innovation Through Trial and Error." Film Library Quarterly, Fall 1969, p. 14.

23. Rice, p. 18.

24. Mannon-Tissot, p. 14.

25. Ibid.

26. Ibid.

27. Library Journal, Feb. 15, 1974, p. 519.

28. Ibid.

29. Library Journal, Jan. 15, 1974, p. 168.

Part II

FINDING AND SELECTING PROGRAMS

Chapter 8

PROGRAM SOURCES
(Where you can find them and how you can get them)

Some libraries are now providing money to pay
speakers and performers who appear at library programs.
In most libraries, however, there is little or no money for
programming. One must, therefore, be prepared to do
some scrounging. There are quite a lot of sources of free
programs, if one gives it some thought. The first thing to
do is to look around you. You may even find the grail in
your own castle. Inquire among your staff, or the families
and friends of staff members. You never know where you
will turn up an expert in some field of knowledge. These
sources have provided discussion group leaders, poets,
musicians, dancers, and people to give demonstrations and
workshops in a variety of arts and crafts such as sewing,
macrame, origami, and gardening. Sometimes one thing
leads to another. One staff member knew a t'ai chi expert
who knew some musicians and a lecturer on Chinese poetry.
The library produced a program using all of these people;
they, later, found other performers and a second program
evolved from the first.

Local colleges are a rich field for exploration; among
both faculty and students there may be actors, poets, musicians and experts in any number of subjects. Furthermore,
they are often willing to perform for a local institution,
such as the public library, without charge. You have nothing
to lose by asking, and we have often been pleasantly surprised at the willingness of such talented individuals, and
even their eagerness, to participate. College faculties on
Staten Island have supplied, among others, a speaker on film
history, a chamber music group and an actor to read a story
by Charles Dickens. Students in a graduate course in children's literature presented some dramatized stories and gave

some puppet shows. Other libraries have found student musicians and students in speech courses to give dramatic presentations.

Zoos and aquariums provide obvious possibilities; a herpetologist we know (who arrived with a boa constrictor that crawled around his neck as he talked, and a rattlesnake that didn't) put on one of the best shows we have ever seen in a library program--or anywhere else, for that matter. Zoos have veterinarians who could give talks on pet care and diseases. Aquariums could supply people to talk to amateur aquarists. Museums will have experts--or they will know people who are expert--in the arts, sciences and local history. They might provide entomologists, microscopists, (an arachnologist would make a great program), anthropologists, archeologists, an expert on the local flora and fauna or an expert in the detection of art forgeries. One museum, known to the authors, has an agrostologist and an expert on diatoms connected with it.

Don't overlook scientific and historical associations and societies. They frequently have members who have become expert in some field, and who are willing to share their knowledge. Such a program may also attract members to their organization. Many people, for example, are interested in local history, and in genealogy which often accompanies it. The Audubon Society or the Sierra Club may have local chapters, or there may be strictly local organizations for such subjects as archeology or geology.

City, state, federal and private organizations in the fields of law enforcement, health, consumer affairs, work with the aged, child care, mental health and business are usually willing to send speakers, and often films, to library programs. City and state police and the Federal Bureau of Investigation may be willing to supply speakers on a variety of subjects. One very popular library program, on protecting the home from burglars, was conducted by local police. In a series of programs for the elderly, a representative of the Better Business Bureau told some fascinating stories of frauds on householders; he also told his audience how to avoid being cheated.

In the same series, a nutritionist talked about food for the elderly and a speaker from the Social Security Administration talked about changes in his field. A psychologist from a mental health society conducted a lively series of discussions on child raising. Films were shown to spark the proceedings. The same mental health society was approached about a program on violence in our society. The program, it could have been a series, never happened, but the Society was interested and would have provided free speakers or discussion leaders.

Many organizations dealing with specific diseases or other aspects of health care are sources of programs. The American Cancer Society, the Epilepsy Foundation, Muscular Dystrophy Associations, heart associations, the Arthritis Foundation, county medical societies, city and county health departments and optometric societies will frequently provide both films and speakers. Drug abuse and drug rehabilitation centers will provide programs; they can send both the people who work with addicts and sometimes the ex-addicts themselves to talk about problems of addicts, methods of rehabilitation and to give information about drugs and their effects. Organizations that work with the physically and mentally handicapped can talk about the training, employment and care of their clients. Organizations that work with the blind can talk about the psychology of the blind, services for them, and their rehabilitation; libraries that serve the blind, for example, can give marvelous demonstrations of their services and of the materials they use.

There are city, county and private agencies that serve the elderly; they can provide speakers on retirement, on activities for the elderly, and on their problems. Human rights commissions can discuss the employment of minorities. City and county planning commissions can discuss zoning, urban renewal, commercial development, public housing and related topics. The League of Women Voters will supply speakers and discussion leaders on a variety of local, national and international topics that are of importance to the citizen.

Local drama groups sometimes attain considerable skill; often they include actors or a director with professional experience. These groups may be willing to perform plays, scenes, or give dramatic readings. There are probably struggling young poets in every community and they often write with power. Many libraries have provided showcases for them. They can be found through the English departments of high schools and colleges and often among your readers. There are music groups that are not affiliated with any institution; among these will be rock groups, string quartets, pianists, singers and chamber orchestras. As with theatre groups, musical societies often include performers with professional experience and a lot of skill. Clubs and organizations such as the American Association of University Women or the Junior League may have a variety of performers among their members; one might find people with expertise in many different crafts, or people who are, or could be trained to be, storytellers, puppeteers and discussion leaders.

There are many clubs in most communities; they all have programs with speakers, demonstrations, performances, and films; often the speakers are drawn from among their members and are experts in some phase of the club's special interest. These clubs--which are often looking for meeting space--can be encouraged to meet regularly in the library, and to have meetings that are open to the public. Such an arrangement benefits the club by stimulating interest in the subject and providing them with publicity and it benefits the library by providing ready-made programs. A geology club, for example, had an interesting series of programs in a library; subjects included caves, fossils, and micromounts; they were presented through the use of speakers, slides and films.

Some businesses are glad to provide programs. They can supply information about a subject without promoting their own businesses; if it is known where they are from, they will regard that as advertisement enough. Stockbrokers, for example, can give informational talks about investments (which often are very popular programs) without drumming up business for themselves. Karate schools have given striking demonstrations to crowds of boys of all ages (including middle-age); they love the board-breaking parts. Garden supply stores or plant nurseries can send speakers to talk about gardening on any subject from azaleas to zinnias. People from pet stores might talk about the care, training or diseases of pets. One library arranged for a butcher to talk to housewives about cuts and grades of meat. Businesses in the arts and crafts are a good source of speakers and demonstrators.

Publishers are businessmen who have a stake in libraries. Their publicity departments may be able to get an author who has a new book on their list to speak in a library--incidentally promoting his book. Publishers can also tell you how to get in touch with an author, if you want to contact one directly. If you can interest him, he may be willing to come for little or nothing. Any local author is certainly worth a try. You may not have the winner of a Pulitzer Prize living in the neighborhood, as we did, but local authors are usually of interest to the local population, and they are usually willing to speak without a fee in their community library.

Ethnic groups often form associations. If you want to put on an ethnic program, and there is a local Italian club or Sons of Norway, they may be able to supply performers or they will know of performers. Two very successful programs on Chinese culture were produced in this way by one library. Often your readers, or other individuals in the community who are unaffiliated with any organization, will prove to be experts in something you can use.

One of the authors worked in a library that was used by a local fireman who had become an expert photographer; he had learned this skill solely through the use of books in the library. He talked to a group on the techniques of photography, and at the same time served as a great advertisement for the library. There are many crafts that lend themselves to this kind of possibility; macramé, needlecraft, Christmas decorations and pottery are some library programs that have developed from contacts with library users. It is useful, in many ways, to know one's readers.

Local newspapers frequently print articles about people in the community who have unusual hobbies or occupations or who have unusual backgrounds. Through newspaper articles, we have discovered two poets, a sculptor, a man who made model ships for a living, a World War I pilot, and an American Indian; they have provided, or will provide, library programs. The American Indian, for example, gave a wonderful performance, talking, dancing and singing before an enthusiastic audience. A great many flyers and brochures come across every librarian's desk. And, although we all regard this kind of mail with impatience, it should be glanced at, if you are looking for program sources; one may as well utilize the groundwork that has been laid by other libraries, museums, and other kinds of organizations that do programming.

Having found all these people, one should record them. A card file or looseleaf notebook is useful; one should record their names, addresses, telephone numbers, specialities, the fee if any, where they have performed, and any observations on the quality of their performance. Naturally, such a file must be kept up to date. Somebody should be responsible for seeking out program sources, and for maintaining a file; some library systems or regions do this centrally and notify their branches or member libraries of available programs.

When asking people to speak or perform on a library program, we have usually found that a telephone call, followed by a confirming letter, worked well. If there are any details or problems to be ironed out, you may want to meet with them, at THEIR CONVENIENCE, to do it; theatre groups may want to measure the stage or confer on lighting, props and dressing rooms; speakers may want a lectern or not want a lectern; and anyone showing slides or films will need to discuss arrangements.

There are several things one must definitely do; speakers and performers should be invited well in advance of the program, sometimes months ahead; they must be notified in writing--a busy person can easily forget--and they should be given one or more reminders, tactfully and without bothering them too much. Several things have to be made clear to anyone you ask to appear on a program. It must be clearly stated that you can't pay them a fee, if that is the case. The library's role in the program and the visitors' role must be clearly defined; some individuals, and groups, tend, consciously or unconsciously, to take over a program for their own purposes, if everything is not spelled out in advance. (They make too many demands or make of the program something you hadn't intended.) Speakers should be given a time limit, which can, of course, be flexible; some speakers will be too brief and most will go on too long. They should be told the purpose of the program and, if possible, indicate the kind and size of audience they might expect. Sometimes, in spite of all precautions, things will get out of hand. Ways of handling such problems will be discussed later.

Now that all those speakers, actors, musicians and poets have been found, is it desirable to invite them sight unseen? If their reputations are big enough or good enough, one might. If possible, however, it is desirable to see a performance first. The contents of the program is important as well as the quality of the performance. One might rely on somebody else's opinion but one must be careful. As E. B. White said somewhere, "One man's Mede is another man's Persian." If no one can see a performance, reading the play or poems may suffice. The programmer will have to judge his sources. These precautions are important for several reasons. There may be something in the content of the program that will make you decide not to use it. The quality of the performance may not be up to your standards; your standards may differ, however, depending on the objective of a particular program; if the program is designed to present new, young poets, high quality and polish can't be expected. Finally, even if you use the program, you will want to be prepared to answer any objections that might arise.

Eventually one runs out of free sources of programs. Or one gets caught up in the excitement and stimulation that programs can offer and wants to do things that cost money. If you are in that predicament, you might consider applying for a grant. At this writing, grant money, both from federal and state governments and from private sources, is much tighter than it was a few years ago. Nevertheless, money is still available. One has only to look at the bulky volume entitled The Foundation Directory, with its thousands of entries, to realize that this is so. Therefore, if you have a good idea and present it in the right way, you have a chance of getting money for your project. The authors have had the very satisfying experience of obtaining such a grant; the money restored a theatre in a branch library and brought hundreds of programs to a neighborhood that had been culturally barren. Now, when the footlights go on and the new, red curtain goes up before an enthusiastic audience, we feel that all the effort that went into library programming has really been worthwhile.

Getting a grant, however, requires some thought and some work. The first thing you need is a good idea that has been thoroughly and clearly thought out. A successful grant-getter and a reader of grants for a foundation have both told us that there are two main reasons that grant applications are not successful. One is that they are cloudy and unspecific; that is, they probably have not been well thought-out. The other is that they are overwritten and overlong. It has been estimated that some foundations receive a thousand proposals a year. Obviously the clear, concise proposal will get more attention.

You have to subject your idea to some close scrutiny, to decide if it is really valuable and is going to benefit

somebody, other than yourself. Other resources and sources
of funding must have been exhausted. And you have to study
the budget very carefully and make sure it is realistic; don't
assume you have to ask for more than you need.

The next step is to find out what foundations might
consider your application. The amount of money they have
to give and the purposes for which they give it are the key
factors. There are several sources of information on foundations. The fourth edition of The Foundation Directory
lists 5454 of the larger foundations. (There are about
26,000 foundations in the United States.) In this directory
you will find the names and addresses of foundations, their
purposes and activities, financial data and lists of their
officers and trustees. It is arranged by state so you will
be able to identify the foundations in your area. Since the
information is not up to date, and since it does not list the
smaller foundations, you will need other sources. The
Foundation Center has offices in Washington, D.C. and New
York City. They also supply materials to regional depository
libraries in eight large cities across the country. These
centers maintain files of tax returns of foundations that show
the grants they have made. Files of annual reports of foundations are also kept. All this information is also available
by mail. You must, of course, pay for it. The Foundation
Center also publishes Foundation News, a bimonthly periodical
that keeps information up to date. It is also possible to see
the tax returns (IRS Forms 990 and 990-AR) of foundations
by visiting the office of the director of Internal Revenue for
the district in which the foundation is located. For information on smaller foundations, consult the Cumulative List of
Philanthropic Organizations Filing as Private Foundations.
Consult the Bibliography for further information on these
publications.

After the project has been thought out, and likely
foundations identified, it must be put in writing for submis-
sion to the foundation. As we said above, these applications
should be clear and concise. In giving guidelines for the
writing of applications, one foundation begins each of the
major points with the word brief. Another foundation speci-
fies a short letter. Proposals should be typed (double-spaced)
on white paper. The project should be described, and the
need for the project should be indicated; your own observations and any documentation should be included. You should
also indicate the qualifications you have for carrying out the
project. The objectives should be spelled out and the

procedures you intend to use as well as the methods you
plan for evaluating the project described. A budget must be
carefully prepared and it should be compared to the written
proposal to make sure they go together and all points are
covered.

There are several other ways by which libraries can
raise money for programming. In both New York City and
Dallas a musician's union has paid the fees of musicians
performing on library programs. Also in Dallas, volunteers
have been used to raise funds for special programs. In
Brooklyn (N.Y.), the Junior League funded a program on
"The Sculpture of Black Africa." Service clubs, women's
clubs and other organizations often have special projects to
which they are devoted; if you can find out what these projects are, you may decide that a program on these subjects
would be useful. So....

"Friends of the library" groups can be very helpful
in programming in several ways; they can supply money,
refreshments, speakers and performers. The Plainfield
(N.J.) Public Library has a very active Friends group. In
their brochure, they describe their activities as follows:
"We sponsor musical and dramatic programs, lectures, art
exhibits and films, including programs for children. We
offer tours of the library to interested groups. We work
with the Library and community organizations on matters of
common concern. We provide funds for special needs outside
the normal library budget."

All this searching for programs may seem like a lot
of work, but there is a positive aspect. After you have had
a number of programs, groups and individuals will begin to
call you and ask if they can perform in the library.

Chapter 9

CHOOSING THE RIGHT PROGRAM

After you have found out what programs are available,
you must decide which ones would be desirable and useful,
and which will fit into your particular library. No matter
how worthy a program may be, if it won't work in your library, you might better concentrate on something else; a
program on welfare rights in a wealthy suburb or one on
investments in an urban or rural slum just won't play.
Don't be too quick to judge, however. There may be scattered people in your community who are interested in a particular subject, and sometimes audiences can be built up
over a period of time.

When selecting a program, there are two main areas
for consideration: the first is the subject matter; one must
find out what subjects a group of people in the community is,
or might be, interested in; the second area for consideration
is the equally important, but more mundane, matter of
physical accommodations--plus a few nagging little problems
that are related.

Ask them what they want

One way to find out what people are interested in is
to ask them. And one way to do that is to form a club or a
group of people with something in common and let them
select the kinds of programs they would like. This has been
done with various age groups. A librarian working with
teenagers suggested the formation of an advisory group of
teenagers. This could be either a formal or an informal
group. Librarians would then talk with them about the programs they wanted the library to present. She says you will
be able to tell easily whether they are interested in a subject

189

or are merely being polite; their enthusiasm will burst
forth.

At the other end of life, the Cleveland Public Library
organized the "Live Long and Like It Library Club" to do
programming specifically for the elderly. This group was
organized, not because all the programs were of interest
only to the elderly, but because that group seemed more at
ease with each other and more willing to attend programs.
Meanwhile, for those of us "Nel mezzo del cammin di nostra
vita" the Plainfield (N.J.) Public Library has organized a
Mother's Club. This group, as do similar groups in other
libraries, meets while their pre-schoolers are having a
program in the children's room. The mothers decide, in
conjunction with the librarian, what programs they want.
They have had programs with titles like "Helping Young
Children Form Healthy Attitudes Toward Sex" and "Sex Education for Adults." But it's not all sex in Plainfield. They
have also wanted to find out what their schools were doing,
about the pros and cons of abortion, how to help their children with music, about television programming for children
and about gardening and various other arts and crafts. The
library has been able to provide programs on these subjects.
One advantage of such groups is that they also may be the
source of the contents of a program, as well as suggesting
the subject. As with the more general friends of the library
groups, these clubs can supply or find speakers, performers,
money or materials.

Have them fill out forms

Another way of asking people what programs they
want is to devise a form that can be filled out and that can
be distributed to all kinds of people in all kinds of places.
This form can be given to library users; it can be distributed at meetings of clubs or other organizations at which one
is speaking, or merely attending; and when one has started
to have programs, it can be given to those attending. Libraries that do a lot of outreach work have even taken them
door-to-door along with other library publicity. Such a form
should be simple and easy to read and to fill out--otherwise
people won't bother. The following is a sample of what one
library used. Depending on your library, you may want to
include other subjects, kinds of programs, or categories of
people. Remember, many people who say they want a particular program won't show up when you have one. Still, a
form like this is useful, and it serves several purposes.

1. Underline below the subjects which interest you.

Animal life	Dance	Photography	Travel
Art	Drama	Poetry	Other ___
Cooking	Music	Pollution	
Crafts	Occult	Sports	

2. What kind of performance would you like to see?

Discussion   Film   Lecture   Workshop

3. Would you like to receive notices of programs?

YES   NO

4. If yes, underline age levels which apply.

Adult   13-17   under 13 years

5. What day of the week would you attend a program?

Mon.   Tues.   Wed.   Thurs.   Fri.   Sat.

6. What time would you attend a program?

Morning   Afternoon   Evening

PLEASE PLACE YOUR NAME, ADDRESS, AND ANY
HOBBY OR SKILL ON OTHER SIDE.

    Another kind of survey, specifically designed for teen-
agers, was tried. From part of a book stack, facing the

JOHN DEGREGORY JR.

front door of the library, some shelves were removed. A
poster was put in that space. At the top of the poster were
the words: TEENAGERS! WHAT TYPE OF PROGRAM
WOULD YOU LIKE? Below were listed many subjects, with
a row of boxes next to each subject for checking preferences.
A wide range of subjects from candle-making to horseback
riding and drag racing were included. A head and hands
were drawn and cut out, and they were placed as if looking
over the top of the stack at the poster; the teenagers especially liked this feature. Their response was excellent,
and for some subjects very great.

What do they read?

But it is not necessary to form a club or take a
survey before having programs. Every librarian knows
what subjects interest his readers. If any sizeable group
is taking out books on a particular subject, that is also a
good subject around which to build a program. This should
be the easiest and most successful kind of program to have;
library patrons are the most used to going to a library;
they are the easiest group to reach with publicity, and they
usually have a variety of interests. If the readers take out
a lot of books on antiques, they will be interested in a
speaker who brings along a Queen Anne tea table or an 1884
Britannia chafing dish. Civil War buffs may be interested
in seeing films like "The True Story of the Civil War"
(McGraw-Hill) or "Some of the Boys" (Hank Newenhouse)
which would supplement their reading. People who take out
books on sewing, crocheting, and macramé will always be
interested in demonstrations, and certainly anyone that reads
poetry will want to hear it read.

Current interests

As everyone who selects books for a library knows,
readers do not have only long term interests; there is always
some new subject that becomes popular for a time. These
subjects may be essentially frivolous or they may be of tremendous importance. Responding to these current interests,
not only in materials, but in programs, is an important
service. The American Indians, the occult, ecology, women's
liberation, breadmaking and acupuncture are just a few of the
subjects that have become popular in the last few years.

There are also needs, as opposed to mere interests, that surface from time to time. These needs have usually always been there, but interest in them grows from time to time, and as interest grows, more materials become available. These subjects should also make useful programs, and they will attract audiences when interest is high. Venereal disease, abortion, welfare rights, the rights of minorities are a few subjects of this kind. Programs that respond to current needs or interests may have the added benefit of attracting people who have not been library users.

Reaching the unserved

That leads us to consider an important group, or groups--the people you are not serving. The community must be examined to see what groups are in it. Then one must think about what those groups might want in the way of programs. If there are large high schools or colleges in the area, or the library is in a retirement community, these things will influence your choice. The kind of high school or college will also be a factor; if it is a vocational school or a high school devoted to special subjects, that will be important. If a large group of elderly people is served, that will not only influence the subject matter, but the time of day and the place in which the program is held.

If blacks, American Indians, people of Italian or Albanian descent, parents, housewives, or a large group of Zoroastrians is served, those facts will help you decide on your program. Within those groups there will also be differences; there will be different levels of sophistication, language problems, income, educational, and occupational differences. Large numbers of people on welfare will be a consideration. Do they live in private houses or apartments? Are the apartments public housing? Are they rent-controlled? What are the industries in the area and how do the people make a living? What problems do these industries present? What part of the country are you in? All these things should be taken into consideration when planning programs.

They also have to be thought about; one can't make superficial judgments. If your library mostly serves people who live in apartments, you may not want to have a gardening program (except for house plants), but you can not necessarily make that assumption. One of the authors worked in a library that exclusively served people who lived in apartments; many of them, however, had summer homes and they used gardening books extensively. Industries that pollute the environment also support the population; programs about such local problems need to present all the alternatives. If you are serving black people, do they want to hear a black poet, or do they want jobs, or do they want both? Knowing the statistics is important, but one must also know things that never appear in a census report.

What is being done?

One must also look at what other programs are being presented in the community. Museums, community centers, colleges and all kinds of organizations are putting on programs. The question to be decided is whether to duplicate what is already being done, or to do something different. Your town may be garden clubbed to death, but have no poetry readings. On the other hand, maybe they don't want poetry readings. And you can't assume that because there are already a lot of programs on a subject, more won't be needed; the garden clubs may not be reaching everybody. Indeed, we have found that the subjects most presented are the programs best attended. It sometimes seems as though everybody is interested in the same thing at the same time.

Recently, a program on Chinese culture (dance, poetry, music) was to be presented at a branch library. It was discovered that a local college was doing almost the same thing on the evening before the library program. The interest, at this date, in things Chinese caused large crowds to turn out for both events. We have sometimes assumed that certain films, or subjects, that had recently been shown on television would have been seen by all who wanted to see them. We have been proved wrong in those assumptions. The television programs merely stimulated interest.

--and what is not?

It may be just as interesting, and more useful, to explore those subjects about which nothing is being done. In any community, there will be plenty of those. Libraries can, as most other institutions cannot, provide programs for small groups; those interested in spiders or--as Ezra Pound said--the 23 persons interested in the Provençal poets. If

the readers of poetry are few and far between, they can
nevertheless be found and brought together to hear poetry
readings. It just takes some time and effort. One can't
expect instant success in such endeavors, but audiences can
be built up as the programs become known.

When deciding on what programs to have, there are
many mundane details to think about. How much staff do
you have and how many will you need for the program? Will
they object that all, or some, of the jobs connected with producing a program are not part of their work? (It has happened.) Will the staff have to work overtime? Might you
have problems with the custodial staff? Union contracts as
well as personalities have to be considered. You will have
to think about the need for ticket takers, ushers, the charging
out of books, and someone to introduce the program, among
other things.

Not having enough staff does not necessarily mean you
can't have a program. Volunteers can be used for many
purposes. They have been used as discussion leaders, story
tellers, ushers and servers of refreshments. Libraries have
frequently also trained these volunteers to tell stories or lead
discussion groups. Friends of the library groups in libraries
throughout the country serve refreshments and do other jobs
connected with programs.

The available space

The amount of space available, and its location in the
library, will help to determine the type of program; discussion groups don't need much space but a Chinese ribbon
dance does. Don't necessarily give up if the space seems
too small. One theatre group presented dramatic productions
in an unbelievably small space; the director was imaginative
and used the space in ways we hadn't thought of. Think
about the different parts of the library and how they can be
used. A library that had only a small story-hour room
available for programs used it for discussion groups during
the morning. Another library with no separate space ran
film programs on mornings that the library was closed
for borrowing. Children's rooms can often be used, when
they are closed. A combination stack area and work room
was used for evening discussion groups, in one case. Sometimes there are basement areas that can be transformed with
some light and paint and by getting rid of accumulated junk.

Noise may be important during library hours; libraries don't want to chase out the readers they already have. This is another reason for having some kinds of programs when the library is closed. Otherwise, some experimentation may show you that you can even find space for a rock music concert. When thinking about the location--in the library-- of the program, one must think about security. Library materials, purses, and even persons may have to be guarded. The condition of the program space is important. In a karate program that we watched, participants were hampered by slippery floors. Dancers in bare feet may not want to pick up splinters. For all these things, the performers are, naturally, the best guide. They should be brought in to test the space, before the program is decided upon.

Furniture and equipment

There are even more mundane matters to think about, when selecting a program. Are there enough tables, chairs, or other furniture? If not, can you get more? Can you transport them, or have them transported, if you can get them? We have been offered wonderful programs that needed a piano; transporting and tuning it, however, turned out to be too expensive. What equipment do you have, or can get? You may be able to beg, or borrow (we don't recommend stealing unless you are eager to work in a prison library) movie projectors, slide projectors and other equipment. Performers may need, or want, lecterns, microphones, screens, blackboards or other items. Those needs have to be determined beforehand, and you have to decide if you can get what they want.

Complaints

When selecting a program to present, as when selecting library materials generally, one must be aware of the possibility of complaints. A program, unlike a book in the collection, sticks out like a sore thumb. And like a sore thumb, it is likely to get hit. It is produced on a stage and presented in front of (one hopes) a large crowd. It is also publicized throughout the community. These features bring the program to the attention of many people who would never think about the library, which is why you are having it in the first place.

When the Salt Lake City Public Library produced a series of programs in an effort to reach the Spanish-speaking community, word reached the local newspaper. They didn't like the whole idea; they said it was the work of "slick-talking racist agitators disguised as librarians and university professors" who were out to make "a pitch for armed revolution among loyal and patriotic Americans of Mexican descent."[1]

Another library was visited one calm morning by a young man who said he represented the John Birch Society. He complained about their showings of films about David Harris, Malcolm X, W. E. B. Dubois and Angela Davis. He asked why they didn't show films about George Washington Carver and Booker T. Washington. The librarian told him that they had shown such films in the past, but now they were showing films about people of interest today. The young man replied that these people were communists, pimps and anti-Americans. He said the John Birch Society had films of positive, pro-American approach for rent. He also said he would attack the library's choice of films in the newspapers. There are some other points the librarian might have made. She could have said that the films in question were only four of forty nine being shown. She could have pointed out that the program was really balanced; the film on Angela Davis was paired with "The Weapons of Gordon Parks," a film with a decidedly different point of view.

The point is that one must be aware of the possibility of complaints, and be prepared to handle them; if the material has been carefully chosen, and one has sound reasons for having chosen it, self-defense is a lot easier. Librarians shouldn't self-censor their programs any more than they would the books on their shelves, but they have to be ready for attacks when they come.

Nothing further came of this complaint, which is what happens to nine-tenths of complaints, but if it had, the librarian could have taken some steps. If the incident seemed likely to grow, she could have contacted her state Intellectual Freedom Committee. Failing that she could have contacted the Office of Intellectual Freedom of the American Library Association. These groups can help librarians decide how to handle such situations.

One case, of a program that did blow up, is fully

described in <u>Film Library Quarterly</u>.[2] It concerns a film program for teenagers in the Los Angeles Public Library that became a community-wide issue. Typical charges of Communism, corrupting youth, etc. were made, and the article describes all the action. It is a good example of the kinds of things that can happen and it tells how one library handled a difficult situation.

NOTES

1. <u>Library Journal</u>, July 1972, p. 2326.
2. Sigler, Ronald F. "A Study in Censorship: The Los Angeles 19," <u>Film Library Quarterly</u>, Spring 1971, pp. 35-46.

Part III

PRODUCING THE PROGRAM

Chapter 10

PLANNING, SCHEDULING, SUPERVISING

When you have committed yourself to a program, or
to programs, you may experience a slight sinking sensation;
it is normal, and not to be worried about. But, careful
planning is now necessary. (Publicity, an essential ingredient in the planning, will be treated separately in Chapter
11.)

Where to have the program

The first thing to think about is where to have the
program. Formerly, this wasn't much of a problem. Librarians had programs, if they had any, in libraries. Now
they are presenting programs wherever they seem to be
needed. Stories have been told on the front steps of apartment houses, and films have been shown in vacant lots;
sidewalks, streets, parks, neighborhood centers, drug rehabilitation centers, old age homes and nursing homes, hospitals, churches, housing projects and doubtless other places
have been used for library programs.

Outreach

There are several good reasons for taking library
programs out into the community. Many members of
minority groups feel that the library is not for them; it is
often a forbidding, official-looking building, with, all too
often, a forbidding staff. So, even if you think you have
the materials they want or need, how are you going to get
them inside to look? You take the materials to them.

On Staten Island, a few years ago, a storefront
neighborhood center, called the Dr. Martin Luther King, Jr.,

Heritage House, was about to open. Many of the residents of that area were not library users. One of the authors met with the board of directors of that institution; after two very dry martinis, he committed the library to co-producing six programs in one week; they were to be held in the Center, during its first week of operation.

We obtained some posters with giant photographs of Martin Luther King, Malcolm X and others. We also borrowed an exhibit of pictures and other materials relating to black inventors, explorers, doctors and others who had made important contributions to civilization. With these items, and with books and recordings devoted to black history and culture, we set up a large display that was to run through the week. A large supply of special booklists devoted to those subjects was also on hand, to be given out to the audiences at the programs.

A program was planned for each weekday evening, and for Wednesday afternoon, it being Lincoln's birthday and a school holiday. Films were selected to appeal to a variety of ages and interests. Library staff members showed films of black history, and films about black political leaders, athletes, musicians and various professional men. There were poetry readings, book talks, dance and drama programs, and lectures given by both librarians and members of Heritage House. Several hundred people attended the week's activities, in spite of a heavy snow on the day before the opening that had almost halted transportation. Many booklists were distributed, library card applications were taken, and reserves for books were taken. Much information about the library was disseminated, informally, by staff members.

As a result of these programs, a black music discussion group was organized, and held in the library; we were invited back to Heritage House to give a series of story hours, some more poetry readings and more book talks. We also know that one direct result of this activity was that a number of persons began using the public library for the first time. And, not the least benefit was that several hundred persons enjoyed a variety of cultural and recreational activities that would otherwise have been unavailable.

The New York Public Library's South Bronx Project, which deals primarily with Spanish-speaking people, has conducted many programs outside the library, in almost every

conceivable place, and frequently under very trying circumstances. Puppet shows have been given in parks, at a street
festival, and on the sidewalk at a bookmobile stop. One of
their most trying, and probably most rewarding experiences,
was giving a puppet show in a vacant lot.

"One of the high points of the summer came in
early July when Dr. Eismann, a psychologist at Lincoln
Hospital, contacted us. He said that he had obtained
permission from a Baptist Church in the Hunt's Point
area to use their adjacent vacant lot as a gathering
place for the young people in the area. He was looking
for an evening outdoor program with some sort of
stimulation for the children. We decided to do our puppet show as well as show the film 'Puppets' which gives
excellent ideas on making various types of puppets.
The children on the block were expecting us as we
drove up to the lot on Fox Street in Mr. Hampton's
red VW bus. They were all, of course, more than
willing to help us with the puppets. The lot was fairly
large, sloping downwards from the street and covered
with dirt, broken glass, sticks, stones and tin cans--
although there had been an evident attempt to clear it
out. It was surrounded on two sides by high metal
fences topped by barbed wire and on the other two by
high brick walls. Neither the height nor the barbed
wire deterred the children from climbing all over the
place. We set up the theater at the far end and used
electricity from a nearby apartment to hook up the
microphones. The children were remarkably good
during the show, and many of them also watched the
film. Others, of course, succumbed to the outdoor
temptations of fences to climb, rocks to throw and
fights to fight. Dr. Eismann enthusiastically told me
afterwards that though I might have thought it chaotic,
he had never seen the children so well behaved or so
enthusiastic."[1]

Other innovative outreach programs include telling
stories on the front steps of apartment houses--in competition with traffic noises, street games and open fire hydrants--
and showing films in a vacant lot next to the library and in
another underneath an elevated train. (It was discovered to
be under the flight path of airplanes also.) This last program was successful in spite of the difficulties. The films--
which had proven successful in other outdoor programs--were
"Liquid Jazz" (Joseph Kramer), "Judoka" (Contemporary/

McGraw-Hill), ¡Que Puerto Rico! (Contemporary/McGraw-Hill), "Anatole" (Contemporary/McGraw-Hill), "Glass" (Contemporary/McGraw-Hill) and, what turned out to be the surprise hit of the evening, "Pigs" (Churchill).

The Plainfield (N.J.) Public Library has taken their outreach programs into a great variety of places. They have gone to neighborhood centers, senior citizens' centers, convalescent homes, housing projects, YM and YWCA's, playgrounds, churches, barbershops and laundromats. Wouldn't people waiting in a laundromat welcome a film program, though? It seems to us they would welcome almost any relief from that most boring of jobs. And there are many good, short films available for showing to people who are waiting for the washer or dryer to stop spinning. You can always tie it in with an announcement or even a sign about the library's other services.

Another Staten Island library is little-used by residents of the immediate area, but there is a heavily-used park across the street. During the summer, the library staff have begun taking their programs into that park. In some cities, street fairs, sponsored by block associations and other neighborhood groups, have become popular. Libraries can participate in these events to advantage. They can set up tables with books, recordings, booklists and any special materials. They can play cassettes (even without electrical outlets), tell stories and give puppet shows. If there are electrical outlets, they can show slides, or films with a rear screen projector. Above all, they can talk about the library.

Another group that doesn't go to libraries is that group confined to institutions; prisons, drug rehabilitation centers, homes for the mentally retarded, hospitals, nursing homes and homes for the elderly are all desirable places to have library programs; all the more desirable, because many of the residents of these places desperately need and want the kinds of recreational activities that libraries can provide. A number of years ago, a drug rehabilitation center was established in a suburban, middle-class community. It was met by overt hostility and a campaign to get rid of it on the part of the community's residents. Since it was hoped that the former addicts would be able to return to a normal life as members of a community, this reception was exactly what they didn't need. The authors decided at least to introduce them to the library's services. They gave an afternoon program to about eighty of the center's residents, showing a film, "Rhinoceros" (Contemporary/McGraw-Hill), playing a recording of poetry and jazz, and giving two book talks. This program resulted in the establishment of a bookmobile stop at the center, and eventually bookmobile stops at a variety of other institutions; these bookmobiles now also give programs in some of those institutions.

The New York Public Library's South Bronx Project also gives programs in institutions. They have regularly had film programs in the children's ward of a hospital and they gave a program of two films and two puppet shows to a combined audience of adults, teenagers, and children.

In addition to minority groups, and people in various kinds of institutions, there are many people who would be able to go to a library, and who would feel free to go to a library, but who do not go. They may never go. But if you take a program to them, they may learn something; they might find out that you have a record or a film collection, a financial service, or a book that will help them repair their leaky pipes. And the program itself may benefit them. Librarians have long given book talks to community groups, but many of the programs that are done in libraries could be done elsewhere in the community. The public library of Elyria, Ohio, developed a series of slide-lectures that they take to groups; a staff member prepares a script and the audio-visual department makes up the slides. They have done programs on local history, local culture and other subjects. [2]

Most librarians have seen worthy books on foreign relations or Congressional reform sitting on their shelves untouched, or they have waited with increasing disappointment while few or no people showed up to see a powerful film on the evils of stripmining or on the dangers of the invasion of privacy. A Detroit librarian expressed this disappointment when she said, "Detroiters were showing themselves more responsive to programs of a cultural nature than those concerned solely with public issues." [3]

Maybe if you take those worthwhile books and films (they can also be interesting, even engrossing, as you know but the public doesn't) to a Rotary Club meeting, a church group, or a PTA meeting, maybe, just maybe, a few members of your captive audience will be shocked, startled, amazed, or made to think about something new; and maybe

one or two of them will go to the library. And think of the
broad field you have to choose from; there are innumerable
meetings in every village and town in the country, not to
mention the alabaster cities.

If a program, or programs, are to be held outside
the library, a lot of trouble can be avoided by thoroughly
checking the situation before the program. The first thing
to do is to make sure you have a thorough understanding
with the people who actually run the place. The president
of a club or the central administrative office of a large
organization may make plans that are not practical or they
may neglect to inform local people. One library in New
York State indicated some of these problems in a recent
report. They planned a summer storytelling program for
the playgrounds. The times and places for the whole
summer were planned centrally. Unfortunately, the
central playground planner did not say anything about
the plans to the local people. Furthermore, the librarians
were not given the names of the local people and had difficulty contacting them when things went awry. Even the
schedule proved inaccurate. In one case, the librarian
went to the first afternoon program--in the rain--only to
discover that it had been held that morning. There were
several other delays, because the planning had not been
coordinated with local officials.

The premises should be checked for electrical outlets,
chairs, and other equipment. The timing of the program
should be discussed with members of the organization. If
it is an institution, such activities as lunch, recreation,
the rounds of doctors and nurses, and others will have to
be considered when planning the program. Subject matter,
the length of the program and other factors will have to be
carefully thought out. Old people and sick people may not
have the attention span of those who are younger or healthier.
Although it is difficult to generalize about a subject when a
large group is involved, some subjects may be more, or
less, suitable or interesting for the old, the sick or other
groups. Talk to various people who deal with those groups.
When we planned a program for a drug rehabilitation center,
for example, we discovered that they wanted materials
dealing with moral and philosophical problems, because they
tied in with the rehabilitation program.

Radio and television

Radio and television are means of reaching out to
everybody in the community, and libraries have been using
them for many years.   Their use for library programs has
been given new life with the development of videotape and inexpensive equipment, and, of course, cable is now the magic
word.   Libraries, in the past, used these media primarily
for book talks.   A glance through the recent volumes of
Library Literature shows the many uses to which they are
now being put.   Almost any program that can be produced
in a library can be videotaped and used as a television program.   (In fact, one of the charms of having anything taped
is that it can be used many times.)   There are, of course,
all kinds of programs that a library can produce especially
for radio or television; the differences between the two media
should be kept clearly in mind.

People are often frightened by the mysteries of television, and, horror of horrors, the prospects of producing
a live program.   You have nothing to fear but fear itself.
There will be experienced people in a station who will,
figuratively at least, take you by the hand.   A good television floor manager can lead a novice through a book talk
so that he'll feel like an old pro.   Timing is, of course,
the most essential element, but with a couple of practice
runs you can fit a script into the allowed time.   And you
soon get to know how long a script should be.   For example,
on a 15-minute radio program of book talks, one of the
authors found that a six-and-a-quarter page, double-spaced
typescript fit into the time almost exactly, leaving about
two minutes for opening and closing announcements.

One kind of program that works well on both radio
and television is the interview.   Poets, novelists, dramatists, authors of all kinds of non-fiction books, musicians,
and lexicographers might all be worth interviewing.   An
editor or book designer, showing examples, and talking
about the physical book, would be the basis of a good television program.   One library, in a kind of expanded interview program, has a group of teenagers and a librarian/
moderator discuss a book with the author.   Other variations
might include, along with the interview, a scene from a
play (which could have been videotaped previously), the
reading of some poems, the performance of music, and the
display and use of objects related to the book or subject.
One library television program, involving an interview with

a naturalist, put the television camera to extremely good use; the naturalist had brought a toad which he put on a table in front of him and, as the camera zoomed in for a closeup, the toad snapped up flies with its long tongue; it was effective theater.

Storytelling can certainly be effectively used on both radio and television. So can reading aloud; although it is usually thought of as being for young children, reading aloud can make a very nice program for adults. Short stories are obviously suited for this activity, as are episodic novels such as Pickwick Papers. The answering of reference questions could make an interesting radio program--possibly including a description of the librarian's search, as a kind of story of detection--and it could, at the same time, show one of the library's services in action.

If the library has a collection of recordings, many radio programs could be built around it. One could adjust the program to play whatever music was not usually available on local radio stations. And, of course, non-musical recordings can make fine programs. One could play Gregorian chants, ragtime, Chinese folk songs, the music of Prokofiev and Copeland, a Bill Cosby record, Robert Frost reading his poetry, and a Sherlock Holmes story, not to mention

> Masses and fugues and ops
> By Bach, interwoven
> With Spohr and Beethoven,
> At classical Sunday pops.   - W. S. Gilbert

If the library has films, that too would be an easy source for television programs. Again, to provide a special service, the emphasis could be on what is not available elsewhere in the community. To add to these programs, the librarian could provide some background commentary on the music or film. This wouldn't be a lecture, but a few remarks that would enhance the viewing or listening. And, as always, one should use the opportunity to plug the library's services. One could merely mention a book that is related to the film or music, or one could make an announcement about a forthcoming program.

The public library of Mobile, Alabama, has had two television programs that illustrate some other possibilities.[4] One program entitled "Yesteryears" is built around a collection of 30,000 photographs that cover Mobile's history from 1869 to 1940. Another program is entitled "Golden Years." A librarian introduced senior citizens with interesting experiences, showed travel films, and described library resources of interest to the elderly.

Of course, the best way to insure a lot of good programs is for the library to have its own radio or television station. Some libraries have done this successfully. The public library of Nashville and Davidson County, Tennessee, has a radio station that has been operating for 12 years, and they broadcast 18 hours a day.[5] Most of this time is used for the playing of classical music, but they also have a regular program of interviews with local citizens and they use syndicated radio programs. The public library of Huntsville, Alabama, was planning to play classical, folk, and jazz music on its radio station, and to present programs using local groups involved in the performing arts.[6]

An exciting new program is taking place in Erie, Pa., where they are reading books and newspapers over the radio to blind people. These programs are broadcast on a special frequency, and special receivers are rented by users for a small fee. Volunteers do the reading, and funds come from the Lion's Club and from federal sources.[7]

"The Answer Man"

This was the title of a radio program of thirty years ago, and the libraries of the Northwestern Region of North Carolina have come up with a modern library-based version.[8] They call it "Information Sleuths." The public calls or writes in questions to the reference department and librarians answer them on the air. The best questions are saved for the program. Instead of merely trying to answer a long list of questions, they try to build interest in special questions. People have asked how to identify antiques, how to find the number of acres in an irregular piece of land, and asked for help in dealing with the problems of raising horses and dogs.

Quiz programs

These programs have, of course, always been very popular on both radio and television, and again the libraries

of northwestern North Carolina have created a library
version. This one is called the "Book Bowl." The schools
select those three students, in each grade, that they consider the best readers, and one school can challenge another
to compete. The program, usually half an hour, is heard
throughout the schools on the intercommunication system.
Librarians prepare short questions with a definite answer,
and they try to emphasize questions that will stimulate
reading and at the same time be fun. The questions are
from books they would expect most children of a particular
age to have read.

Cable television [see also Chapter 6]

Much has been written about cable television and its
future, but at this writing there seem to be more words
than action. (A lot of libraries are buying videotape equipment and making plans, but it will, no doubt, take time to
explore the potentialities.) There are great possibilities for
a broader scope and greater flexibility in programming than
libraries have had before; the portable videotape equipment
can be taken almost anywhere to tape a program; furthermore, libraries can, and in some cases do, control the
programming. The Monroe County Public Library of
Bloomington, Ind., for instance, has leased a cable channel
and has regularly scheduled programming; they telecast from
6 to 8 p.m., Monday through Friday.[9] In such a case, the
library would need to have the technical expertise to produce
an entire television program. Otherwise they might make
an agreement with the cable company (to present programs
using station personnel) just as one would make with any
commercial radio or television station. The difference in
cable television is that FCC regulations make provisions for
public access, in some cases.[10]

Some libraries are already producing a wide range of
programs on cable television. Most of these are traditional
library programs, but, in some cases, new kinds are being
presented. The combination of portable videotape equipment
and cable television, for example, allows one to respond
quickly to current needs and interests. These needs might
be transitory but important, such as coverage of local poli-
ticians or a controversial community problem that needs an
immediate solution. A community in New York City was
faced with a garbage disposal problem that had become very
controversial. A branch library made a videotape showing

scenes of the area and interviews with community residents
and city officials. They could thus illuminate the problem
for a large number of people.

On the other hand, the needs might be immediate but
of longer duration. The same library in Bloomington, Ind.,
for example, presented a demonstration of food canning and
freezing, which would be particularly useful in difficult
economic times. In Framingham, Mass., the public library
has presented a bilingual program of survival information for
the Puerto Rican neighborhood.[10] They have also presented
news and cultural events for the same group, information
that group would not get in any other way.

Bloomington, Ind., has also done some interesting
interviewing. One interview with a resident was entitled,
"I'm Poor and It's Damned Unhandy." There were also
interviews with local artists whose work was displayed in the
library. Interviewing people for the collection of local oral
history would also be useful and could be of great interest
to many. One might interview elderly people who are long-
time residents, or one could collect the history of minorities
or ethnic groups whose backgrounds have usually, in the
past, gone unrecorded.

The presentation of local events or places is another
aspect of this kind of programming that would be useful, because these things, again, go unrecorded. In Bloomington,
public library staff members toured, with their camera, a
new medical care facility for low-income persons. The Tri-
County Regional Library of Rome, Ga., does documentaries
of local agencies, as well as taping local cultural and social
events.[11]

For more traditional programming, Bloomington has
presented a demonstration of backpacking, and an adult story
hour entitled, "Fireplace Fiction." In the Georgia library
they have a daily children's story hour and they have taped
children's music and drama classes.

In the library

Meanwhile back at the branch (library), is where
most programs will be held. After all, that's where the
books are, and the films, and the records, and everything
else. And if you can get people to go there, that is still
the ideal.

Whether you are having the program in the library, or anywhere else, many things must be taken into consideration. One of the first things to think about is what time of day to have it. The physical space, the location of the library in the community, the kind of community, and what people do with their spare time are all considerations.

Time of day

One library felt the need for a program, but the small staff and small meeting room, which adjoined a busy children's room, severely limited their choices. Evening programs would mean scheduling staff to work extra evenings, and afternoons were too busy. Mornings, however, were not busy and a full staff was in attendance, in any case. Furthermore, since children would not be there, the meeting room would be quiet. They decided on an adult book discussion group, which would fit into the small room, and would require the attendance of only one staff member. The choice of mornings limited the kinds of people who could attend, but since the investment in time was small, it seemed worth trying. It was. The group, consisting of housewives and one or two men, has grown over the years to about twenty participants, and, judging from the evolution of their readings, their horizons have expanded considerably. As of this writing, it is in its seventh year and going strong.

A similar library, with an equally small staff, and no meeting space, has run morning film programs in the rear of the public area. The small inconvenience to the few morning readers was worth it in an area where such attractions were non-existent.

Another library had tried a number of evening programs with little response. Late afternoon programs, however, drew both adults and young people. Apparently people had been afraid to go out in that area after dark. Some libraries have had success, in business areas, with noontime programs. The point to remember is that one must be flexible, and think of the time that fits your conditions. We haven't heard of a midnight program, in a library, but don't count it out. Even the exact hour is important. If many of the potential audience are commuters returning to your community, a later start in the evening would be desirable.

The day of the week and the season of the year must

be considered. People may shop on Friday evenings or on
Saturdays. During good weather, they may garden on
Saturdays and weekday evenings. Sunday afternoons should
be considered as potential program times. The days preceding major holidays may be bad times for programs.
School and church activities might occupy your public at
certain times; examination periods, for example, or the
evenings of regular church group meetings, may be important in a community. Find out about any special events
before you do any scheduling and decide if they will take
people away from your program. In some towns there are
community calendars, so that events can be coordinated.

Regular schedule

If there is going to be a series of programs, a
regular schedule is important. The difficulties involved in
canceling a program or changing a date are great, so the
schedule should be carefully thought out beforehand. When
something has been widely publicized, it is difficult to
counteract it. And if people come to a program that isn't
there, they will be annoyed, undoing the goodwill that would
have been created by the program. Rather than cancel a
program, or change a date, it might be better to find a
substitute speaker, performer or film. It will be best if
you have thought of that before it becomes necessary to
cancel, and have a substitute program ready. If the particular speaker or film was what the public was coming to
see, it would then be better to change the date. Unfortunately, such things often happen at the last minute, so it
is always wise to have alternatives. A small group, like a
discussion group, can be more easily notified of changes,
but even then you never know who will show up for a publicized program and angrily confront you. It is better to
think carefully about changes.

Details

Forgetting to pay attention to detail can spoil a good
program. All equipment should be checked beforehand, and
it should be checked early enough so that you can have it
replaced if necessary. You can't buy a light bulb if the
stores are closed. Extras should be provided for everything,
like a projector bulb, that might give out during the program. If projectors, films, props or display materials are

going to be delivered, a pre-program check must be made; one can't count on messages being delivered, records being kept correctly, or mail being delivered promptly. Performers and speakers need to be reminded, and any necessary transportation arranged for. Remind them a day or two before the program. A tactful way to do it is to ask them if they need transportation, or if there is anything else you can do for them. If the speaker has a secretary, a check with him or her will be sufficient.

Think about audience comfort. Rest rooms are important. Are they conveniently located, or will a staff member have to conduct people to them? Are they unlocked, or has the custodian locked them and gone off for the evening with the key? If you are going to allow smoking, ash trays must be provided. You may want to provide coat racks, especially if the room is likely to be crowded. Ventilation and temperature are important. A room full of people can get very hot. On the other hand, you don't want a cold breeze blowing on the necks of the audience. Exits and exit lights must be checked. When P. T. Barnum wanted to get people out of his show quickly, he is said to have put up a sign that read, "This Way to the Egress." You will want to have your egresses clearly marked and unlocked.

Related exhibits and displays

These can give a program an added dimension. They might be put into outside display windows, or in various parts of the library during the weeks preceding the program; then they would give the event extra publicity. A display might be set up at the site of the program for the audience to look at or handle. Sometimes understanding is helped if an audience can examine objects that a speaker is talking about or if they can look closely at pictures, maps or other visual materials. Books, periodicals and recordings related to the subject are especially useful to display, particularly when there is a how-to-do-it program. If library materials are displayed, you may want to charge out books and recordings on the spot, or take reserves for them. This will create some small problems, but hack away the red tape; public service is more important than a charging system. There will have to be enough staff on hand to take care of the routines. Pencils, daters and whatever else you need will have to be ready. Extra time must be allowed. Objections from the staff may have to be overcome (We can't do that! It's against the rules!). In spite of these minor annoyances, such service is worthwhile for the goodwill it creates, and such a display is worthwhile; it will bring to the attention of the audience materials they may never have otherwise discovered.

Lists of appropriate books, recordings and films can be distributed to the audience, introducing them to a wider range of materials than can possibly be brought together for display. Such lists might already be in existence (a list might even spark the idea for a program) or you might want to compile one for the occasion.

Speakers and performers

A number of things must be arranged with speakers and performers. Speakers may want, or not want, a lectern or a microphone. They might want lights turned on or off at particular times. Someone might be needed to run a slide projector. The length of the performance must be discussed. The speaker should be told what kind of talk (formal, informal) you would like, and the level of the potential audience should be discussed. One lecturer, on Chinese poetry, in a library program, not only went on much too long, but talked above the heads of most of the audience, marring what was otherwise an excellent and enjoyable program. Musicians, actors and dancers will want to examine the performing space, and they may want to rehearse in that space. Actors need dressing rooms, and since most libraries don't have theatres in them, temporary dressing rooms must be arranged. Workshop leaders will want to make sure there are tables set up, equipment arranged, or other needs filled. At the time of the program, be on hand in plenty of time to greet the performers. Find out if they have additional requests. Make them comfortable; show them where the rest rooms are and where they can hang their hats; offer them a cup of coffee. One group of actors, at a library program, came directly from work, without eating. Sandwiches were bought and the actors were given a room in which to eat them.

There are several things that can be done before, during and after the program. The program, and the performers, have to be introduced. At the same time, books and other materials related to the program can be mentioned, or briefly talked about. The library's services can be described, and future programs announced.

Add to the mailing list; evaluate the program

This is a good time to add to the mailing list. Put a 3x5 card on each chair before the program--have a supply of pencils handy--and announce your intention; tell them to put the essential information (name, address, telephone number and special interests) on the card, and that the cards will be collected after the program. That's one way to do it. This is also a good chance to test the efficiency of various forms of publicity and to ask the audience to evaluate the contents of the programs. Simple forms, the simpler the better, can be devised for the audience to check. (See the two representative forms on the following page, reproduced at about one-half real size. The form on the right was a dark pea-soup green.) If it is a small group, you can ask them directly. Both methods have virtues. It is possible to add to the mailing list, test the publicity, and get reactions to the programs on a single form.

Many comments from the audience, either written or verbal, will be merely polite. But some will be worth noting (It's too hot. The speaker talked too long. The subject was too difficult) and will help you improve future programs. Audience reactions are useful to have when you are writing reports (if you have a grant, you will certainly have to report on your activities) and they help the moral of those giving the program.

In case of mishaps

Try to be ready in case of mishaps. The best-laid plans of mice and men do you know what. In one library program, a speaker telephoned from many miles away to say that he had had a flat tire ("had had" sounds like the bumping of a flat tire) and would not get to the program at all. An actor was in a minor automobile accident on the way to another program and arrived fifteen minutes late. Sometimes, with all precautions, a projector breaks down or a film snaps. The possibilities are, if not endless, certainly numerous. So one has to be prepared as well as one can. If you are losing your head, when all around you are losing theirs and blaming it on you, it certainly won't do.

HELP

US PLAN BETTER PROGRAMS

WHERE DID YOU HEAR ABOUT THIS PROGRAM?

Newspaper _____

Flyer _____

Poster _____

Friend _____

Other _____

HOW DID YOU LIKE IT?

Excellent _____

Good _____

Fair _____

Poor _____

WHAT OTHER PROGRAMS WOULD YOU LIKE?

DO YOU WANT TO BE ON OUR MAILING LIST?

Name _____

Address _____

_____

The New York Public Library

---

please, tell us...

WHAT DID YOU THINK ABOUT THIS PROGRAM?
WHAT DID YOU LIKE OR DISLIKE?

FOR OUR INFORMATION FOR FUTURE PROGRAMS -

What are your special interests, talents, ideas
for programs?

NAME _____

HOME ADDRESS _____

BOROUGH _____ ZIP CODE _____

ORGANIZATION
or SCHOOL _____

WOULD YOU LIKE TO BE ON OUR MAILING LIST? _____

OFFICE OF YOUNG ADULT SERVICES
THE NEW YORK PUBLIC LIBRARY
8 East 40th Street
New York, N. Y. 10016

The speaker with the flat tire was a psychologist who was going to comment on some films about raising children and then lead a discussion on the subject. The audience was large, partly because of the subject, and partly because the psychologist was locally prominent. When the announcement was made, the audience expressed considerable disappointment. But, the librarian, who had had discussion group experience, showed the films and led the discussion himself. The session was lively and the audience seemed satisfied. No one left early and they were promised an attempt to book the psychologist for another appearance.

When the actor was fifteen minutes late, the audience (a very large one) was kept waiting. Again, all went well. A delay of much more than fifteen minutes would probably have been unpleasant, and might have undone much the library was trying to do. Since there were several parts to this program, the order of appearance could have been changed, and the program started. If a late speaker is the entire program, the librarian can begin by talking about the library's services, but should certainly explain the problem. People wait better if they understand the reason. Recorded music is useful with a waiting audience, if the music is picked for the particular audience. If it is the audience that is late, don't panic. Audiences have a habit of materializing at the last minute, and inevitably some will be a few minutes late.

We don't want to scare you out of a year's programming, but other things can happen. Most librarians have had to deal with drunks, troublesome children and obnoxious adults. The same people sometimes go to programs. Potential trouble of this kind can often be foreseen. In any case, don't leave yourself shorthanded; enough staff should be on hand to take care of such situations. Young troublemakers are often bored. They can sometimes be transformed by involving them in programs as ushers, ticket-takers or stagehands; this is especially true if they can be interested in something that is real (not just makework), such as stage lighting or movie projector operation. One library solved some very difficult discipline problems by getting just such a group of teenagers involved in a videotape workshop. They learned how to handle delicate and expensive equipment, and they learned how to do something that must have seemed real and useful. After that experience, some of them, at programs, tried to quiet other disturbers.

If the material in the program is potentially explosive, mentally or emotionally, one has to think of possible objections beforehand, and be ready with answers, just as one must be ready to answer objections to material on the shelves. Troublemakers who are drunk or otherwise extremely objectionable will simply have to be ejected. The audience will appreciate it and so will the performers.

Anyone who has ever been to a meeting of any kind knows that speakers frequently go on much too long. Your programs will face the same potential problem. Speakers should certainly be given time limits beforehand. One cynic has suggested that they be given a time limit of ten or fifteen minutes less than you really want, on the theory that all speakers talk too long; he says if they don't, the audience will be glad to have a break anyway. If the speaker does exceed his allotted time, you can try to catch his eye; maybe a signal should be prearranged. If that doesn't work, walk across the stage and stand beside him. He should, of course, be allowed some leeway.

Recording the program

With the program running smoothly--and most of them do--you might find it useful to record it in some way. The medium used to record the program will depend on the kind of program, the equipment available, and the uses you intend for the record. You can take still photographs that can be used for further publicity and for reports; they are useful for help in obtaining grants. Children and adults like to see themselves in pictures, as performers or as members of the audience. A photograph album of programs will build goodwill among those who participated and stimulate the interest of others. A children's librarian who keeps such an album says the children are constantly asking to see the pictures. You could record the sound alone or you could record both the sound and the picture on film or on videotape. Such records can be used in future library activities or for radio or television programs; they can be sent around the community for use with groups or they can be used for the training of librarians. The actual recording, sound or visual, must be carried on unobtrusively so that neither audience nor performers will be disturbed. Fortunately, they quickly become accustomed to cameras, cables and lights. As with other aspects of programming, plan ahead and try to create a minimum of fuss.

Receptions

For some special programs, you might want to try a reception after the event, and serve refreshments. It will add work, difficulties and probably expense to the program, and you probably won't want to do it every time. But, such a reception serves several purposes; it allows the audience to meet and talk to speakers and performers; it lets you and your staff talk to the audience about the program and about the library; and it lets them look around the library. Not incidentally, eating, drinking and talking informally with the public creates goodwill. A reception is really an informal continuation of the program. For a program on Chinese culture, shrimp chips, lotus pastries, lichee punch and jasmine tea were served, and they occasioned a discussion of Chinese food. A t'ai chi demonstrator was questioned further about his subject, and the musicians were asked about their instruments. Thus, the program was given added depth. In another library, the auditorium is used as an art gallery. The refreshments, served after the program, allow the audience to have a leisurely look at the paintings, drawings and photographs that have surrounded them during the program.

In this same library, the Friends of the Library organization takes care of the preparation and serving of the refreshments, as well as cleaning up, and that eases the staff burden. Extra staff for such an event can be a problem, but in our experience staff members are often eager to be involved in a special event. Food, drink and utensils should be kept very simple to avoid problems in serving and cleaning up. A reception need only cost a few dollars. Sometimes interested staff members, performers or members of the public will offer to bring in utensils or prepared food, and the reception will cost even less.

Long-term scheduling

All the foregoing has been concerned with planning one program or a series of programs. For several reasons, it is desirable to plan programs for a period of time, say a year or a season, depending on the type of library. If programs are a regular occurrence in a library, people will get in the habit of going to them and watching for them. If planning is not done, scheduling tends to be haphazard; there may be several programs in a month, and then none for several months. Of course planning should be flexible enough to allow for the inclusion of unexpected programs and the removal of others. Frequently one hears of a new program source, or a subject becomes popular, and these things cry out to be included in your schedule.

Another reason for planning a year ahead is that everything has limits; projectors, films, rooms, and staff members must be scheduled, and there will be fewer disappointments if they are scheduled well in advance. If money is involved, its spending must also be scheduled. If several people are involved in planning programs--adult and young adult librarians, for example--the overlapping or repetition of programs can be avoided by planning ahead.

A year's plan should provide for all ages, any other significant groups in the community, a variety of subjects, and several types of programs. One might want to have a discussion series for adults, several series of film programs for different age levels, two different musical programs or series, some poetry readings or plays, one or two craft workshops for different ages, two or three puppet shows and a story-hour series. For particular kinds of audiences (film, music) it is useful to have the programs on the same day and time, so that audience comes to expect them; one might, for example, have concerts once a month on Sunday afternoons at 2:30, or have films for children on the first Saturday of every month at 10:30 a.m.

NOTES

1. Conwell, Mary K. The New York Public Library. South Bronx Project. Children's Services Report, June-Dec. 1969, pp. 19-20.
2. Library Journal, April 15, 1969, p. 1570.
3. Mansfield, Jewell. "A Public Affairs Program--The Detroit Public Library," Library Trends, July 1968, pp. 58-61.
4. Sager, Donald J. "Mobile and the Cable," Library Journal, Feb. 15, 1973, pp. 501-4.
5. American Libraries, Jan. 1973, p. 12.
6. American Libraries, March 1973, p. 130.
7. American Libraries, Sept. 1973, p. 467.
8. McRae, Jane Carroll. "Radio-Free Library Power," Wilson Library Bulletin, Nov. 1974, p. 228.

9. Cable Libraries, vol. 2, no. 4, June 1974.
10. There are two qualifications: the cable company must
    have one of the 100 largest markets and must have
    been licensed after March 1972.
11. Televisions, vol. III, no. 1, Jan./Feb. 1975.
12. Ibid.

Chapter 11

PUBLICITY

Successful attendance at a program has two ingredients; some group of persons must be interested enough in the content to go to wherever the program is being given, and that group must find out about it in time to plan to attend. The second ingredient is not as easy to supply as it might seem. Invariably, after a program is over, somebody will tell you they hadn't heard about it in time, and if they had known they certainly would have come. Although such remarks must be taken with several grains of salt, it is true that reaching people with publicity is difficult. One has only to think of the number of flyers, posters, signs and notices with which one is bombarded, and the radio and television that assault one's ears, to realize what sensory overkill we face; one also realizes that the defense against these assaults is to block much of it out.

Publicity, therefore, requires some careful thought and some hard work. We have seen too many libraries that put inconspicuous flyers on the charging desk and thought they had done their publicity work; that might do for some programs in some places, but most programs would die of malnutrition in such circumstances. In contrast, the libraries of the New York Public Library's North Manhattan Project used every available means of publicity. For teenage programs, for example, announcements were made in the New York Times, the New York Amsterdam News (a community newspaper), and on a local radio station. Posters and fliers were placed in the library and in community agencies. Fliers were mailed to teenagers, to teachers, to persons in charge of community organizations and to other libraries. Fliers were distributed on the streets near the library. Every teenager who registered for a library card was told about the programs. On the day of the program, telephone calls were made to individuals in community agencies and schools, as reminders.

222

The audience to be reached

One would not necessarily need publicity that wide-spread. But one must think about the potential audience and how they can be reached. The audience may be the general public. Or it may be a specific segment: the young, the old, housewives, blacks, whites, radicals, reactionaries, farmers, artists, or bubble gum salesmen. The pitch should, primarily, be made to that group; the publicity should be designed to appeal to them, and it should be distributed in places where it will reach them.

When we were fortunate enough to get Edward Field for a poetry reading, we were sure he would appeal to the young. His photograph--sweat shirt, beads, long hair--confirmed that opinion, and we used it on a poster in the library. (The photograph of another poet made him look like a middle-aged insurance salesman and we knew we wouldn't use that one with a young audience.) For the Field program, we also used excerpts from some of his poems, "Frankenstein" and "Curse of the Cat Woman," on fliers; these too we thought would appeal to teenagers, and they might draw the attention of those not familiar with his work.

For a program on Charles Dickens, we aimed at, and drew, a largely older audience. Publicity was sent to literary societies, women's clubs, college faculties and similar groups. Some general publicity is also necessary, since one can never be really sure who will show up. One poetry discussion group was led by a young, bearded poet and discussed no one much older than John Ashberry; it was attended by mostly elderly people, thus proving the wisdom of assuming nothing.

Physical form of publicity and its design

Having decided on the probable audience, one must decide what forms the publicity will take (fliers, posters, newspaper articles, etc.), and who will design it and who will execute the design. As with other aspects of programs, there is probably no, or little, money available for publicity. Fortunately there is some free material available. If an author is part of your program, or you are featuring the books of a particular author, call the publicity department of his or her publisher. They can usually send you photographs, book jackets or other promotional materials. The

author may have some of these items himself. Sometimes
performers, or cosponsoring organizations, will have their
own publicity, or will agree to create some. That will save
you some work, but you should examine it before it is distributed. You won't want the library's name on anything
that is tasteless, offensive or shoddy, and if it is any of
those things, it won't be good publicity anyway.

If the publicity is not readymade and must be designed,
explore the talents of the library staff, your friends, and
members of the public. There are often staff members who
can do simple lettering or have other art skills, and many
people will have imaginative ideas, when they put their minds
to a project. Sometimes school art classes, or other teenagers, will be interested in such a project; one possibility
is to hold a contest and to offer a small prize; that should
generate interest, give the programs added publicity (you
can also publicize the contest), and get you some reasonably
good art work. Try designing the publicity yourself. Even
if you think you are unoriginal and have no talent, you might
surprise yourself. Designing it yourself will also insure
that you get it the way you want it.

Materials, design sources, reproduction

Although you may be able to get somebody to design
your publicity for nothing, the materials and the reproduction
will probably cost something. Fortunately, the cost can be
small. Dry transfer letters and symbols are available from
stationery and art supply stores. Their use makes good-
looking copy a simple matter, and for three or four dollars
you can get a good supply in a variety of sizes and styles.
There are several brands on the market and they vary somewhat in quality, so you might want to experiment.

There are some simple ways to get ready-made elements for the copy. If you are working with a group that
has a letterhead or a publicity brochure, you can cut, from
them, pictures, symbols, decorations and unusual lettering;
these items can be pasted on the mock-up and can be reproduced, if they don't have fine shading or more than one
color which make reproduction expensive. Discarded library
books and periodicals can be useful for this purpose, provided the items are not subject to copyright. For a program
on Charles Dickens, several sources were used. A flier
that evoked a Pickwickian atmosphere was wanted. A

Christmas card was found with a black and white scene from Pickwick Papers, and we cut that out. Then we searched through a book of designs, bought for the purpose, and found one that seemed Victorian in style; we cut that out too, and pasted both these items on our mock-up. Dry transfer letters were used for the large print. A striking flier had been produced, with no artistic talent--fortunately, since none was available.

Sometimes pictures or symbols will be found that can't be clipped from their source. When we found a silhouette of Charlie Chaplin on the cover of a book, we also found a staff member with drawing ability. The silhouette was so successfully copied, and was such a useful symbol for film programs, that it has been borrowed many times by other libraries. Another way of using unclippable pictures is to have them photocopied; the photocopy is then pasted on the mock-up. They must be illustrations that will reproduce well. The paper should be very white, and the drawing dark with little shading. We had good success, for example, with a line drawing of a hand that we found in a book on how to draw.

There are books of designs and illustrations that are made to be cut up. Dover Publications issues a series entitled The Dover Pictorial Archive. There are 62 books in the series and the illustrations are no longer copyrighted (which is something to watch out for). The illustrations are of every conceivable kind and style, and they are mostly line drawings so that they can be easily reproduced. When you cut out the illustration, you can save the master copy of the flyer, or other form of publicity, so that the illustration can be used repeatedly. Dover Publications issues a catalog for this series. Large art supply and stationery stores also often issue free catalogs that describe various methods and supplies that are available for designing and reproducing all kinds of art work.

When creating the copy, a few simple rules should be followed. Use a carbon ribbon electric typewriter, if possible. Second best is a cloth ribbon electric typewriter. A manual typewriter produces uneven copy. Clean the typewriter keys before starting, and use a very black ribbon. For pasteups, use rubber cement so the copy won't wrinkle. Remove excess cement with rubber cement pickup. Excess cement may show up as a smudge on printed work. Clean the pasteup with an art gum eraser after removing excess cement.

Methods of reproduction for flyers and posters can also be fairly inexpensive. If you want to reproduce your own posters, a complete silk screen outfit can be purchased for little more than $20 and the process, we are told, is not difficult to learn. If only occasional flyers and posters are to be reproduced, there are in most cities and towns shops that will make inexpensive copies and they will do it quickly. One such shop, for example, which advertises printing while you wait, will make 500 flyers for about $6, using offset lithography. There are a variety of printing methods and there are varying qualities of work. Probably the best thing to do is to experiment; consult printers about your specific problems, get sample copies, and compare prices.

Writing the copy

There are several points that we have found to be important when designing flyers and posters. They should be clear and simple. If there are too many words, people aren't going to take the time to read them, or they won't remember them, or they will become confused. Avoid the temptation--we know it can be strong--to be fancy or clever, if by your cleverness you sacrifice clarity. Make sure that all the essential facts are included before the copy is sent to the printer. When the printer returns the copy, check everything again; do this immediately so you will have time to have corrections made. Such items as the time, date, place (with address and possibly telephone number), ticket information, and who is doing what are sine-qua-nonical. It is often important to include, and perhaps emphasize, the word free; many people do not seem to understand that a public library's services are free. Finally, make sure no eager staff member puts even one piece of publicity out before it is checked.

In short, trust no one (not even yourself), and assume nothing. In one press release, somebody changed the spelling of John Donne's name to Dunne, because they assumed it was incorrect. In another flyer, the time, schedule of events and details of the program were attractively presented, but the location was omitted entirely. Both pieces of publicity had been widely distributed by large organizations, and they had been prepared by experienced people.

Make the most interesting word or phrase stand out,

and the public may stop to pick up a flyer or read a poster.
Names such as Charlie Chaplin, D. W. Griffiths, Robert
Flaherty or Ingmar Bergman will attract film enthusiasts.
If the names are not well known, just the words FILM,
DANCE, or POETRY in very large letters will catch the
eye of those interested in the subject. To attract the attention of a particular group, you might want to emphasize
some special aspect of an art form, such as rock music,
horror films or black poetry. Sometimes the subjects or
titles are important or attention-getting; venereal disease
and narcotics are words that should stop the interested
passer-by, and titles like No Exit, Under Milk Wood,
Hiroshima, Mon Amour and The Perils of Pauline will attract those persons who are interested if the words stand
out sufficiently.

Even the day of the week or the time of day may be
the significant item. Certain times and days attract the
most people, and if nothing else seems more important,
you might want to feature Saturday Films or Sunday Afternoon Concerts. Symbols can be useful devices for attracting
attention. Drawings of musical instruments, film reels, or
a silhouette of Charlie Chaplin are all symbols that convey
messages to interested persons. Photographs of speakers
or performers can be helpful, particularly if you want to
emphasize some aspect of those persons, such as their
dress, race or age. Other pictures that indicate the content of the program may be good, if they are dramatic. A
close-up of a tarantula's face, a rattlesnake's fangs, or dead
fish in a polluted river should be stoppers. Nude bodies of
women, or even men, are too common. Don't use them.

Once you have caught attention, you have to keep it,
so the copy should also be intriguing. Biographical information can help.

If a singer has sung at La Scala,
or a filmmaker's "shot" an impala,
or a dancer learned dancing in Bali,
or a painter has studied with Dalí,

you would certainly want to put those facts into your publicity.
If, as often happens, the name of the performer or speaker
isn't well enough known to attract attention, you can emphasize any prizes or awards that she or he has won, any
performance she, he or they have given, or any writings
they, he or she have published. Quotations from their

writings, when carefully selected, can give a special flavor to the publicity.

If films are being shown, mention any special techniques or effects that are used in the film. Describe the intention of the producer of the film, or point out any special feature of the content. Such words and phrases as computer-made, electrovideographic technique, experimental, rarely seen or synaesthetic cinema might help.

When planning for publicity that must be printed by somebody else, allow plenty of time for the printing, allow for delays in the mail, and allow for the unforeseen. A printer getting sick has caused us problems more than once, and one of them died at a time that was inopportune for us (as well as for him). Again, the principle of checking on everything must be stressed. Call the printer before the delivery date to remind him and to make sure everything is going all right.

Distribution

When publicity has been designed, printed, received and rechecked, it must be distributed. Unless the program is a sure-fire success and you are afraid of being swamped, putting a poster in the lobby of the library or flyers on the charging desk probably won't be enough. Mailing lists are one of the most effective means of distribution. They are made not born. They must be compiled, usually over a long period of time, and they take staff time and cost some money for postage. But, if much programming is to be done, they are important, if not essential.

Most effective are mailing lists to individuals, but one can begin by compiling a list of schools, colleges, churches, clubs and other institutions and organizations. Mailings to them will draw some persons who can become the basis for a list of individuals. Continue to mail to organizations after compiling a list of individuals because some different people will see each new mailing. The library's readers can also serve as a basis for a list. Staff members can be trained to ask the readers if they want to receive mailings, while they are talking to them at charging desks, doing floor work, and in other situations. Another method is to take names and addresses from books that have been charged out. For a series of films on artists, one

librarian compiled an instant mailing list by taking readers'
names from books on art. This proved to be an effective
method--the response was high--and it became the basis for
an all-purpose list.

Use a card file for mailing lists. Lists are worse
than useless if they are not weeded and kept up to date; the
use of cards makes that easier. Also if a list is not weeded,
the postage bill will become excessive, and much staff time
will be wasted. Put names, addresses, telephone numbers
and special interests on the card. If subject interests are
indicated, selective mailings can be made, further cutting
down on work and postage.

One way to keep mailing lists up to date is to peri-
odically ask people on the list to return a form verifying
their addresses, telephone numbers, interests and other information. The cards of those not responding can be with-
drawn. A simple method, insuring a higher rate of return,
would be to include a stamped, addressed post card in a
mailing for a program. The following notice could also be
included:

Dear Library User,
    The Klondike Public Library is updating
its mailing list. If you wish to continue re-
ceiving announcements of programs and other
library mail, please fill in the enclosed post
card and drop it in the mail box, or bring it
with you when you next come to the library.

And the post card might read:

Name _____

Address _____

Organization you represent (if any):

Kinds of programs that interest you:

Take advantage of the mailing lists of other institutions and organizations. Libraries can often have notices
of programs of special interest to the members of such
organizations inserted in their newsletters or other mailings.

Word-of-mouth
_____

Word-of-mouth advertising is very effective, especially

if it is reinforced by a printed reminder such as a flyer.
Have the staff talk across the desk, to library users, about
the program, handing them flyers at the same time. However, don't count on staff members doing this automatically.
We have seen libraries where half the staff was unaware of,
or only vaguely conscious of, a program. The staff--all the
staff--must be trained to do these things. The first thing
to do is to make sure they know all about the program; they
must know the day it is to take place, the right time, where
it will be held, and what it will be about. They can and
should be made enthusiastic about the program. One way to
do that is to get them involved; involve them in the planning
and the production, talk to them about the subject and the
problems, and get their ideas which will often be very helpful. As with other areas of library work, your own enthusiasm and good example are probably the best leadership.

In some cases, you may want to telephone a few
selected persons that will probably be interested in the subject, following the call with a mailing of a flyer.

Librarians frequently speak at meetings of women's
clubs, church groups, parent-teacher associations and other
organizations. They also frequently belong to local groups
of various kinds. These meetings are good places to distribute publicity and to talk about the programs. Even if
you are not personally in attendance, arrangements can often
be made to have announcements at meetings and in schools.
One large New York City high school regularly announces a
library's programs through its loudspeaker system, during
the home room period. About four thousand students and
many teachers are reached at once, in this way.

Although individual contacts and mailings are the most
effective publicity methods, don't overlook any means.
Posters and flyers can be put on the bulletin boards of
colleges, schools, churches, stores, museums and other libraries. Since there is not unlimited money or time for
publicity, they should be placed selectively. A poster advertising a poetry reading might be put in a garden supply
center and attract some attention, but it would probably do
better in a college.

Outreaching

Many times you will want to attract, to a program, a

group of people who never use the library. Frequently they
will be people who because of language or other reasons
can't be reached through normal publicity channels. Some
libraries employ a very direct approach: they go out, or
send out others, to talk to people where they are. During
The New York Public Library's North Manhattan Project,
located in Harlem, staff members distributed flyers on street
corners and at bus and subway stops. The Chicago Public
Library and the public library of Plainfield, N.J., among
others, enlist children and other residents of particular
neighborhoods to distribute flyers door to door and to invite
their friends and neighbors to programs. Other libraries
have found teenagers very good for this purpose.

A Staten Island librarian demonstrated the effectiveness of going into the streets and she did it by herself. The
library was having its first Spanish-language program, but
very few Spanish-speaking people had ever used that library.
The children's librarian roamed the streets of the community
for a few days before the program, and during the morning
before the program. She had with her some very colorful
flyers, in both Spanish and English, and she felt that they
attracted much attention. She spoke mainly to children and
teenagers who understood English (she does not speak
Spanish, which is something to think about) and they brought
their families. Eighty-five children and adults attended,
and almost all of them were Spanish-speaking non-users of
the library. She believes that her approach was important
in her success. She says she quickly learned that they
didn't want to be regarded as "Spanish-speaking people," or
they were suspicious when approached in that way; but, when
she asked if they understood Spanish, they responded well.
A librarian in Maryland also found going into the streets
effective. She walked around ringing a cowbell, to gather
children for a storytelling session.

Undoubtedly the most direct means of getting people
to programs is to transport them, and some libraries are
now using buses for this purpose. The Chicago Public Library, in a state and federally funded program, takes children to its Neighborhood Library Centers by bus and a New
York state library takes groups of elderly people to programs in that way. Although it is expensive, libraries with
a lot of programs could find this method useful. Parking
and transportation problems, and the fear that many people
have of going out at night or even in the daytime have
eroded library use.

Press releases

Newspapers provide a very important means for distributing publicity, and the press release is the primary means for pre-program publicity, in many communities. Local newspapers are usually read from cover to cover by a large segment of any community, and they will print-- sometimes giving excellent coverage--items about local activities. When sending out releases, don't disregard the small papers or the special interest papers. Although the number of major city newspapers has been shrinking in recent years, many small papers have been springing up. Frequently they serve a small area of a city. Sometimes they cater to a particular group such as black people. And there are many papers serving various ethnic groups, usually in the language of that group. In addition to newspapers, press releases should go to radio and television stations; they also serve both the general public and special interests.

Given the importance of the press release in attracting the attention of the community, it is also important to attract the attention of the editor. Newspaper editors are flooded with mail, and they make their decisions in seconds. Therefore, it is important to catch the eye of the editor by getting the most important or interesting point up front, just as with flyers and posters. Press releases have other points in common with flyers and posters. Strive for clarity. Avoid being fancy. Make sure the who, what, where, when and how are included; these facts should be rechecked, not only for your benefit, but for the benefit of the publication. A publication using a release becomes responsible for its accuracy, and it intensely dislikes being tripped up by someone else's mistake. So for the sake of future relations with the news media, check everything twice.

In writing the press release, give it some depth. Then the rewriteman won't be required to keep calling you, or be made to dig out his own information. Depth will also make the release more newsworthy. The kind of information that was described for flyers would be relevant here. If there is a newsworthy picture, that can be included too. Newspapers like their local stories to have some connection with the community, in addition to the fact that the event is taking place there. It would be helpful if some person connected with the program lived in the area or formerly lived there. Otherwise one could try to make a connection with

NEWS

May 17, 1975

The Klondike Public Library
110 Bonanza Avenue
Tel. Yukon 5-0000

For Release:
Immediate

Contact:
Bill Snow
Yukon 5-0000
Ext. 3

GOLD PANNING DEMONSTRATION

Gold panning techniques will be demonstrated at the
Klondike Public Library, 110 Bonanza Avenue, on
Saturday, May 24, 1975 at 3 P.M. The demonstration will be conducted by Joe Oldtimer, proprietor
of the Whitehorse Saloon. Oldtimer has panned for
gold all over the Northwest Territories for the past
seventy years and he will show how it is done. He
will also tell some stories of the rough, tough
early days, and why his motto is "All that glitters
is not gold." Admission is free, as it is to all
library programs.

(a sample press release)

---

some local place or event. If the subject of the program is
timely, that is important. The release should be as concise as is consistent with a good story. If you make it too
long, it might end up in the editor's wastebasket.

Timing is important. Be certain the release gets to
the publication at least several days ahead of the day you
want it published. Editors like to schedule the handling of
even small stories. And don't forget that mail is often delayed. Personal delivery is the surest way. The story
should not be published too far ahead of the date of the program or too shortly before it. The timing will also depend
on whether you are requiring tickets. One editor of a daily

newspaper has told us that Monday and Tuesday are good
days for getting stories printed because the news tends to
be lighter on those days.

There are a number of other pieces of information
that should go into every press release. The name, address,
and telephone number of the library must be included, and
the name and telephone number (including extension) of the
person to contact for further information should be there.
Two dates should appear; the date the release is sent out
and the date of the requested release for publication; one
can either request immediate release or ask for a specific
date. If a story has special news value, the same release
can be sent to all media. If you want announcements to
appear in calendars of events, or you want spot announcements on radio and television, you can send those places a
separate release giving only the basic information.

Another use for the press is having them cover the
program with reporters and photographers. If the program
has news value, if they have room to print the story, and
if they have the staff to send, they will probably cover it.
Telephone the city editor if time is limited, but it is better
to send him a memorandum about three days in advance of
the event. Tell him the place, time and subject, and include
a brief description of the program, being sure to mention
local angles, names of well-known performers, or other eye-
catching information. Press coverage of a library program
can serve several purposes: it helps to build a good image
of the library and to alert people to the possibility of future
programs. Press clippings and photographs are useful at
budget time and when applying for grants or seeking funds in
any manner.

Libraries are shy, if we can be permitted to indulge
in a little bit of anthropomorphism. They are discreet,
dignified and reserved (that is, most of them are in outward
appearance). Even if all kinds of exciting things are going
on inside, outwardly they remain, or appear, the same.
One way to temporarily transform a cold exterior is to hang
out a banner. One library made an effective banner, simply
and cheaply. Two bed sheets were donated by a staff member, and they were stapled together. Stencils were made
from newspaper and cardboard and the letters, proclaiming
a week of Puerto Rican cultural activities, were painted with
a can of spray paint. This 12-foot banner, with foot-high

red and blue letters on a white background, was easily legible a block away.

Such a device is certainly helpful when a series of programs or a festival is planned, and an all-purpose banner or flag might be made to be hung out whenever programs were to take place. In Elizabethan days, because rain or an outbreak of the plague would cancel the play, all the playhouses flew flags when a performance was scheduled. Rain or the plague are unlikely to cancel a library program, but the plague of library anonymity is almost as bad.

Tickets

Directly related to publicity, and in a sense part of it, is the use of tickets for programs. Although admission will almost always be free for library programs, the use of tickets can be valuable. If you are afraid the crowd might overflow the space, tickets can be used to limit the size of the audience. Not everyone who takes a ticket will come and the amount of attrition can vary greatly. This is partly dependent on how they are given out. If they are put on the charging desk, they will be put to all kinds of uses, including the making of paper airplanes. People, especially teachers, frequently ask for large batches of tickets to give to friends, enemies, students and others. If, on the other hand, tickets are carefully handed out to those persons requesting them, they do give some guide to the number of people likely to attend. Another, and in a sense contradictory, use of tickets is that they may increase attendance. There is something about even a free ticket, if it is attractively printed on good paper, that enhances the value of an event in the eyes of the public.

When tickets are used, indicate that on the publicity. It is usually best to say that they can be picked up at the library. Other pickup points can be designated but that makes them harder to keep track of and to control. Post cards can be included with individual mailings asking people to request the number of tickets they would like held for them, or mailed to them.

Tickets were put to good use by one library when its budget was severely limited. A Scandinavian multimedia program was being presented and there was no money for

THE NEW YORK PUBLIC LIBRARY
OTHER PEOPLE'S MAIL

A Lecture
by
DR. LOLA L. SZLADITS

Tuesday, April 2, 1974 at 7:00 p.m.

ST. GEORGE LIBRARY CENTER
10 Hyatt Street
Staten Island

FREE ADMISSION TICKET

THE NEW YORK PUBLIC LIBRARY
You are cordially invited to hear

Mrs. Virginia Sloan, Arden Antique Shop
give a lecture - demonstration on

ANTIQUES

Monday   May 24, 1971   7:30 p.m.

TOTTENVILLE BRANCH
7430 Amboy Road, Staten Island

Admission Free

Two sample NYPL tickets (at three-quarters real size)

flyers. An 18-inch high straw goat, the Swedish Jul Tomte, was placed on the charging desk and hand-lettered tickets (using catalog card stock) were hung from the goat so that children could take them. This unusual, attractive object drew considerable attention and was a good publicity device. Some thought would bring to mind similar devices for other kinds of programs.

Chapter 12

ONE EXEMPLARY LIBRARY PROGRAM

<u>Paul Zindel and Some of His Friends</u>
<u>Visit with Their Staten Island Neighbors</u>

We began to be aware of Paul Zindel in the mid-
sixties. He was teaching science at a local high school,
and some of his plays were appearing on New York's educational television channel. They were original, humorous
and compassionate, and were bright spots on otherwise
generally tame television. When in 1968, his first teenage
novel, <u>The Pigman,</u> was published, we realized that we had
a library patron and neighbor who was a very good writer.
Then <u>The Effect of Gamma Rays on Man-in-the-Moon-Mari-</u>
<u>golds</u> opened in an Off-Broadway theatre to general critical
and public acclaim, winning the New York Drama Critics'
Circle Award. We began talking about how nice it would be
if we could persuade him to appear on a library program.
We continued to talk about it for more than a year.
"Wouldn't it be great if Paul Zindel came to talk," we
kept saying. We did nothing.

Ads started to appear in the <u>New York Times</u>. His
new play, <u>And Miss Reardon Drinks a Little,</u> was to open on
Broadway with a star cast. His books, it was reported,
were being made into films. He was suddenly big time. It
was too late. We could never get him now.

We decided to try anyway. The worst we could get
was no answer. So we dreamed up a program and wrote
him a letter. We suggested that if he would come and talk
about his work, we might be able to get some actors to perform scenes from his plays. We also said we would like to
have a big display in the library during the month of the
performance, and asked him if he could lend us some pictures,

manuscripts and other material. A few days later, during
a coffee break, the word came. "Paul Zindel is on the
phone." Raced through the building. Up the stairs. Out
of breath. Answer. He would be glad to do it. This
month if possible. He would be busy later.

Now we needed actors. We had been in touch with
the Staten Island Civic Theatre, talking about possible programs, and decided to try them. It happily turned out that
Mrs. Elaine Boies, whom we called, was a friend of Mr.
Zindel's and would be glad to work on such a program.

After some more telephone calls, a meeting was arranged with Mr. Zindel and Mrs. Boies. Mr. Zindel was
better than his word. He arrived with two shopping bags
filled with manuscripts, galley and page proofs, photographs
of scenes from his plays, copies of his books in Danish,
Swedish, French and English, his awards, and various other
material for display. We agreed on a date, April 29, that
didn't conflict with anything we could think of and a time,
8 p.m., that was late enough for the commuters and early
enough to be finished at a reasonable hour. Scenes from
the plays were discussed, and it was suggested that scenes
from the novels be dramatized. A reception after the program was suggested, and Mr. Zindel said he liked receptions.
Life was becoming more complicated but we decided to go
ahead. Mrs. Boies measured the stage and would decide on
the scenes. They departed, leaving the staff in a state of
euphoria mixed with trepidation. The trepidation was to
increase as the day came closer.

A committee was set up to plan, buy, prepare, and
serve the refreshments for the reception, and we were
promised $25 (the only cash we spent) for the food. We
decided on two kinds of punch, one with wine and one without, and canapes and cookies. All were fairly easy to prepare and serve. We would have the reception in the children's room which was easily accessible, by two entrances,
from the auditorium.

Publicity was the next problem. Flyers, newspaper
publicity, and a poster in the branch along with the exhibits
would be enough. We knew that for this one, unlike some
past programs, we wouldn't have any trouble filling the
house. What we didn't yet realize was how overwhelming
the response was to be. Tickets were necessary to control
the size of the audience. In the past, the number of tickets

taken had been a fairly reliable guide, although it is often difficult to tell how many ticket holders will show up, the tickets being free. It seemed likely that the percentage coming would be higher for this one, and we would have to be careful about giving out tickets.

No matter how far ahead one plans a program, publicity inevitably seems to be rushed. We wanted flyers two weeks before the program to allow time for mailing them out and getting back requests for tickets. We had to figure on the time for printing and allow for delivery time. A final decision on the scenes to be performed and the rounding up of the actors delayed us somewhat, but a flyer was finally designed by the staff and printed in the Library's Letter Shop.

Meanwhile back at the branch, more mundane chores remained to be done. Mr. Zindel wanted a microphone which had to be brought from another branch. The cast needed screens at the edge of the stage which had to be found and brought in. Seating was a major problem. Only 80 folding chairs were available. Enough chairs were available in other branches, but their programming schedules proved to be so tight that they had to be transported in the last two days before the program. The cast wanted two rehearsals in the library, and the schedule was cleared. We were ready to go. All the preliminaries had been taken care of.

The publicity arrived on time, with all the spelling and information correct. Meanwhile an item had appeared in a column of the local newspaper announcing the program, with the wrong date. Fortunately only three people showed up a week early. We had compiled a mailing list of high schools, colleges, organizations, churches, and individuals, and we sent them all flyers, as well as sending flyers to all libraries. We wrote a press release, trying hard for clarity and good timing. The newspaper gave us some good space, but neglected to mention tickets. A faint foreboding of doom flickered feebly in our esophagi. Or it may have been heartburn.

Then came the tsunami of requests. Before we had time to turn around, a hundred tickets had gone. Soon it was 150. Fear struck deep within us. Fear? It was more like panic. Maybe we could leave the country. Visions of not sugar plums, but the Beatles at Shea Stadium danced in

(cont. on p. 243)

PULITZER PRIZE WINNING PLAYWRIGHT AND NOVELIST

PAUL ZINDEL

MONDAY, MAY 24th
8:00 P. M.
PORT RICHMOND BRANCH LIBRARY
75 BENNETT STREET
STATEN ISLAND, N. Y. 10302

THE NEW YORK PUBLIC LIBRARY

Program flyer advertising the Zindel evening emphasized his
name because he was the recognizable element (he had just
won a Pulitzer Prize). Contents of this program/flyer shown
on next page. Both reproduced at 75 per cent of original size.

PAUL ZINDEL .... TALKS TO THE AUDIENCE

MEMBERS OF THE STATEN ISLAND CIVIC THEATRE, DIRECTED BY ELAINE BOIES .... PERFORM SCENES FROM:

THE EFFECT OF GAMMA RAYS ON MAN-IN-THE-MOON MARIGOLDS

I NEVER LOVED YOUR MIND

AND MISS REARDON DRINKS A LITTLE

MY DARLING, MY HAMBURGER

MOLLY SHEREN
ANGELO DeSIMONE
SARAH MODEN
PAM MAMAY
JOHN CARLSON

THE AUDIENCE .... TALKS TO PAUL ZINDEL

PAUL ZINDEL, a native of Staten Island and former science teacher at Tottenville High School, is the author of three novels for teenagers and has had his plays performed on and off-Broadway and on television. He has won the Drama Desk Award, the Village Voice Off-Broadway Award, and the New York Drama Critics Circle Award.

In May 1971 Mr. Zindel was awarded the Pulitzer Prize in Drama for The Effect of Gamma Rays on Man-in-the-Moon Marigolds.

Novels:

I Never Loved Your Mind

My Darling, My Hamburger

The Pigman

Plays:

And Miss Reardon Drinks a Little

Let Me Hear You Whisper

The Effect of Gamma Rays on Man-in-the-Moon Marigolds

our heads. People kept calling. Begging for tickets. Can't
I just have three? Five for my students? One for my aunt
from Tottenville? Why don't you get a bigger auditorium?
It had never happened to a library program before. Almost
200 tickets had been given out a week before the program,
and the most we had ever been able to seat was 150. For
a normal program, attrition would have taken care of the
difference. But we weren't so sure for this one. Every
movable object had to be cleared from the auditorium. With
some careful scheming we managed to put in 170 chairs,
even putting two in the projection booth for some staff members who were clamoring for tickets.

The Big Night came. Two strong-willed, stout-
hearted staff members were stationed at the doors to collect
tickets and to keep out those without them. The thought had
formed, and was now growing, that we should repeat the
program if the principals were willing. We decided to take
the names and addresses of people without tickets, just in
case we could pull it off. Not to keep you in suspense,
everything turned out all right. About thirty people were
turned away, although many who had telephoned had been
discouraged. All seats were filled and a few standees
managed to crowd in. There was some, slightly warm,
discussion with one man who left because he didn't like the
plays we were presenting. The auditorium was pretty warm,
too. We must remember to open more windows next time.
The performances went off almost without a hitch, considering the crowded conditions, and some difficulties with
the directions for switching on and off the lights. The performances and the reception, with some heroic work by the
staff, were enjoyed by all.

Four days later, Mr. Zindel was awarded the Pulitzer
Prize for drama. There is a sequel. We hesitantly asked
Mr. Zindel if he would be willing to give a repeat performance. He was again most agreeable and willing. The whole
thing was repeated in another branch, with better facilities,
in front of about 230 people. This second performance had
to be presented within a month, because of various commit-
ments. As it was, two new members of the cast had to be
found, and rehearsed. After we were sure of them, the
publicity had to be rewritten and reprinted. The only
hitches this time were one member of the cast who had an
automobile accident on the way to the performance, which
only caused a ten-minute delay, and a heckler in the back of
the auditorium, who was taken in stride by everybody. We

taped the entire performance and had pictures taken, since, in Mr. Zindel's remarks, and particularly in the dramatizations from the novels, we had a unique program.

There now seemed to be nothing left to do but retire. We had run out of Pulitizer Prize winners.

APPENDICES

A. SAMPLE LISTS OF BOOKS FOR DISCUSSION

Women's Rights
  Ibsen: A Doll's House
  Strindberg: The Father
  Woolf: A Room of One's
    Own
  Greer: The Female Eunuch

War
  Heller: Catch-22
  Brecht: Mother Courage
  Killens: And Then We
    Heard the Thunder
  Vonnegut: Cat's Cradle

Conscience of the Playwright
  Eliot: The Cocktail Party

Brecht: Galileo
Dürrenmatt: The Visit
Ionesco: The Rhinoceros

Lure of the East
  Hesse: Siddhartha
  Bhagavad-Gita
  Watts: Spirit of Zen
  Lao-tzu: Way of Life

Love or Will
  May: Love and Will
  Albee: Who's Afraid of
    Virginia Woolf?
  Nabokov: Lolita
  Friedan: Feminine Mystique

Following are the lists for the Adult Great Books Discussion Program, which is sponsored by The Great Books Foundation, 307 North Michigan Ave., Chicago 60601 and is reprinted here by permission. Librarians can order paperback sets of these readings from the Foundation, or they might wish to use these lists as bases for compiling their own lists of readings. The Foundation also sponsors the Junior Great Books Discussion Program. The asterisk * denotes selections only.

FIRST SET
1 The Declaration of Independence
2 Sophocles: Antigone
3 Plato: Apology; Crito
4 Thoreau: Civil Disobedience;
    Walden*
5 Machiavelli: The Ruler
6 Plutarch: Pompey
7 Shakespeare: Macbeth
8 Locke: Of Civil Government
9 Aristotle: Politics*

10 The Federalist Papers*
11 Adam Smith: The Wealth
    of Nations*
12 Marx and Engels: The
    Communist Manifesto
13 Tocqueville: Democracy in
    America*
14 The Gospel of Matthew
15 Tolstoy: The Death of
    Ivan Ilych
16 Joyce: Dubliners*

SECOND SET

1 Melville: Billy Budd, Fore-
   topman
2 Plato: Euthyphro
3 Sophocles: Oedipus Rex;
   Oedipus at Colonus
4 Aristotle: Ethics*
5 St. Augustine: The Confes-
   sions of St. Augustine*
6 Shakespeare: Hamlet
7 Freud: A General Introduction to Psychoanalysis*
8 Racine: Phaedra
9 Homer: The Odyssey
10 Descartes: Discourse on
   Method
11 Hobbes: Leviathan*
12 Pascal: Pensées*
13 Mill: On Liberty
14 Swift: Gulliver's Travels*
15 Poincaré: The Value of
   Science*
16 Gogol: The Overcoat

THIRD SET

1 Freud: Civilization and Its
   Discontents
2 Dostoyevsky: Notes from
   Underground
3 Mann: Death in Venice
4 Aeschylus: Oresteia
5 Thucydides: The Pelopon-
   nesian War*
6 Aristophanes: Peace; The
   Birds
7 Aquinas: Treatise on Law*
8 Rousseau: The Social
   Contract*
9 Kant: Perpetual Peace
10 Voltaire: Candide
11 Aristotle: Poetics
12 Shakespeare: King Lear
13 The Book of Job
14 Gibbon: The Decline and
   Fall of the Roman Empire*
15 Nietzsche: Twilight of the
   Idols
16 Shaw: Heartbreak House

FOURTH SET

1 Chekhov: The Three Sisters;
   The Cherry Orchard

2 Veblen: The Theory of the
   Leisure Class*
3 Montaigne: Essays*
4 Mill: The Autobiography
   of John Stuart Mill*
5 Henry James: The Pupil;
   The Beast in the Jungle
6 Henry Adams: The Educa-
   tion of Henry Adams*
7 Molière: The Misanthrope;
   Tartuffe
8 Berkeley: The First Dialogue Between Hylas and
   Philonous
9 Diderot: Rameau's Nephew
10 Plato: The Republic*
11 Hume: An Enquiry Con-
   cerning Human Under-
   standing*
12 Calderón: Life Is a Dream
13 Bernard: An Introduction
   to the Study of Experimental Medicine*
14 Vergil: The Aeneid
15 The First Letter to Corinth;
   The Letter to Rome
16 Conrad: Heart of Darkness

FIFTH SET

1 Ibsen: The Wild Duck
2 Epictetus: The Manual
3 Chaucer: The Canterbury
   Tales*
4 Dante: The Inferno
5 Euripides: Medea; Hippolytus
6 Bergson: Time and Free
   Will*
7 Goethe: Faust
8 William James: Psychology:
   Briefer Course*
9 Spinoza: On the Improvement of the Understanding
10 Plato: Symposium
11 Kierkegaard: Works of
   Love*
12 Boccaccio: The Decameron*
13 Kant: Foundations of the
   Metaphysics of Morals*
14 The Book of Genesis
15 Darwin: The Origin of
   Species*
16 Turgenev: Fathers and Sons

SIXTH SET
1 Aeschylus: Prometheus
 Bound
2 Plato: Phaedrus
3 Aristotle: Metaphysics*
4 Longinus: On the Sublime
5 St. Augustine: On Nature
 and Grace; On Grace and
 Free Will
6 Aquinas: Existence & Simplicity of God*
7 Chaucer: Canterbury Tales*
8 Shakespeare: Richard II
9 Cervantes: Don Quixote*
10 Spinoza: Ethics*
11 Hume: Dialogues Concerning
 Natural Religion
12 Voltaire: Philosophical
 Dictionary*
13 Hegel: Philosophy of History*
14 Darwin: The Origin of
 Species*
15 Melville: Billy Budd; Fore-
 topman
16 Henry James: The Turn of
 the Screw

SEVENTH SET
1 Plato: Gorgias
2 Aristotle: On the Soul
3 Bhagavad-Gita
4 Boethius: Consolation of
 Philosophy
5 Maimonides: Guide for the
 Perplexed*
6 Donne: Holy Sonnets
7 Molière: Tartuffe; The
 Misanthrope
8 Leibniz: Discourse on Metaphysics
9 Kant: Fundamental Principles
 of the Metaphysics of
 Morals
10 Goethe: Faust
11 Schopenhauer: The World as
 Will and Idea*
12 Kierkegaard: Concluding Un-
 scientific Postscript*
13 Dostoyevsky: Notes from
 Underground
14 Conrad: Heart of Darkness
15 Freud: The Interpretation of
 Dreams*

16 Shaw: Man and Superman

EIGHTH SET
1 Aristophanes: The Birds;
 Peace
2 Plato: Phaedo
3 Aristotle: Physics*
4 St. Paul: Epistle to the
 Romans; First Epistle
 to the Corinthians
5 Galen: On the Natural
 Faculties*
6 Shakespeare: Henry the
 Fourth, Part One
7 Shakespeare: Henry the
 Fourth, Part Two
8 Harvey: On the Motion of
 the Heart and Blood
9 Descartes: The Passions
 of the Soul
10 Milton: Samson Agonistes
11 Fichte: The Vocation of
 Man
12 Byron: Don Juan*
13 Mill: Utilitarianism
14 Nietzsche: The Genealogy
 of Morals
15 Henry Adams: The Education of Henry Adams*
16 Yeats: Fourteen Poems

NINTH SET
1 Homer: The Iliad
2 Herodotus: The History*
3 Plato: Sophist
4 Aristotle: Posterior Ana-
 lytics*
5 Tacitus: The Annals*
6 Plotinus: The Fifth Ennead
7 Luther: A Commentary on
 St. Paul's Epistle to the
 Galatians*
8 Galileo: Dialogues Con-
 cerning Two New Sciences*
9 Racine: Phaedra
10 Vico: The New Science*
11 Balzac: Père Goriot
12 Marx: Capital*
13 Ibsen: The Wild Duck
14 William James: The Principles of Psychology*
15 Baudelaire: Flowers of Evil*
16 Poincaré: Science and Hy-
 pothesis*

N.Y.P.L.'s Significant Modern Books

Abe, Kobo. Woman in the Dunes

Albee, Edward. American Dream
& The Zoo Story; Who's
Afraid of Virginia Woolf?;
Zoo Story (see Kernan)

Baldwin, James. Another
Country

Baraka, Imamu Amiri. Black
Music; Blues People;
Dutchman, the Slave [plays]

Barth, John. The End of the
Road

Beckett, Samuel. Molloy;
Malone Dies; The Unnamable
[novels]; Waiting for Godot

Bellow, Saul. Mr. Sammler's
Planet; Seize the Day

Berube, H. R. Confrontation
at Ocean-Hill Brownsville

Betti, Ugo. Corruption in the
Palace of Justice (see
Kernan)

Bhagavad-Gita

Bolt, Robert. A Man for All
Seasons

Brecht, Berthold. The Cauca-
sian Chalk Circle; Galileo;
The Good Woman of Set-
zuan; Mother Courage and
Her Children (see Kernan)

Buck, Pearl S. The Good
Earth

Bulgakov, Mikhail. The Master
and Margarita

Bullins, Ed. Goin' a Buffalo
(see Couch)

Burgess, Anthony. A Clockwork
Orange

Camus, Albert. The Fall; The
Myth of Sisyphus; The
Stranger

Celine, L. F. Death on the
Installment Plan

Cleaver, Eldridge. Soul on Ice

Commoner, Barry. Science
and Survival

Confucius. Sayings of Confucius

Couch, William, ed. New
Black Playwrights: Bullins,
Ed, Goin' a Buffalo;

Elder, Lonne, III, Cere-
monies in Dark Old Men;
Kennedy, Adrienne, A
Rat's Mass; Mackey,
William, Family Meeting;
Ward, Douglas Turner,
Happy Ending; Day of Ab-
sence

cummings, e.e. The Enormous
Room

De Bell, Garrett. Environmental Handbook

Della Femina, Jerry. From
Those Wonderful Folks
Who Gave You Pearl
Harbor

Dubos, René. So Human an
Animal

Dürrenmatt, Friedrich. The
Visit

Ehrlich, Paul. Population
Bomb

Elder, Lonne. Ceremonies in
Dark Old Men (see Couch)

Eliot, T. S. The Cocktail
Party

Ellison, Ralph. The Invisible
Man

Fanon, Frantz. Wretched of
the Earth

Faulkner, William. Absalom!
Absalom!; The Sound and
the Fury

Fitzgerald, F. Scott. Tender
Is the Night

Forster, E. M. Passage to
India

Friedan, Betty. Feminine
Mystique

Fuller, R. Buckminster.
Operating Manual for Space-
ship Earth

Gardner, John. Excellence;
Grendel

Genet, Jean. The Balcony

Godden, Rumer. The River

Golding, William. Lord of the
Flies

Gordone, Charles. No Place
to Be Somebody

Grass, Gunter. The Tin Drum

Greene, Graham. The Potting Shed

Greer, Germaine. The Female Eunuch

Grier, W. H. Black Rage

Hoffman, William, ed. New American Plays, vol. II

Hawkes, John. The Lime Twig

Heinlein, Robert. Stranger in a Strange Land

Heller, Joseph. Catch-22

Herbert, Frank. Dune

Herndon, James. The Way It Spozed to Be

Hesse, Herman. Siddhartha; Steppenwolf

Guares, John. The House of Blue Leaves

Huxley, Aldous. Doors of Perception and Heaven and Hell

Ibsen, Henrik. Ghosts (see Kernan); A Doll's House; The Wild Duck; Hedda Gabler

Ionesco, Eugene. Chairs (see Kernan); Rhinoceros

Jacobs, Jane. Death and Life of Great American Cities

Jacobs, Paul. Prelude to Riot

Jones, Le Roi see Baraka, Imamu Amiri

Joyce, James. The Dubliners; Portrait of the Artist as a Young Man

Kafka, Franz. The Penal Colony; The Metamorphosis; The Trial

Kennedy, Adrienne. A Rat's Mass (see Couch)

Kernan, A. B. Classics of the Modern Theatre: Albee, Zoo Story; Brecht, Mother Courage; Betti, Corruption in the Palace of Justice; Ibsen, Ghosts; Ionesco, Chairs; Lorca, Blood Wedding; Pirandello, Six Characters in Search of an Author; Shaw, Arms and the Man; Strindberg, The Father, Ghost Sonata

Kerr, Walter. The Decline of Pleasure

Killens, Oliver. And Then We Heard Thunder

Koestler, Arthur. Darkness at Noon

Kosinski, Jerzy. Steps

LaFarge, Oliver. Laughing Boy

Lao-Tzu. Way of Life: Tao Te Ching

Leary, P. ed. A Controversy of Poets

Lessing, Doris. The Golden Notebook

Lewin, Leonard. Report from Iron Mountain...

Lewis, Sinclair. Babbitt

Lorca, Garcia. Blood Wedding (see Kernan)

Lorenz, Konrad. On Aggression

Lowell, Robert. Life Studies

Luke, Peters. Hadrian the Seventh

McCullers, Carson. Ballad of the Sad Cafe; The Heart Is a Lonely Hunter

McGinniss, Joe. The Selling of the President

Mackey, William. Family Meeting

MacLeish, Archibald. J. B.

McPherson, J. A. Hue and Cry

Malamud, Bernard. The Assistant

Malcolm X. Autobiography

Malraux, André. Man's Fate

Mann, Thomas. Death in Venice & Other Stories

Mao Tse-Tung. Quotations from Chairman Mao

May, Rollo. Love and Will

Mill, John Stuart. On the Subjection of Women

Miller, Arthur. The Crucible

Murdoch, Iris. A Severed Head

Nabokov, Vladimir. Lolita

Nowlis, Helen H. Drugs on the College Campus

O'Connor, Flannery. Everything That Rises Must Converge; Wise Blood; The Violent Bear It Away; A Good

Man Is Hard to Find and Other Stories

O'Neill, Eugene. The Iceman Cometh; Long Day's Journey Into Night; Desire Under the Elms; Strange Interlude; Mourning Becomes Electra

Orwell, George. 1984

Packard, Vince. Hidden Persuaders

Pinter, Harold. The Homecoming; The Dumb Waiter; The Caretaker

Pirandello, Luigi. Six Characters in Search of an Author (see Kernan)

Piven, Frances. Regulating the Poor

Porter, Katherine Anne. The Old Order

Rand, Ayn. Fountainhead

Reich, Charles. The Greening of America

Sanders, Ed. The Family

Sartre, Jean-Paul. No Exit; Flies; Dirty Hands; Respectful Prostitute [plays]; The Age of Reason

Shaw, Bernard. Arms and the Man (see Kernan); Don Juan in Hell; Man and Superman

Singer, Isaac. The Spinoza of Market Street

Snow, C. P. The Search

Sontag, Susan. Against Interpretation

Sopkin, Charles. Seven Glorious Days, Seven Fun-Filled Nights

Spark, Muriel. Ballad of Peckham Rye; The Comforters; Memento Mori

Steinbeck, John. The Grapes of Wrath

Strindberg, August. Father; Ghost Sonata (see Kernan)

Theobald, Robert. Guaranteed Income

Toffler, Alvin. Future Shock

Von Hoffman, N. We Are the People Our Parents Warned Us Against

Vonnegut, Kurt, Jr. Cat's Cradle

Wakefield, Dan. Addict

Ward, Douglas Turner. Happy Ending; Day of Absence

Warren, Robert Penn. All the King's Men

Watts, Alan. Spirit of Zen

Weiss, Peter. Marat/Sade

West, Nathaniel. Day of the Locust; Miss Lonelyhearts

Williams, John. The Man Who Cried I Am

Williams, Tennessee. A Streetcar Named Desire

Wolfe, Tom. The Kandy-Kolored Tangerine-Flake Streamline Baby

Woolf, Virginia. A Room of One's Own

Wright, Richard. Native Son

Wright, Richard B. Weekend Man

B. SOME FILMS FOR DISCUSSION

Appalachia: Rich Land, Poor People   59m   Indiana University   1969

Study of Appalachian poverty.   Interviews with local family, mine owners, and others.

Banks and the Poor   58m   Indiana University   1970

Probes banking industry and its exploitation of the poor. Variety of viewpoints.

Before the Mountain Was Moved   59m   Contemporary/McGraw-Hill 1968

Efforts of West Virginia residents to have law passed controlling strip mining.

The Black Cop   15m   Indiana University   1969

Explores attitudes of Blacks toward policemen, and attitudes of Black policemen.

Bulldozed America   25m   Carousel   1965

Plea for conservation of America before it is despoiled by mining, lumber and real estate interests.

Constitution and Censorship   28m   Center for Mass Communication 1957

First Amendment issues.   Involves cases of censorship of the film, The Miracle, and restraint of activities of Jehovah's Witness minister.

Cosmopolis/Big City 2000 A.D.   52m   ABC News   1970

Surveys problems of overcrowding and urban sprawl, and some solutions being suggested.   Focuses on Tokyo, Los Angeles, London and planned cities such as Reston, Va. and Columbia, Md.

Crime of Our Courts   50m   Westinghouse Learning Corporation 1972

Report on the problems including plea bargaining and multiple case loads.

Eye of the Storm   25m   ABC News   1970

3rd grade teacher tries to help children understand prejudice.   There were strong community reactions to this teacher's methods.

The Hand   19m   Contemporary/McGraw-Hill   1965

> Animated allegory of totalitarianism.

I Am Somebody   28m   Contemporary/McGraw-Hill   1970

> Record of strike of hospital employees in South Carolina. Most of strikers were black women.

Interviews with Mylai Veterans   22m   New Yorker Films   1971

> Five who participated in the massacre tell what they did, how they felt about it, and how they feel about it now.

It Happens to Us   30m   New Day Films   1972

> Women speak about abortion experiences.   Medical and moral problems.

Mrofnoc   6m   Radim   1965

> Problem of resistance or conformity.

Nell and Fred   28m   Contemporary/McGraw-Hill   1972

> Nell, over 80 and Fred, over 90 must choose between caring for themselves or moving into old people's home.

Of Broccoli & Pelicans & Celery & Seals   29m   Indiana University 1969

> Report on the harmful effects of pesticides.

Red Squad   45m   Pacific Street Film Corporation   1972

> A special N.Y.C. police unit charged with photographing, filming and taping all political demonstrations in N.Y.C. Filmmakers were harrassed and intimidated by police.

This Child Is Rated X   53m   NBC Educational Enterprises   1971

> Treatment of child criminals.

Tokyo: 51st Volcano   52m   Time/Life Films   1972

> Problems of pollution, over-population and consumerism.

Toys   7m   Contemporary/McGraw-Hill   1967

> Children's toys come alive and fight a war.   Intercut with faces of children.

Women Who Have Had Abortions   29m   New Day Films   1972

> American women of all classes discuss their abortion experiences.

C. SAMPLE FILM PROGRAMS (Adults, Teenagers, Children)

ADULTS

AFRICA SPEAKS

Ancient Africans   color   27 minutes
        Review of African history combining animated historical
sequences with location photography of the ruins of Kush and
Axum, life today in the ancient Sudanic kingdoms and Benin,
and the stone walls of Zimbabwe. 1970. International Film
Foundation.

African Girl--Malobi   color   11 minutes
        Presents the experiences of Malobi, a ten-year-old girl
of the Ibo tribe in Nigeria. 1960. Atlantis.

African Craftsman: The Ashanti   color   11 minutes
        Shows the skillful woodcarving of their ceremonial
wooden stools. 1970. BFA

Suite of Berber Dances   10 minutes
        Three folk dances performed among the isolated North
African Berber tribes. 1950. Radim.

FILMS ABOUT GROWING OLDER

Nell and Fred   28 minutes
        Nell, over eighty, and Fred in his nineties, must choose
between doing for themselves as best they can, or moving into
an old people's home. 1972. Contemporary/McGraw-Hill.

Woo Who? Mary Wilson   color   33 minutes
        Portrait of an artist and senior citizen who comes to
New York and tries to make a new life centered on her old
hobby, painting. 1970. Amalie R. Rothschild.

Bubby   5 minutes
        A teenage filmmaker's view of his grandmother. 1968?
Youth Film Distribution Center.

253

TRAVEL--WISH YOU WERE HERE

<u>Pompeii</u>   color   10 minutes
      Tours the ruins of Pompeii and describes life in the Roman Empire. 1965. Out of Print.

<u>Versailles</u>   color   19 minutes
      Aerial cinematography from a helicopter provides a "bird's-eye" view of the splendors of the gardens and architecture of the palace of Versailles. 1968. Kinetic.

<u>Venice: Etude No. 1</u>   color   9 minutes
      Through multiple exposures, experimental filmmaker Ian Hugo has given a highly personal view of the Italian city. 1962. Radim.

<u>Norwegian Folk Dances</u>   color   12 minutes
      Performed in traditional costumes in the remote upper valleys of Norway. 1962. Dance Films.

FANTASMAGORIA

<u>Entr'Acte</u>   silent   13 minutes
      A humorous Dadaist fantasy directed by René Clair. 1924. Radim.

<u>Super Artist</u>   color   22 minutes
      Impressionistic satire of Andy Warhol, his personality, technique of movie making, and on the pop art scene. 1966-7. Bruce Torbet Films.

<u>Un Chien Andalou</u>   16 minutes
      Classic surrealistic shocker by Luis Buñuel and Salvador Dalí containing dreamlike images relating to sexuality and sexual repression. 1928. Pyramid.

<u>Help! My Snowman Is Burning Down</u>   color   10 minutes
      Surrealistic fantasy by Carson Davidson. 1964. Contemporary/McGraw-Hill.

WOMEN

<u>Diane</u>   color   30 minutes
      "Semi-documentary" featuring a young would-be actress from South Dakota who tries to find success in New York and battles loneliness, frustration, exploitation and despair. 1969. Mary Feldhaus-Weber.

<u>Domestic Tranquility</u>   7 minutes
      A young woman, bound by her children and a demanding husband, reflects on what life might have been like, had she

the opportunity to develop her individual talents. 1973. Women Make Movies.

Nobody's Victim   color   20 minutes
     A film on self-defense for women which outlines life-saving precautions and demonstrates simple defense methods that anyone can use to fend off attackers. 1972. Ramsgate Films.

NATURE STUDIES

Birth of the Red Kangaroo   color   21 minutes
     Fascinating description of the reproductive process and birth of this Australian marsupial. 1968. International Film Bureau.

Way of a Trout   color   25 minutes
     Exceptional underwater and nature photography depicts the life cycle of a trout. 1970. James Wilkie.

White Throat   color   10 minutes
     The nature of the forest is explored in this journey in the wake of the whitethroated sparrow. 1965. AV Explorations.

POTPOURRI

Solo   color   15 minutes
     Photographed on twenty-two different climbs, located across the North American continent, climber Mike Hoover captures the beauty, danger, and challenge of this very special sport. 1971. Pyramid.

Frank Film   color   9 minutes
     Superbly animated autobiography of the filmmaker, Frank Mouris. An Oscar winner. 1973. Pyramid.

Popcorn Lady   color   11 minutes
     A gentle lady's popcorn business started at the turn of the century is threatened by modern business enterprises. 1973. Warren Schloat.

It Ain't City Music   color   14 minutes
     A light-hearted celebration of grassroots America and its music. 1973. Tom Davenport Films.

Invasion of the Teacher Creatures   6 minutes
     Designed as a humorous "trailer," young filmmaker, Henry Parke, gives us glimpses of ghoulish teachers rampaging through a school 1974. Youth Film Distribution Center.

ADULT--TEENAGE

THE FAR NORTH

Eskimo Artist Kenojuak   color   20 minutes
        A semi-impressionistic study of Eskimo wife and mother, Kenojuak, her ice bound country, and the art she creates to celebrate it. National Film Board of Canada. 1964. Contemporary/McGraw-Hill.

Land of the Long Day   38 minutes
        The life of an Eskimo family living near Baffin Bay. National Film Board of Canada. 1952. International Film Bureau.

THE DANCE AND THE DANCER

Behind the Scenes with the Royal Ballet   30 minutes
        Margot Fonteyn, Rudolf Nureyev and Christopher Gable rehearse Romeo and Juliet. 1965. Warner Bros. /Seven Arts.

Capriccio   color   6 minutes
        A special effects film made with TV equipment, producing multiple exposures of two modern dancers. 1969. James Seawright.

Nine Variations on a Dance Theme   13 minutes
        Brilliantly imaginative photographic exploration of the movements of modern dancer Bettie de Jung. 1966. Radim.

THE RACES

Wild Water   color   20 minutes
        Stunning photography records the excitement and beauty of competitive canoe and kayak racing. Schloat Productions.

Spider and the Frenchman   color   22 minutes
        Downhill ski racing competition in various locales around the U.S. 1974. Film Forum.

Lizzies of the Field   silent   12 minutes
        A Mack Sennett comedy ending with a free-for-all road race. 1924. Blackhawk.

MOVIE CLASSICS

Leave 'Em Laughing   silent   20 minutes
        A Laurel and Hardy classic, in which Laurel develops a toothache that results in a wild bout with the dentist and laughing gas. 1927. Blackhawk.

Musketeers of Pig Alley   silent   13 minutes
          Lillian Gish plays her first feature role in this story of
the slums and rival gangs. 1912. Blackhawk.

Cops   silent   15 minutes
          Buster Keaton tangles with the police department, and
the resulting riot is the grandest chase scene ever filmed.
1922. Blackhawk.

Rudolph Valentino--Idol of the Jazz Age   10 minutes
          The life of this famous star with scenes from his most
famous films. Creative Film Society.

SILENT HORRORS--Drop in and Shiver [Both by Blackhawk]

Dr. Jekyll and Mr. Hyde   silent   45 minutes
          John Barrymore plays the split personality in this first
great American horror film, made in 1920.

The Phantom of the Opera   silent   25 minutes
          "Great Moments" from this famous film, starring Lon
Chaney as the phantom who unleashes a reign of terror.

SHADES OF THE BLUES

Roberta Flack   color   29 minutes
          The popular singer-pianist rehearsing, performing, re-
laxing. 1971. Indiana University.

Black Music in America   color   38 minutes
          Sachmo, Leadbelly, Count Basie, Nina Simone, Billy
Holiday, and a scene from an early film by Bessie Smith.
1970. Learning Corp.

TEENAGERS

SPORTS--BASKETBALL

Fabulous Harlem Globetrotters   9 minutes
          A humorous and fast-paced demonstration of the dexterity
of this famous basketball team. Blackhawk.

Sports Action Profiles: John Roche   color   22 minutes
          Action-cameras reveal the skills of this young basket-
ball player as he heads his team the New York Nets to victory
over the Utah Stars. Oxford.

Willis Reed: Center Play (Pts. I & II)   color   10 minutes
          Willis Reed demonstrates some of the basketball tech-
niques that have made him famous. Schloat Productions.

THE (YOUNG) WOMEN'S MOVEMENT

A to B   color   35 minutes
A young girl's conflicts with strict, conservative, middle-class parents. By Nell Cox. 1970. Time/Life Films.

Lucy   color   13 minutes
An unwed, pregnant teenager tells her story. 1970? Pictura.

Operator   color   15 minutes
A lively, humorous look at the modern telephone operator. 1969. AT&T.

To Hear a Whistle   8 minutes
A teenage girl tries to fight off make-up and Mom. 1972. Youth Film Distribution Center.

TREK THROUGH THE STARS

La Jetée   27 minutes
A gripping science-fiction fantasy. 1963. Pyramid.

The Intruder   color   6 minutes
A clay monster disrupts the peaceful life of a planet and gobbles up everything in sight. Animated by Scott Morris. 1970. Youth Film Dist. Cnt.

K-9000: A Space Oddity   color   11 minutes
A dog transported through space in a spoof on 2001: A Space Odyssey. 1971? Creative Film Society.

PRE-SCHOOL CHILDREN
(three 4-film programs)

The Smallest Elephant in the World   color   6 minutes
The adventures of an elephant the size of a house cat and his attempt to find a home. Based on the book by Alvin Tresselt. 1964. Sterling.

Gilberto and the Wind   color   6 minutes
Harry Belafonte reads from Marie Hall Ets' book in a warm and pleasant manner with pictures from the story interwoven into the visuals. 1967. McGraw-Hill.

I Know an Old Lady Who Swallowed a Fly   color   6 minutes
Burl Ives sings this animated version of the popular folk song. 1964. International Film Bureau.

Curious George Rides a Bike   color   10 minutes
Led by his curiosity, a small monkey gets into trouble but emerges triumphant. 1958. Weston Woods.

Patrick   color   7 minutes
        A man buys an old violin and discovers that his music
transforms everything it reaches; fish fly through the air, become multicolored; cows dance, their black spots become colored stars.   1973.   Weston Woods.

Dick Whittington and His Cat   color   15 minutes
        An animated puppet film about Dick Whittington and the
fortune that he receives as a result of his kindness to a cat.
1965.   Sterling.

Fiddle-de-dee   color   4 minutes
        Gay color combinations form an abstract design to the
Mocking Bird.   1947.   International Film Bureau.

Ashlad and His Good Helpers   color   15 minutes
        Puppet animation of Norwegian folk tale.   No date.
Modern Learning Aids.

Madeline   color   8 minutes
        The popular picture book by Ludwig Bemelmans about
Madeline and her appendectomy is animated for the screen.
1955.   Columbia.

Cirkus, The Merry Circus   color   10 minutes
        An interpretation of circus acts animated by Jiri Trnka.
1951.   Contemporary/McGraw-Hill.

Hen-Hop   color   4 minutes
        Animated film by Norman McLaren in which a hen and
an egg dance to barn-dance music.   1943.   International Film
Bureau.

Morning Zoo   color   10 minutes
        A young woman zoo keeper talks about her work and
shows us the animals she looks after.   1972.   Trend Films.

SCHOOL-AGE CHILDREN

HALLOWEEN FILMS

Dragon Stew   color   14 minutes
        A con man cook whose speciality is dragon stew is put
on the spot when a dragon is captured.   A delightful cartoon
for middle to older children.   Bailey Film Assoc. (BFA).

The Seventh Master of the House   color   13 minutes
        Puppet animation of Norwegian folk tale in which a lone
traveler deep in a forest asks for shelter from a strange family
of men who live there.   U.S. release 1969.   Modern Learning
Aids.

<u>Dr. Jekyll and Mr. Hyde</u>   silent   10 minutes
    This early silent version of the classic tale was made in 1911.   Blackhawk.

FEATURE STORY

<u>Blind Bird</u>   color   45 minutes
    A young Russian boy takes his blind pelican to an eye specialist in Moscow who restores the bird's sight.   1963. Contemporary/McGraw-Hill.

WINTER-CHRISTMAS STORIES

<u>Snow</u> (British Railways)   color   10 minutes
    Rhythmic film-poem of train moving through snow-covered countryside.   1969.   ACI.

<u>Snow White and Rose Red</u>   10 minutes
    One of Lotte Reiniger's charming silhouette films based on the Grimm fairy tale.   No date.   Contemporary/McGraw-Hill.

<u>Ti-Jean Goes Lumbering</u>   color   16 minutes
    A little boy mysteriously appears on a white horse at a lumber camp, performs remarkable feats and then rides away.   1953.   International Film Bureau.

CHILDREN AND CITIES

<u>Tadpole Tale</u>   color   16 minutes
    A warm tale about a boy who catches a tadpole in a pond in New York's Central Park but finds he must let it go when it becomes full-grown.   1967?   Universal Education.

<u>My Own Yard to Play In</u>   7 minutes
    An unusual and moving document of children playing, singing and talking among the tenements and cluttered vacant lots of New York City.   1959.   Contemporary/McGraw-Hill.

<u>The Red Balloon</u>   color   34 minutes
    The moving and beautifully photographed story of a young boy in Paris who makes friends with a magic red balloon.   1956.   Audio/Brandon.

AFRICAN FOLK TALES

<u>Anansi the Spider</u>   color   10 minutes
    An African folk tale from the Ashanti tribe about the origin of the moon.   1969.   Texture.

<u>Why the Sun and the Moon Live in the Sky</u>   color   11 minutes
    This Nigerian legend relates how the Sun and the Moon,

who used to live on land, were forced to move into the sky.
1970. ACI.

The Magic Tree   color   10 minutes
        Animated version of a tale from the Congo about an
unloved son who runs away and finds a magic tree whose
leaves become people. 1970. Texture.

AT THE CIRCUS

Circus Town   color   48 minutes
        Follows non-professional youngsters through training to
the final performance in a circus in Peru, Indiana. NBC.

NATURE AND MYTHOLOGY OF THE NORTH AMERICAN INDIAN

The Loon's Necklace   color   11 minutes
        The Indian legend of how the loon, a water bird, ob-
tained his neckband of white feathers. 1948. EBEC.

Navajo Rain Chant   color   2 minutes
        Animation based on the designs of Navajo blankets which
shows how these patterns were inspired by natural phenomena.
1971. Creative Film Society.

Paddle to the Sea   color   28 minutes
        The adventures of a little wooden Indian in a canoe,
carved by a young boy in Northern Canada. 1966. National
Film Board of Canada.

COMEDY AND SLAPSTICK

Apple Thieves   color   9 minutes
        A very sophisticated but funny cops and robbers spoof
acted out by inanimate objects, animated. Brandon.

One A.M.   14 minutes
        A Charlie Chaplin classic. 1916. Blackhawk.

The Ride   color   8 minutes
        A chauffeur's dream about putting his employer on a
runaway toboggan comes true in part when he allows the car
brakes to slip. A slapstick comedy. 1963. Contemporary/
McGraw-Hill.

When Knights Were Bold   color   20 minutes
        The Magnificent 6-1/2 in a slapstick adventure full of
screaming women and pies in the face. 1972. Sterling.

STORIES TO START A VACATION

Three Pirates Bold   color   15 minutes
        Two boys and a dog embark upon a somewhat hopeful

search for treasure in the West Indies.   No date.   Out of Print.

<u>Kumak--The Sleepy Hunter</u>   color   13 minutes
    A humorous Eskimo folktale enacted by puppets.   1953. Radim.

<u>Captain Stormalong</u>   color   13 minutes
    An iconographic treatment of the tall tale hero from American folklore.   1972.   BFA

D.   FILM SOURCES

Below are some of the major sources of free-loan films, filmstrips, slides and recordings.   One should also try some of the more general and more local sources that are mentioned in Chapter 2, "Film Showings."   The three following companies are the major distributors:

Association-Sterling Films
866 Third Avenue
New York, N.Y. 10022

Their free catalog lists 16mm films, filmstrips, slides and recordings (there is also a section of rental films).   Gives running times, color, a descriptive paragraph and terms of borrowing.   Subject and title indexes.   Subjects of films include Americana, conservation, science, sports, travel, and women's interests.   Of interest to all ages.   There are regional offices in various parts of the country.

Modern Talking Picture Service
2323 Hyde Park Road
New Hyde Park, N.Y. 11040

The free catalogs list running times, color, give brief annotations and terms of borrowing.   There are catalogs for adults and for schools covering many subjects.   There are regional offices in many cities in the United States and some in Canada. These are 16mm sound films.

West Glen Films (A division of West Glen Communications, Inc.)
565 5th Avenue
New York, N.Y. 10017

The free catalogs for high schools and for adult organizations list running times and color, give annotations and terms of borrowing.   Includes sports, travel and films dealing with contemporary problems.   Lists are shorter than the first two companies but many good films are available.   They also have an automatic booking service of interest to anyone having regular showings.

The following two books are guides to the sources of free films:

Educator's Guide to Free Films $12.75
Educators Progress Servicing
Randolph, Wisc. 53956

> This is a very useful guide for anyone running regular film
> programs, and not having access to a large film library.
> The emphasis is on school age but some films would interest
> adults.   The entries indicate whether the film is 8 or 16mm,
> sound or silent, title, running time, date of release, terms
> and conditions of loan, booking time required, probable availa-
> bility, and names and addresses of sources.   There are
> indexes by title, subject, source and availability.   Almost
> 5,000 titles are included in the 1974 edition.   Publication is
> annual.   Films are from government agencies at all levels,
> industry and many other sources.   Subjects include arts and
> crafts, consumer education, environmental education, history,
> science, music and religion.

United States Government Films; A Catalogue of Motion Pictures
and Film Strips for Sale by the National Audiovisual Center, 1969;
supplement 1971.
National Audiovisual Center
Washington, D.C. 20409

> When one finds a title of interest listed in this book, it may be
> borrowed--in many cases--free, directly from the agency that
> owns it.

FILM DISTRIBUTORS

There are a vast number of film distributors.   The following
are those that we feel would be the most useful to libraries.

ACI Films
35 West 45 Street
New York, N.Y.   10036

> A variety of films, including a good series of art media
> films.

Benchmark Films
145 Scarborough Rd.
Briarcliff Manor, N.Y.   10510

> A small collection containing films of high quality on social
> issues.

Carousel Films
1501 Broadway
New York, N.Y.   10036

Films on social issues, including many CBS news documentaries.

Churchill Films
662 North Robertson Blvd.
Los Angeles, Calif. 90069

Specializes in films for the classroom.

Contemporary Films /McGraw-Hill
1221 Ave. of the Americas
New Yor, N.Y. 10020

The largest collection of films in the country that are appropriate for public libraries. Includes all kinds of subjects; strong on cultural subjects (the arts, archaeology, etc.); strong on children's films. Contains many National Film Board of Canada films.

Film Images
17 West 60th Street
New York, N.Y. 10023

Strong on films relating to French art and culture.

Films, Inc.
1144 Wilmette Avenue
Wilmette, Ill. 60091

An excellent large collection of documentaries on a wide range of subjects. Also, a large collection of American feature films for rental.

Grove Press
53 East 11 Street
New York, N.Y. 10003

A large collection of avant-garde films.

International Film Foundation
475 Fifth Ave., Rm. 916
New York, N.Y. 10017

Specializes in films on countries around the world; particularly strong on Africa.

Learning Corp. of America
711 Fifth Ave.
New York, N.Y. 10022

A large collection specializing in films for the classroom.

Macmillan Films
34 MacQuesten Pkwy. So.
Mt. Vernon, N.Y. 10550

A vast collection of features especially foreign films, including the Russian classics. Distributor for Brandon films.

National Film Board of Canada
1251 Avenue of the Americas
16th Floor
New York, N.Y. 10020

Most of their films are now distributed by a variety of U.S. companies such as Contemporary Films/McGraw-Hill.

New Yorker Films
43 West 61st Street
New York, N.Y. 10023

The unusual and socially committed feature film. Many films on the Third World.

Oxford Films
1136 N. Las Palmas Ave.
Los Angeles, Calif. 90338

Sure-thing, good quality sports films, among others.

Phoenix Films
470 Park Ave. So.
New York, N.Y. 10016

Issue-oriented films (rape, aging, etc.) of high quality.

Pyramid Films
P.O. Box 1048
Santa Monica, Calif. 90406

A large collection of well-made, "sure-fire" films.

Texture Films
1600 Broadway
New York, N.Y. 10019

A high quality collection of films on cultural subjects and on sex education.

Time-Life Films
Time & Life Bldg.
Rockefeller Center
New York, N.Y. 10020

An important collection, containing documentaries on all

kinds of topics (social, political, cultural, etc.) and BBC TV film documentaries.

Weston Woods Studios
Weston, Conn. 06880

The largest collection of children's films.

Youth Film Distribution Center
43 West 16 Street
New York, N.Y. 10011

The largest collection of films made by teenagers and children.

E. SAMPLE FLYERS AND POSTERS

The following pages show various sample promotional materials developed by Prince George's County Memorial Library System, the New York Public Library, and others.

JUDO
demonstration

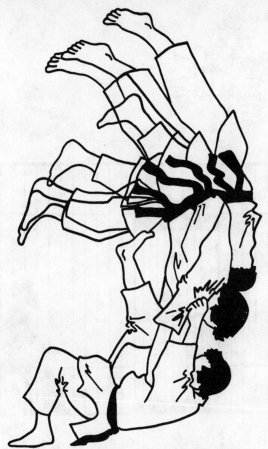

Laurel Branch Library
Wednesday, Oct. 17
7:30 p.m. Meeting Room

PRINCE GEORGE'S COUNTY
MEMORIAL LIBRARY SYSTEM
Laurel Branch Library
Young Adult Department
507 7th Street
Laurel, Maryland 20810
Phone   776 - 6790

The Night Thoreau Spent In Jail

This flyer/program (contents on facing page) was for a presentation of this play in a library. The cover was designed and drawn by a staff member with no artistic training.

THE FARRELL PLAYERS PRESENT

The Night Thoreau Spent In Jail

by

Jerome Lawrence and Robert E. Lee

Cast of Characters

THOREAU	CHARLES CATANESE
EMERSON	CHARLES SULLIVAN
JOHN THOREAU	KEVIN CALLAGHAN
BAILEY	AIDAN ROONEY
LYDIAN	ELLEN ROBERT (St. Joseph by the Sea)
ELLEN	NOREEN MOSS (St. Joseph Hill Academy)
SAM	BILL ENDROM
EDWARD	CHARLES LOFFREDO
DEACON BALL	AL MITCHELL
MOTHER	VAL SANGUEDOLCE (St. Joseph Hill Academy)

TOWNSPEOPLE:
Dan Peterson, John La Femina,
Dennis O'Brien, Mike Portantiere,
Marty Orlano, Richard Grasso, Mark Bennaci
Thomas Sorrentino, Tony Mazza, Donna Hartel
Liz Endrom.

DIRECTED BY	JOSEPH GERAGHTY
DESIGN	PAUL DIETY
COSTUMES	EAVES
LIGHTING	HENRY WOHLTJEN
THE MODERATOR	FATHER CARROLL

"Any man more right than his neighbors
constitutes a majority of one."

"It takes two to speak the truth— one to
speak, and another to hear."

"That man is the richest whose pleasures
are the cheapest."

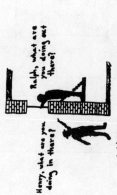

Ralph, what are
you doing out
there?

Henry, what are you
doing in there?

Ralph W. Emerson visits Henry Thoreau

Tuesday November 27, 1973 at 7 P.M.

The New York Public Library
SAINT GEORGE BRANCH
10 Hyatt St.
S.I., N.Y., 10301   442-8560

"The frontiers are not east or west,
north or south, but wherever a man fronts
a fact."

Admission Free

A YOUNG ADULT PRESENTATION

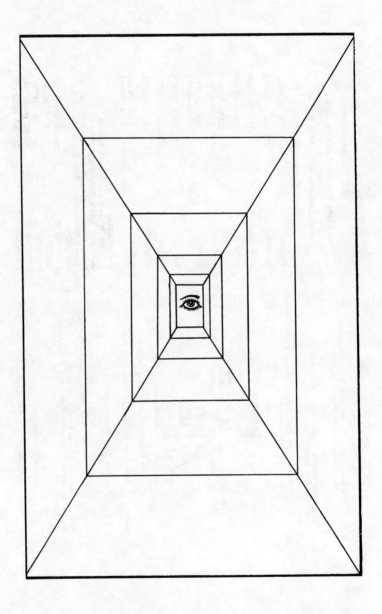

Inside contents of this flyer/program, which was drawn, hand-lettered and typed by a staff member, are shown on facing page.

A Poetry Jam Session

MONDAY
MAY 15 7:30 PM

Admission Free

Admission Free

Admission Free

Joel Scherzer

The New York Public Library

The Chinese Playhouse

Port Richmond Library

75 Bennett St.

442-0158

has been writing news professionally for the last four years. At the moment, he is the man behind the never ending news report which circles the Allied Chemical Building on Times Square. Poetry and short stories are his forte. His topics are drawn from his vast knowledge of trivia and his surrealistic view of life. While attending Lehman College, Scherzer and Kovler jointly authored the "Eatery", a screenplay of visual madness. Their friendship dates back to Alexander's Warehouse in the Bronx. Mr. Scherzer has one of the most complete Rhythm and Blues record collections in the Northeast and plans to incorporate a few "Oldies" into the program.

Allen Kovler

Immigrated to Staten Island in his 1948 Cadillac which you may have spotted by the Gypsum Factory. He is currently a reporter on the Staten Island Advance, and spends his free time working out on his guitar. His poetry and prose reflect the absurd. His mind focuses on unnoticed details. He is an authority on the art of turning parsnols, and chili. Mr. Kovler intends to read a poem of special interest to Islanders: "Rider, Written While Riding the Mary Murray". She was built in 1936".

Dennis Piana

(alias Detroit Denny) lives on a farm in Mehoopany, Pennsylvania. He's a traveller who has spent time living in Africa, Spain, Greece, and New York City. His poetry has appeared in *Telephone*, a periodical published by the St.Mark's-in-the-Bowery Poetry Project. He is currently preparing a book of poems about country life and working on a novel with a friend. Last winter he wrote for *Changes*, an underground rock paper, but has given it up to work on his organic garden.

T H E N E W Y O R K P U B L I C L I B R A R Y

Teenage Crafts Workshops

at the

ST. GEORGE LIBRARY CENTER

10 Hyatt Street

Staten Island, New York 10403

SELECT FROM:

_____ JEWELRY MAKING

_____ MACRAME

_____ PUPPET MAKING

_____ CERAMIC TILING

_____ NEEDLE WORK

_____ CANDLE MAKING

ADMISSION FREE. SIGN UP ON REVERSE SIDE OF PAGE.

I would like to participate in a workshop on

☐ JEWELRY MAKING   ☐ MACRAME   ☐ PUPPET MAKING

☐ CERAMIC TILING   ☐ NEEDLE WORK   ☐ CANDLE MAKING

(Indicate your first, second, third choices).

NAME: _____

ADDRESS: _____

PHONE: _____

SCHOOL: _____ GRADE: _____

I am available on _____ from _____ to _____ .
                (Day of week)   (time)

Please return this form at front desk. We will contact you.

THE SILENT SCREEN

-

DOUG FAIRBANKS
WM. S. HART
HAL ROACH
PEARL WHITE
MACK SENNETT
D. W. GRIFFITH

THE NEW YORK
PUBLIC LIBRARY
PORT RICHMOND BRANCH
75 BENNETT ST.
442-0158

AUGUST 12, 19, 26   7:30 P.M.

ADMISSION FREE

PROTECT YOURSELF

SELF-DEFENSE
FOR WOMEN

An informal talk and demonstration
by Susan Lenaerts
Representative of the D. C. Rape Crisis Center

Tuesday   7:30 P.M.

March 5, 1974

Meeting Room

PRINCE GEORGE'S COUNTY MEMORIAL LIBRARY SYSTEM
New Carrollton Branch Library, Young Adult Department
7414 Riverdale Road
New Carrollton, Maryland 20784
Phone 459 - 6900

ASTROLOGY: WHAT'S IT ALL ABOUT?

Guest Speaker:
Ms. Deborah Diroll,
Practicing Astrologer
and Teacher of Astrology

TUESDAY, NOVEMBER 27
7:30 P.M.

HYATTSVILLE BRANCH LIBRARY

HOT NUMBER

YOU'RE ALL WOMAN

DIZZY BLOND

OLD MAID

WOMEN DRIVERS!

NAG

HYSTERICAL FEMALE

GIRLIE

MY OLE LADY

BABE

JUST A HOUSEWIFE

FEMME FATALE

THAT'S WOMEN'S WORK

DUMB BROAD

CHICK

THE WOMEN'S MOVEMENT: A PANEL DISCUSSION

TUESDAY JANUARY 9, 1973
7:30 P.M.

NEW CARROLLTON BRANCH LIBRARY MEETING ROOM

PRINCE GEORGE'S COUNTY MEMORIAL LIBRARY SYSTEM
Young Adult Department
New Carrollton Branch Library
7414 Riverdale Road
New Carrollton, Maryland 20784
Phone 459 - 6900

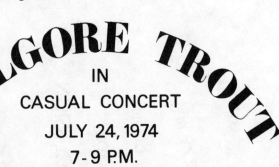

KILLGORE TROUT

IN
CASUAL CONCERT
JULY 24, 1974
7-9 P.M.

Avondale Mill Recreation Center
26 Avondale Avenue
Laurel, Maryland
(off Main Street in Laurel)

BRING A BLANKET TO SIT ON AND A FRIEND!

Co-sponsored by:

City of Laurel Department of Parks and Recreation
Avondale Mill Recreation Center
26 Avondale Avenue
Laurel, Maryland 20810

and

PRINCE GEORGE'S COUNTY MEMORIAL LIBRARY SYSTEM
Laurel Branch Library, Young Adult Department
507 7th Street
Laurel, Maryland 20810
Phone 776 - 6790

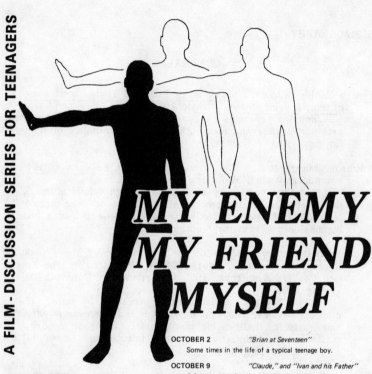

A FILM-DISCUSSION SERIES FOR TEENAGERS

MY ENEMY MY FRIEND MYSELF

OCTOBER 2   *"Brian at Seventeen"*
Some times in the life of a typical teenage boy.

OCTOBER 9   *"Claude," and "Ivan and his Father"*
A funny and serious look at the generation gap.

OCTOBER 16   *"Changing"*
A young family changes its lifestyle.

OCTOBER 23   *"Bunny," "Tom," "Guy," and "Teddy"*
The youth culture from four different viewpoints.

OCTOBER 30   *"Nobody Waved Goodbye"*
At odds with his family, Peter strikes out on his own.

TUESDAYS

7:30 P.M.

MEETING ROOM

PRINCE GEORGE'S COUNTY MEMORIAL LIBRARY SYSTEM
New Carrollton Branch Library, Young Adult Services
7414 Riverdale Road
New Carrollton, Maryland 20784
Phone 459 - 6900

BIBLIOGRAPHY

GENERAL

Boston Public Library. Idea Source Book for Young Adult Programs; a preliminary edition, 1973, 61p., $2
Includes programs on sports, theatre, women in America,
arts and crafts, and many other ideas. Examples of flyers
for publicity.

Edwards, Margaret A. The Fair Garden and the Swarm of Beasts,
rev and expanded, Hawthorn Books, 1974, 182p.
Excellent section on book talks to high school students -
the objectives of giving book talks, how to prepare them and
techniques of delivery. Also section on how to lead a book
discussion program for teenagers.

Foundation Directory, The. Edition 5, Compiled by The Foundation
Center, Marianna O. Lewis, Editor, Published by The Foundation Center, New York, 1975, Distributed by Columbia University Press
Lists thousands of foundations, arranged by state. Includes purposes, financial data, high and low grants, officers
and trustees. Indices include: fields of interest; donors,
trustees and administrators; list of foundations. Essential for
successful grant-getting.

Golden, Hal and Kitty Hanson. Techniques of Working with the
Working Press, Oceana, 1962, 232p.
Contains a full chapter on press releases, as well as
chapters on working with various departments of a newspaper.

Greene, Ellin and Madalynne Schoenfeld, comp. & ed. A Multimedia Approach to Children's Literature; A Selective List of
Films, Filmstrips, and Recordings Based on Children's Books.
A.L.A., 1972, 262p.
In addition to the annotated lists, includes sources of
other materials for programmers, and a list of articles,
books and films of help to those doing programming. Techniques are presented and programs described.

Mayer, Robert A. "Grantsmanship," Library Journal, July 1972,
pp. 2348-50.
Preparing and applying for a grant.

Moore, Vardine. Pre-School Story Hour, 2d. ed., Scarecrow Press, 1972, 174p.
Ideas for story tellers, many ideas on planning programs and related activities. Includes lists of books and recordings.

Pierini, Mary Paul Francis. Creative Dramatics; A Guide for Educators, Herder and Herder, 1971, 166p.
Contains many suggestions and ideas on all aspects of the subject.

Sigler, Ronald F. "A Study in Censorship; The Los Angeles 19," Film Library Quarterly, Spring 1971.
A detailed description of what happened when the censor came to a film program, and how the library handled the situation.

Stroner, Sandra. "Media Programming for Children," "Library Journal, Nov. 15, 1971, pp. 3811-13.
Interesting and imaginative ideas for multimedia programming.

Top of the News, April 1968.
Articles and news items about music, theatre and other activities for teenagers in libraries.

Top of the News, April 1970.
Several articles describing a great variety of activities in libraries around the country.

Vanko, Lillina. "A Metropolitan Library Reaches Out," Illinois Libraries, Sept. 1971, pp. 462-6.
Describes the outreach programs of the Chicago Public Library.

Wilson Library Bulletin, April 1971, pp. 758-62.
Describes many kinds of library programs.

FILMS

Betancourt, Jeanne. Women in Focus, Pflaum, 1974, 186p.
A list of films by a teacher of film, annotated from the feminist point of view. Includes new films by feminists, short documentaries, and choice masterpieces about women by men filmmakers. Recommended for use with teenagers and adults.

Film Library Quarterly, Film Library Information Council, Box 348, Radio City Station, New York, N.Y. 10019, $10.00 per year.
Contains articles, news and reviews of interest to programmers. The Fall, 1972 issue contains a list of 500 core films for a medium-size library, and an article on evaluating films.

The last issue of 1974 is double (vol. 7, nos. 3 & 4) and
the entire issue is devoted to programming. There are
articles on feature films, independent films, children's films
and videotape. Included are sources of information, sample
programs and programming tips. (The bibliography of information sources alone is worth the price.)

Films: A Catalog of the Film Collection of The New York Public
Library. May be purchased by mail prepaid from the Office
of Branch Libraries, 8 East 40th Street, N.Y., N.Y. 10016,
1972, 166p., $3, Supplement, 1976, $2.
An annotated list of hundreds of films for adults, teenagers and children. Gives producer, running time and color.
There is a subject index and an index to directors.

Films in children's programs; a bibliography prepared by the film
committee of the Children and Young People's Services Section
of the Wisconsin Library Association, 1972, Wisconsin Library
Association, 201 West Mifflin St., Madison, Wisc. 53703, $1
to members, $2 to non-members.
For use with grades 3-6. Includes running time, color,
distributor, price and annotation, bibliography and filmography
and directory of distributors.

Friedlander. Madeline S. Leading Film Discussions; A Guide to
Using Films for Discussion, Training Leaders, Planning Effective Programs. League of Women Voters of the City of
New York (817 Broadway, N.Y., N.Y. 10003), 1972, 42p., $2.
A list of free, rental and purchase sources; notes on how
to preview, how to conduct a discussion, training discussion
leaders, planning a program; and an annotated list of discussion films.

Limbacher, James L., comp. and ed. Feature Films on 8mm and
16mm; A Directory of Feature Films Available for Rental,
Sale and Lease in the U.S., with Serial and Director Indexes,
4th ed., Bowker, 1974, $16.50.
Contains 6000 new entries.

Manon-Tissot, Thalia. "Innovation Through Trial and Error," Film
Library Quarterly, Fall 1969, pp. 13-5.
Good ideas for children's film programs.

Previews; Non-Print Software and Hardware News and Reviews.
Phyllis Levy, ed., Bowker, $5 per year.
Reviews 8 and 16mm films, filmstrips, slides, prints,
games and recordings. Describes and evaluates all kinds of
equipment, including projectors, microphones, screens,
splicers and headphones. The January 1975 issue has an
article entitled "The Selection of Audiovisual Equipment; A
Few Basics" by Kenyon C. Rosenberg.

Rice, Susan, comp. and ed. assisted by Barbara Ludlum. Films Kids Like; A Catalog of Short Films for Children. Published for Center for Understanding Media by American Library Association, Chicago, 1973, 150p.

    The introduction contains good, practical information about showing films to children. The body of the book is an annotated list of films that have been used with children. The annotations are outstanding, not only describing the films but also giving the reactions of the children to the film, and many other practical bits of advice.

Spehr, Paul. "Feature Films in Your Library," Wilson Library Bulletin, April 1970, pp. 848-55.

    Lists film distributors, film periodicals and suggested feature films.

Top of the News, Children's Services Division and the Young Adult Services Division of the American Library Association.

    Frequent articles of interest to programmers. The November 1969 issue includes several articles about film-making by teenagers and about creative dramatics in the library.

Sightlines (a quarterly). Educational Film Library Association, Inc., 17 West 60th St., New York, N.Y. 10023, $12 per year (with membership).

    Annotated lists of films and articles of interest to programmers.

PUPPET SHOWS

Batchelder, Marjorie. The Puppet Theatre Handbook, Harper, 1947.

    How to make all kinds of puppets. Design and construction of costumes, stages, scenery and lighting. Choosing and writing plays. Producing the show.

    . Puppets and Plays; A Creative Approach, Harper, 1956.

    Puppetry as drama. Values and use of the puppet theatre. Making puppets. Creating the play. Staging and producing the show.

Baumann, Hans. Casper and His Friends, Henry Z. Walck, 1968.

    Ten non-royalty puppet plays translated from German.

Boylan, Eleanor. How to Be a Puppeteer, McCall, 1970.

    Writing the play, making scenery and stages and manipulating the puppets. Includes six plays from traditional stories.

Bufano, Remo. <u>Remo Bufano's Book of Puppetry</u>, Macmillan, 1950.
Sections on puppets and marionettes, including, for each,
how to make and manipulate them, and how to make the
theatre. Includes four plays.

Cummings, Richard. <u>101 Hand Puppets</u>, McKay, 1962.
Tells how to make many different puppet characters in-
cluding Little Miss Muffet, Goldilocks, Little Red Riding
Hood, Pecos Pete and many others. Includes three plays.

Ross, Laura. <u>Finger Puppets</u>, Lothrop, Lee and Shepard, 1971.
Tells how to make many puppet characters from very
simple materials. Includes rhymes, poems and stories to
use with them.

STORYTELLING

Cathon, Laura, Marion McC. Haushalter and Virginia A. Russell,
eds. <u>Stories to Tell to Children: A Selected List</u>. 8th ed.,
rev., University of Pittsburgh Press, 1974, 145p., $5.95.
One of the standard lists, first published in 1916 by the
Carnegie Library of Pittsburgh. The new edition has section
of stories for preschool, ages six to ten, and one for older
children. There is also a list for holiday programs, and a
classified list that includes such subjects as Afro-American,
American Indians, Ecology, Ethical and Social Values, Blind-
ness, Jews, Action Stories and Tall Tales.

Cincinnati and Hamilton County, Ohio, Public Library. <u>Books for
Mentally Retarded Children</u>, Sept. 1973, 34p.
The books on this list have been tried with one or more
classes in Cincinnati schools. The books have been divided
into four categories of the mentally retarded. Many of the
books would be suitable for storytelling.

<u>Compton's Encyclopedia</u>. F. E. Compton Co., Division of En-
cyclopaedia Britannica, Inc.
The article on storytelling (e.g. in the 1975 ed.) includes a
section entitled "How to Tell a Story." There is also a list
of "Folk Tales from Many Lands."

Hardendorff, Jeanne B., ed. <u>Stories to Tell: A List of Stories
with Annotations</u>, 5th ed., rev. & ed. by Jeanne B. Hardendorff, Office of Work with Children, Enoch Pratt Free Library, Baltimore, 1965.
This collection is based on the stories which have been
successfully used in story hours at the Pratt Library. Includes a section of picture books that are particularly useful
for television storytelling. There are suggested programs for

storytelling, and a subject list of stories. There is also a list of sources of individual stories.

Sawyer, Ruth. Way of the Storyteller, rev. ed., Viking, 1965, 356p., $4.50 (pap. 2.25).

Shedlock, Marie L. The Art of the Story-teller, 3d. ed. rev. (foreword by Anne Carroll Moore, with a new bibliography by Eulalie Steinmetz), Dover, 1951, 290p.
    This title and the Sawyer are the classics in the field. They tell how to select a story and give the tricks of the trade. Both books contain sample stories and lists.

Ross, Eulalie Steinmetz, ed. The Lost Half-Hour; A Collection of Stories (illus. by Enrico Arno), Harcourt, Brace & World, 1963, 191p., $5.50.
    A collection of sample stories for telling, but most valuable for the last chapter which tells you how to tell them.

STORYTELLING--FILMOGRAPHY

The Pleasure Is Mutual 24 min. color $250 rental $30
    Connecticut Films, Inc. Six Cobble Hill Road, Westport, Connecticut 06880.
        Designed to help adults conduct effective picture book story hours. Tells how to present them and how to control the group. Used by libraries in training programs. Comes with a list of sample programs.

Sharing Literature with Children 16 min. color $195
    Orlando (Fla.) Public Library, 10 N. Rosalind Ave., Orlando, Fla. 32801.
        How to involve the community in programs for pre-school children. The authors have not seen. Completed late 1974. No rental, but previews available.

VIDEOTAPE AND CABLE TELEVISION

Cable Libraries [a periodical].
    C. S. Tepfer Pub. Co., Inc., 607 Main St., Ridgefield, Conn. 06877. Pub. 12 times a year, $15 a year. Contains cable regulations, information on library programs, and reviews of hardware.

Harwood, Don. Everything You Always Wanted to Know About Video Tape Recording, VTR Pub. Co., N.Y., 1974, 184p. $3.95.
        Clearly and simply answers almost all technical questions

for beginners and intermediates in video; an ideal handbook for learning or teaching.

Murray, Michael. The Videotape Book, Bantam, 1975, 248p. ($9.95; 1.95 pap).
Basic guide to portable TV production, and the organizing and carrying out of projects; clean, simple presentation.

Price, Monroe E. and John Wicklein. Cable Television: A Guide for Citizen Action, Pilgrim Press, Philadelphia, 1972, 160p. ($2.95).
How citizens can gain access to cable television.

Schwartz, Tony. The Responsive Chord, Anchor Press/Doubleday, 1973, 173p. ($6.95).
This book discusses the ways sounds and pictures affect us, and, for anyone interested in communications, it is fascinating.

Shamberg, Michael. Guerilla Television, Holt, Rinehart & Winston, 1971, 108p. ($7.95; 3.95 pap).
A first book on how to work with videotape in the community.

Tate, Charles, ed. Cable Television in the Cities: Community Control, Public Access, and Minority Ownership, 3d ed., Urban Institute, Washington, D.C., 1971, 184p. ($3.95).
Tells what cable is and does, and discusses its prospects; may be somewhat dated (names, addresses, regulations) but still useful.

Television [a periodical]. Washington Community Video Center, P.O. Box 21068, Washington, D.C. 10 issues a year, $10 a year. Contains news items, regulations, book reviews, articles. Highly recommended.

Videofreex [organization]. The Spaghetti City Video Manual, Praeger, 1973, 116p. ($7.95).
Guide to use, repair and maintenance of equipment. Helpful for those working with young people who are just getting started.

Weiner, Peter Mark. Making the Media Revolution; A Handbook for Video-Tape Production, Macmillan, 1973, 217p. ($8.95).
Much useful information on lighting, special effects, animation; includes tips on preservation; clear, lively style.

INDEX